Indian hemp
&
Mandala
Coloring Book

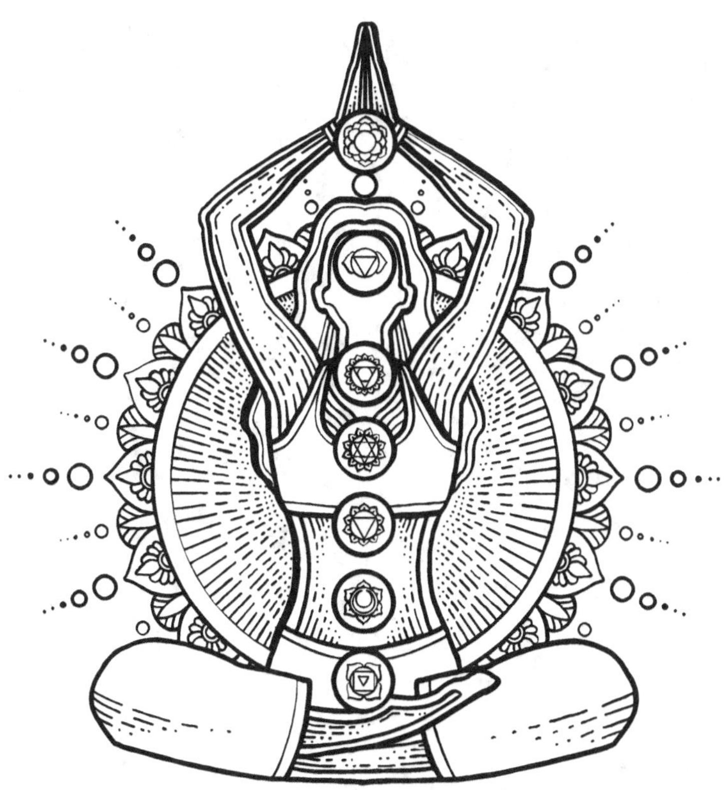

THIS BOOK BELONGS TO:-

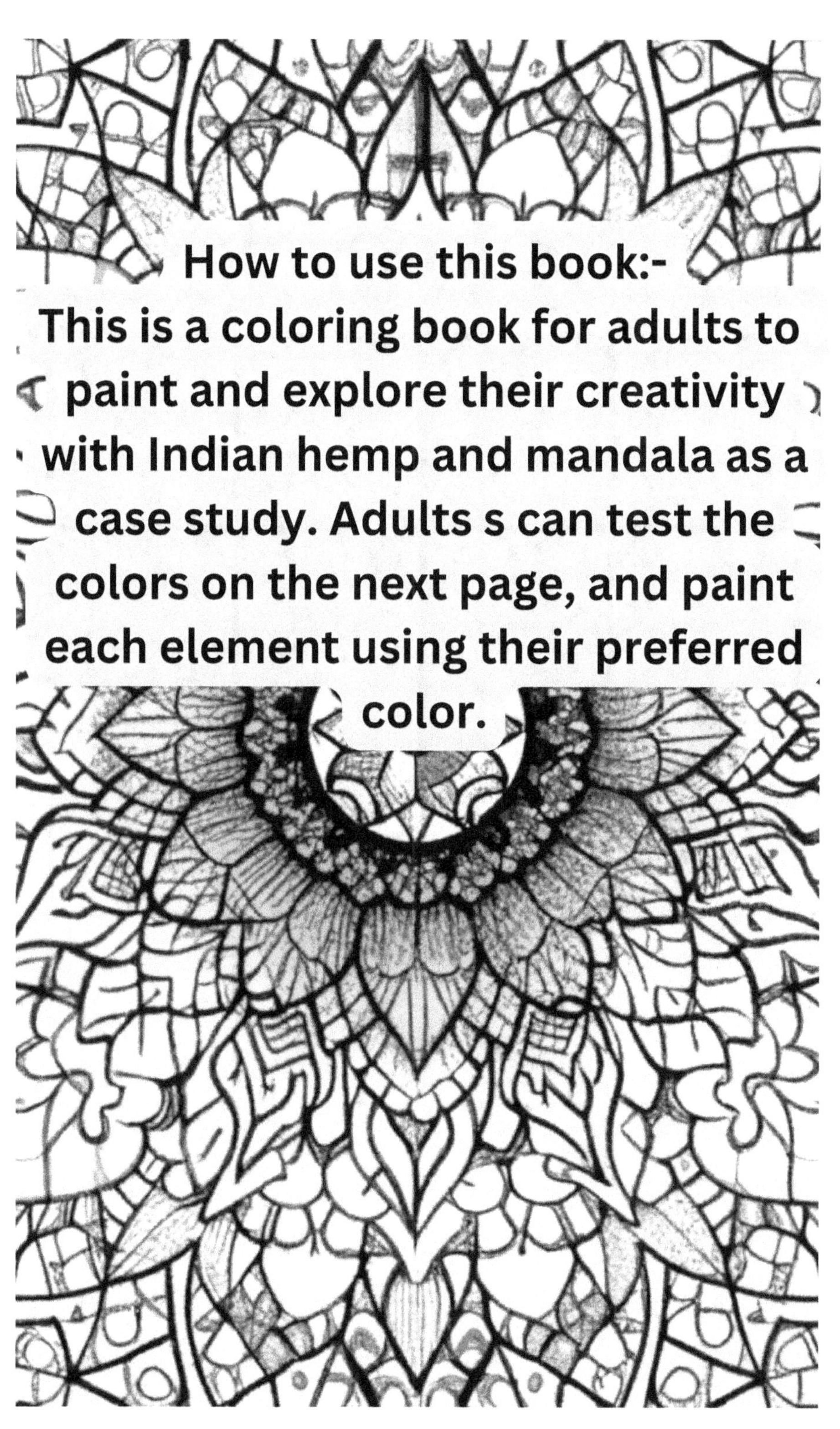

How to use this book:-
This is a coloring book for adults to paint and explore their creativity with Indian hemp and mandala as a case study. Adults s can test the colors on the next page, and paint each element using their preferred color.

TEST YOUR COLOR HERE

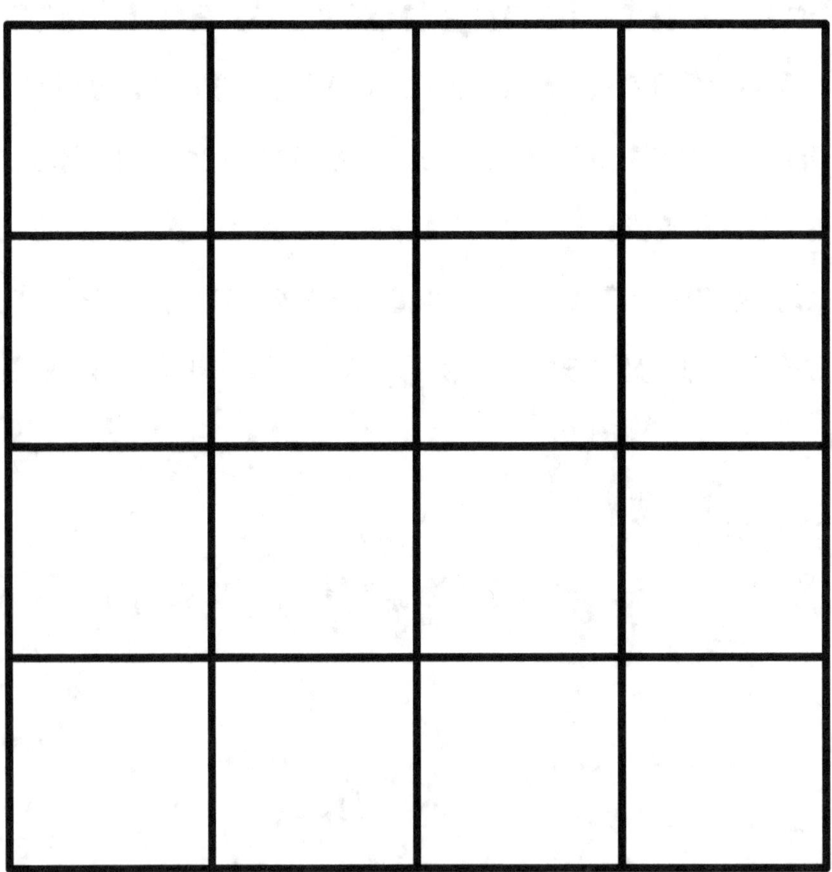

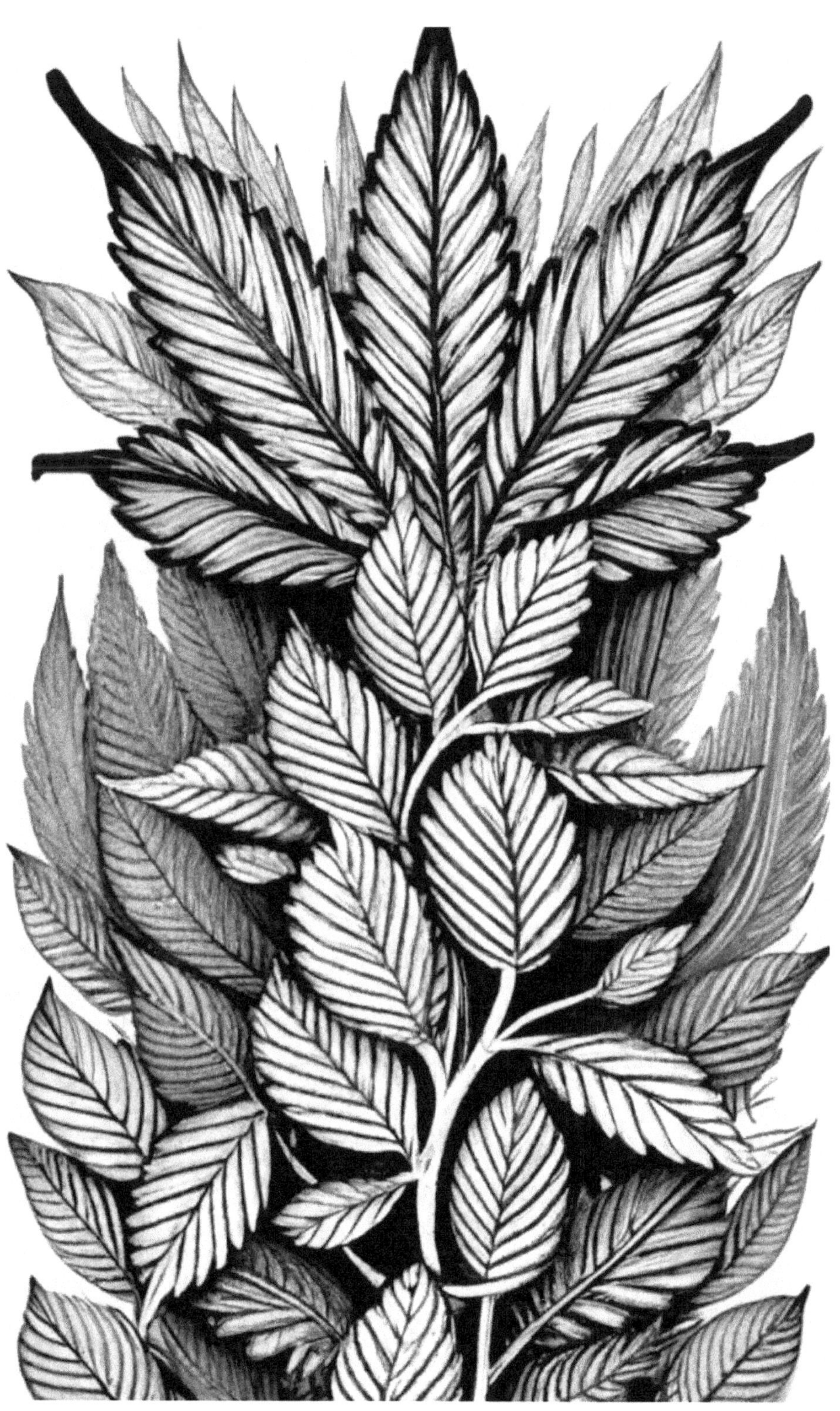

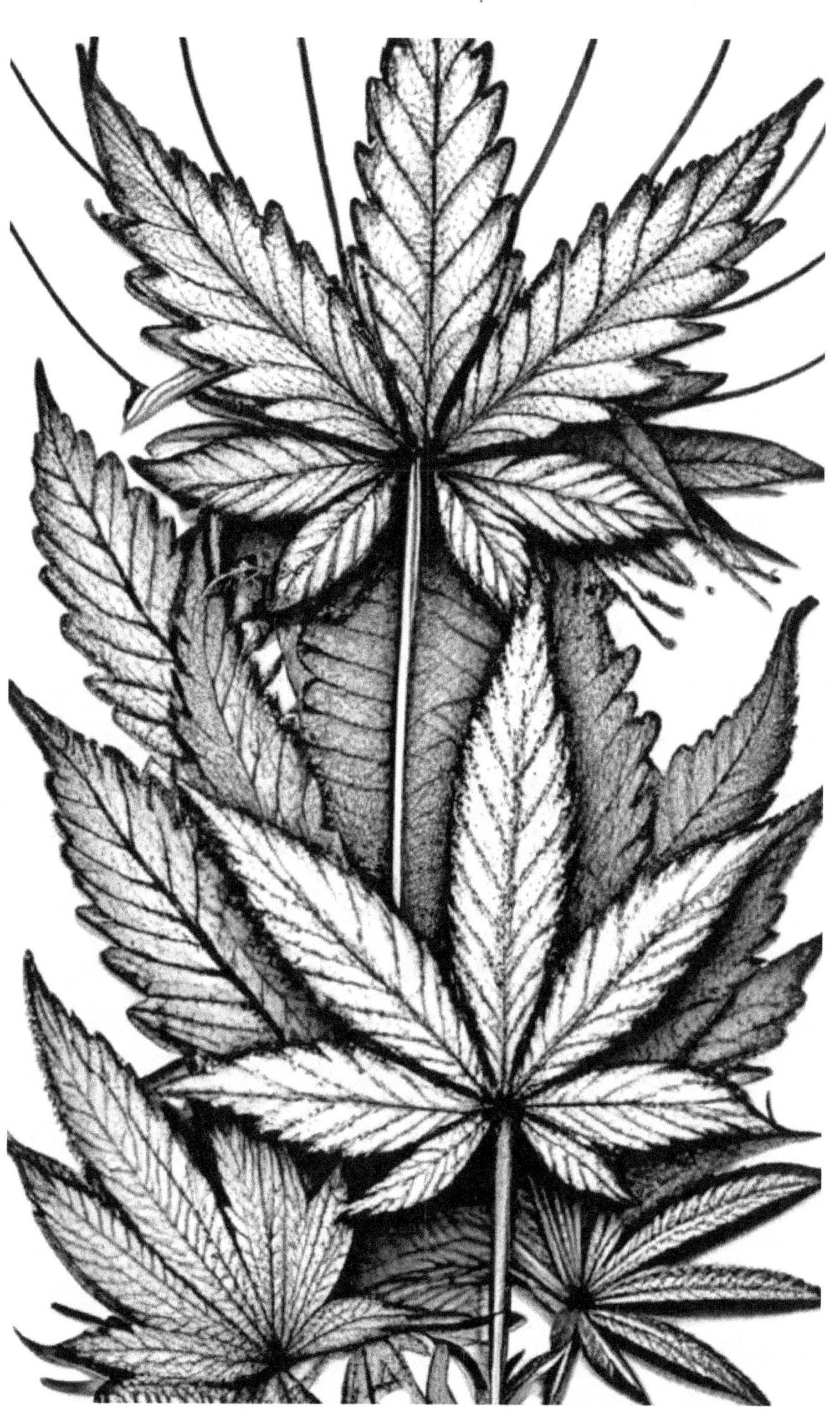

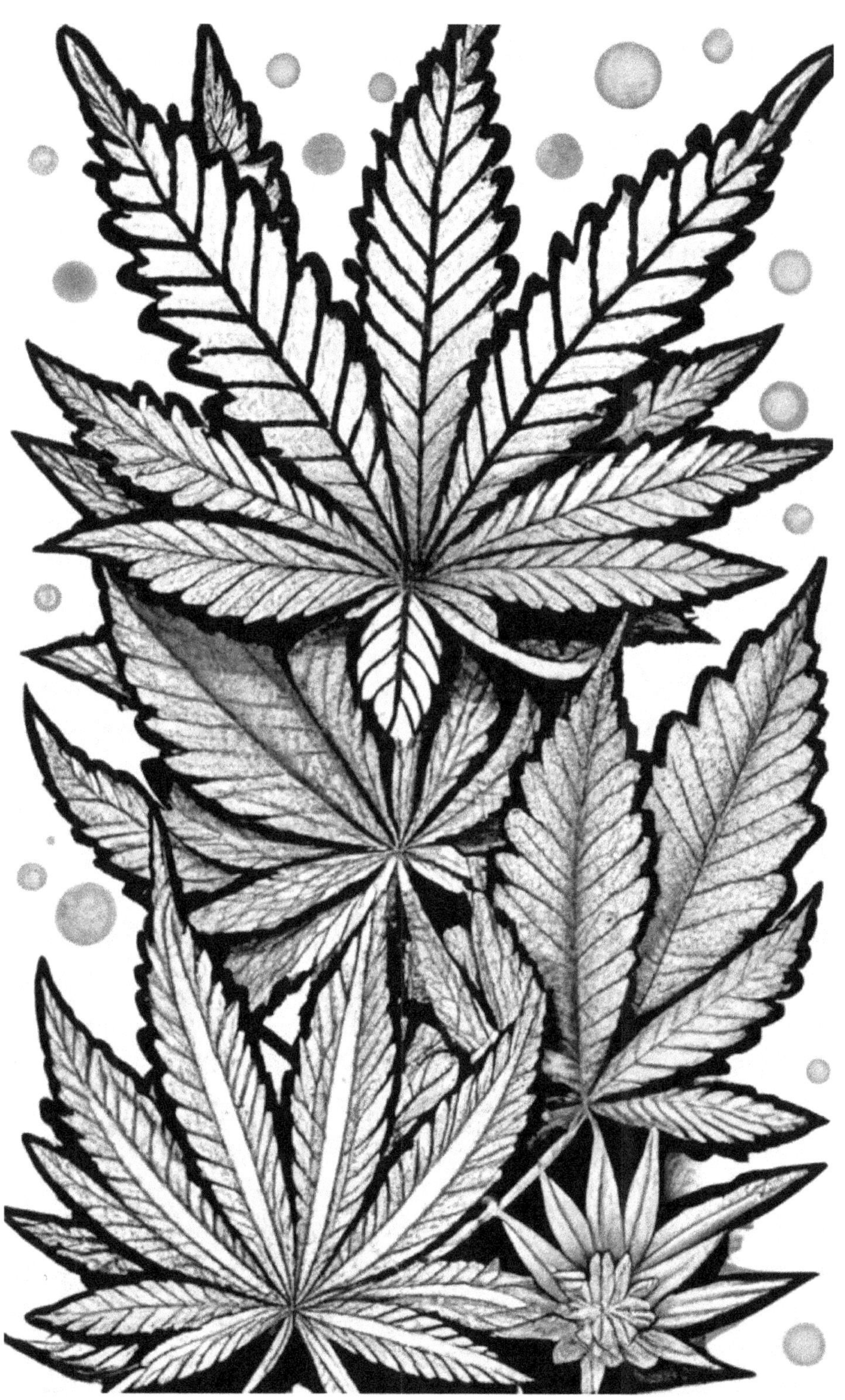

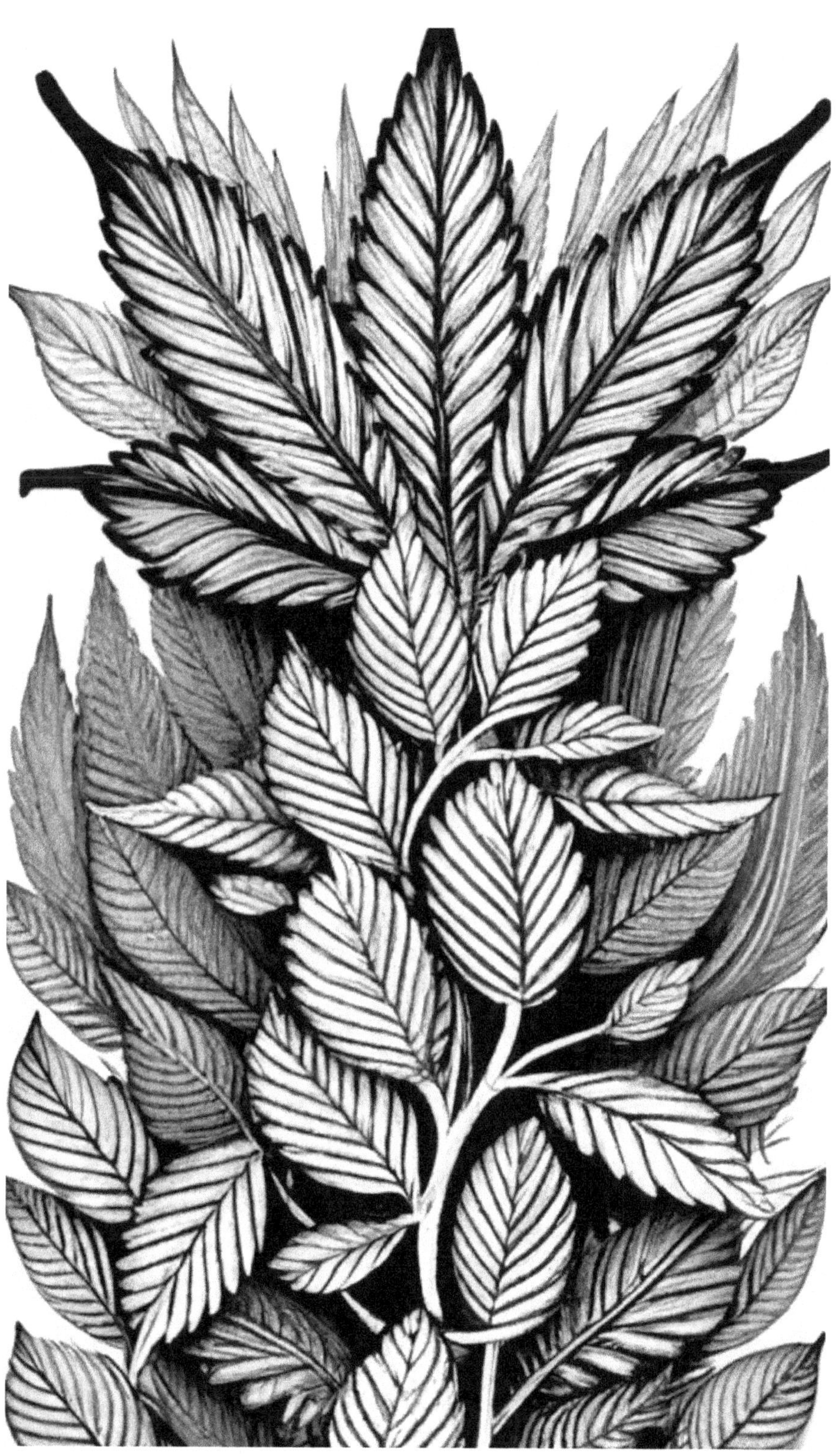

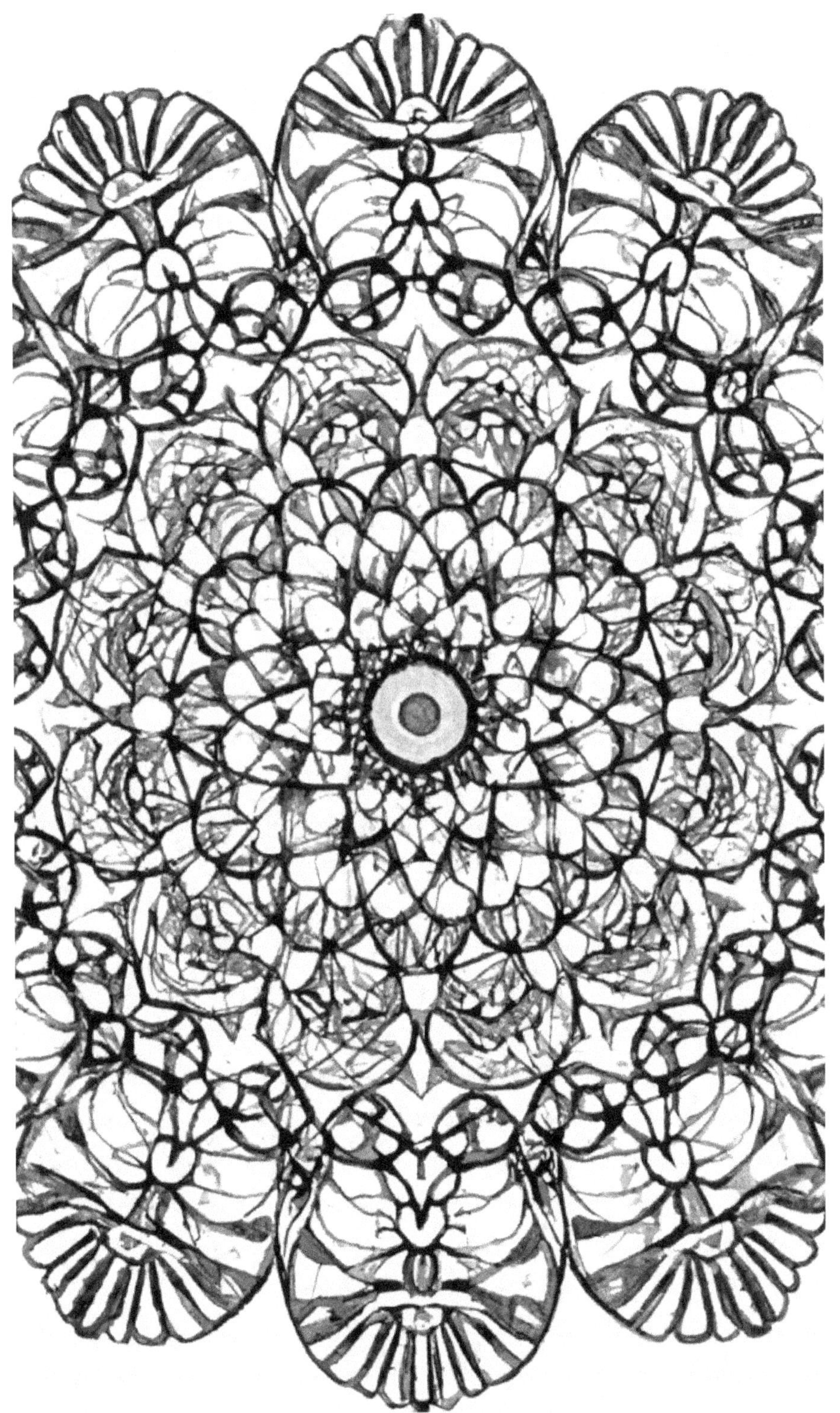

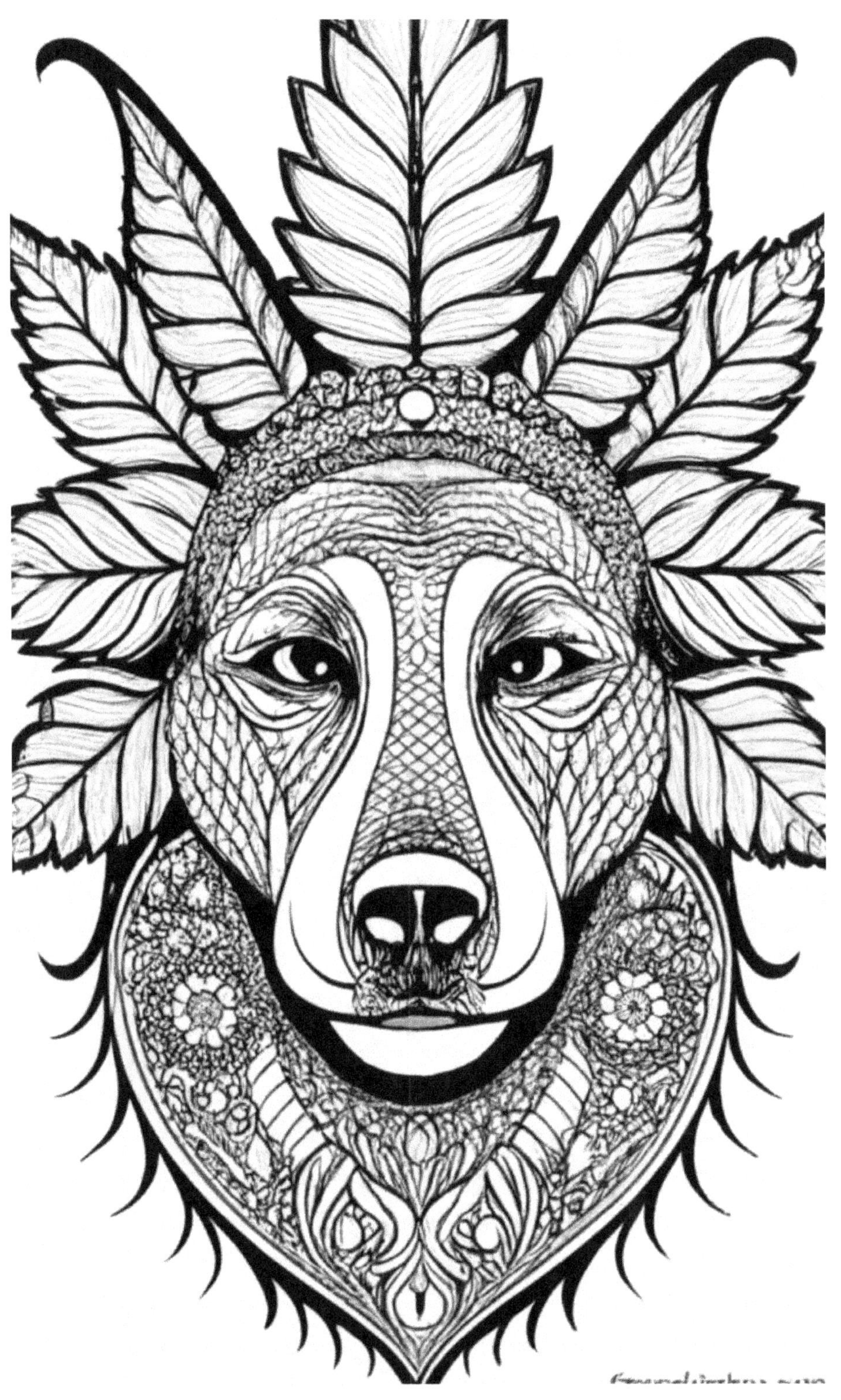

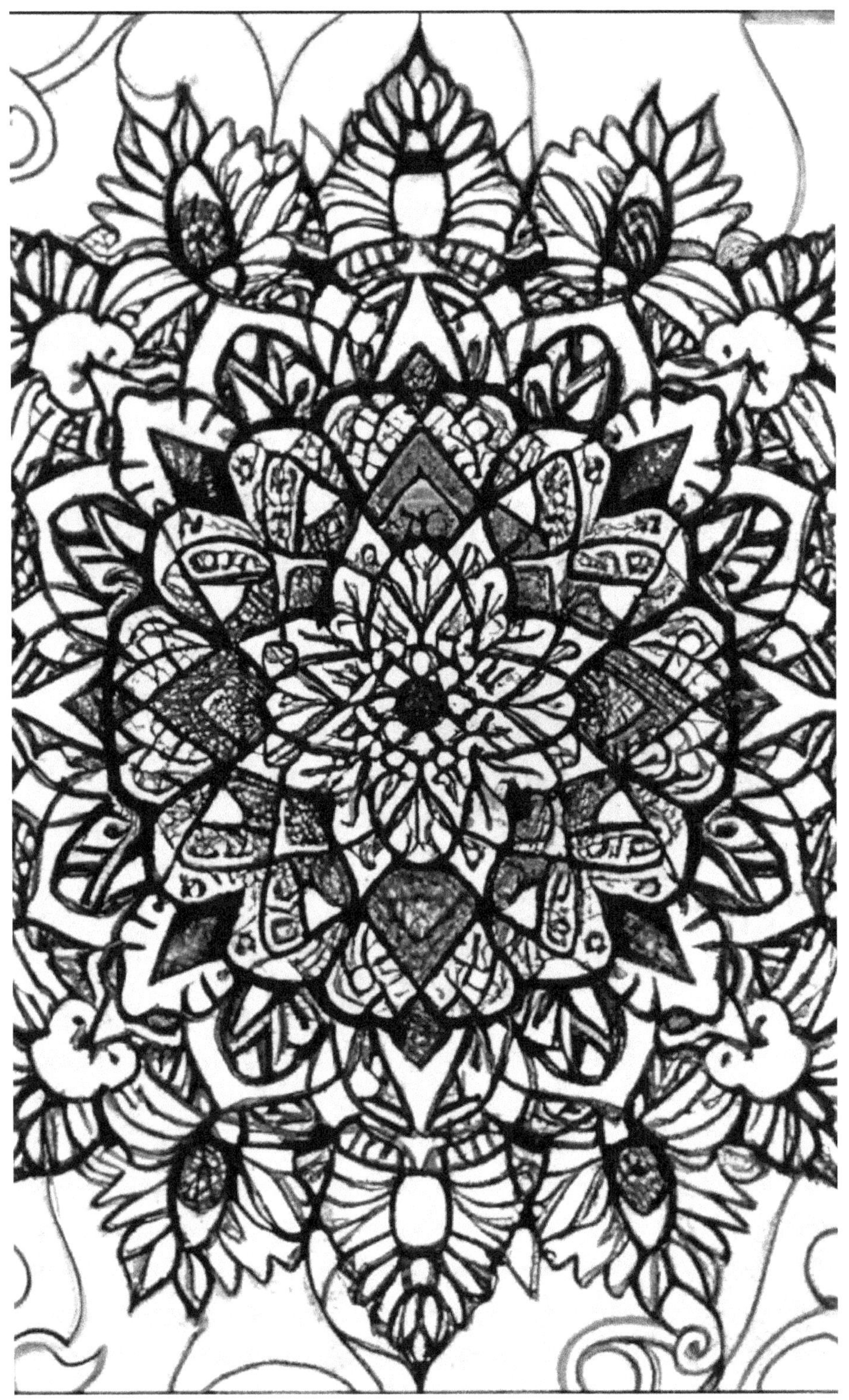

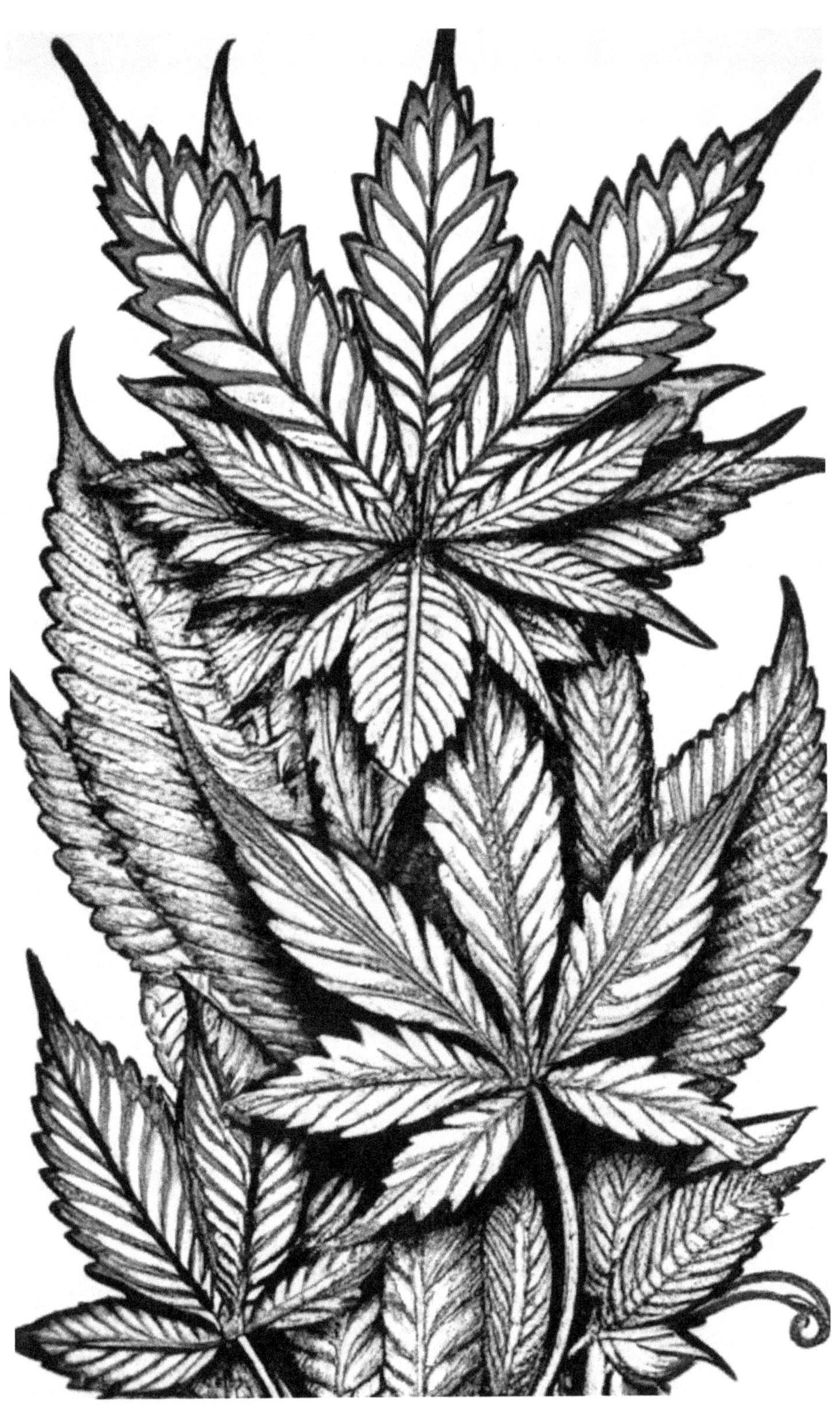

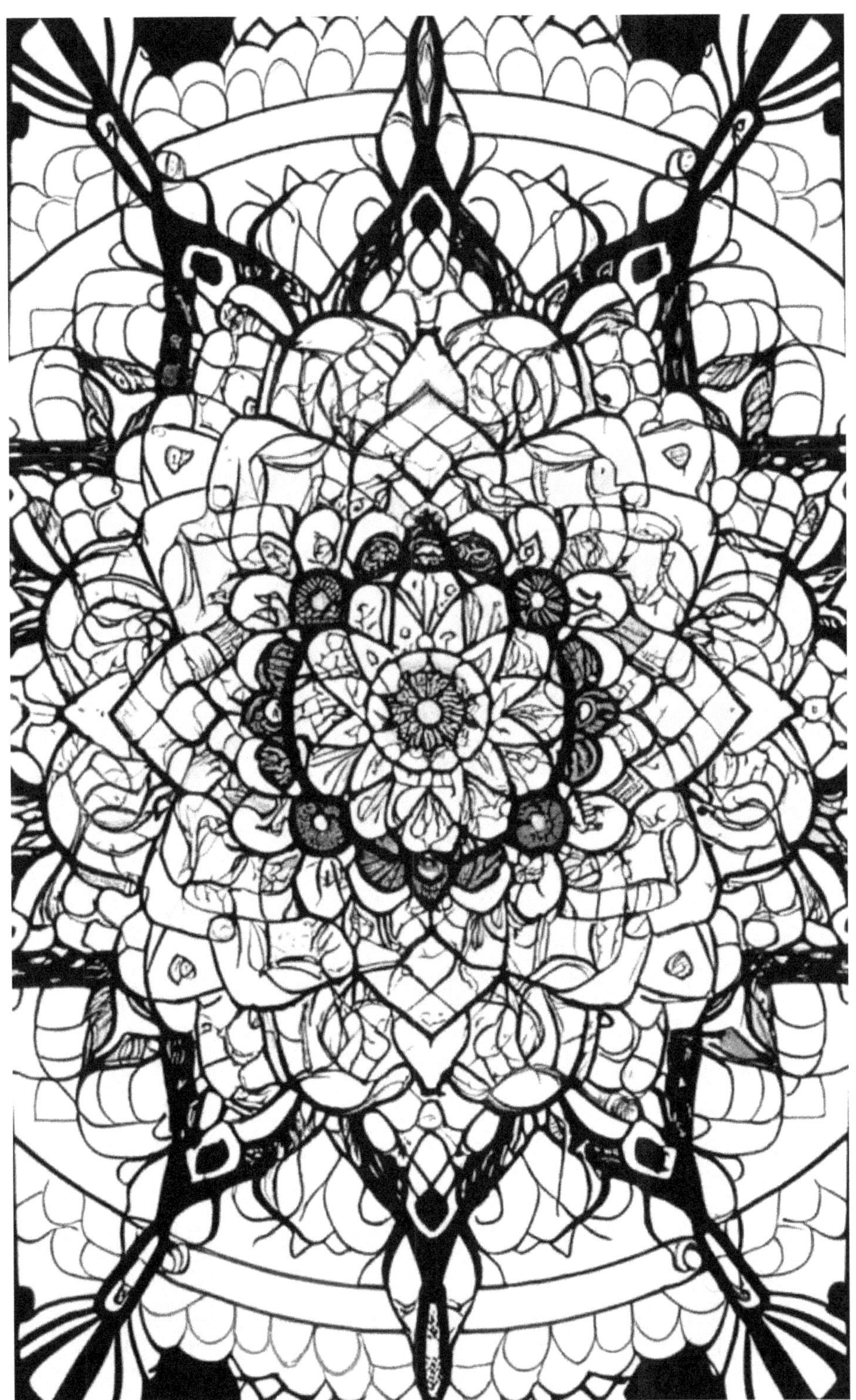

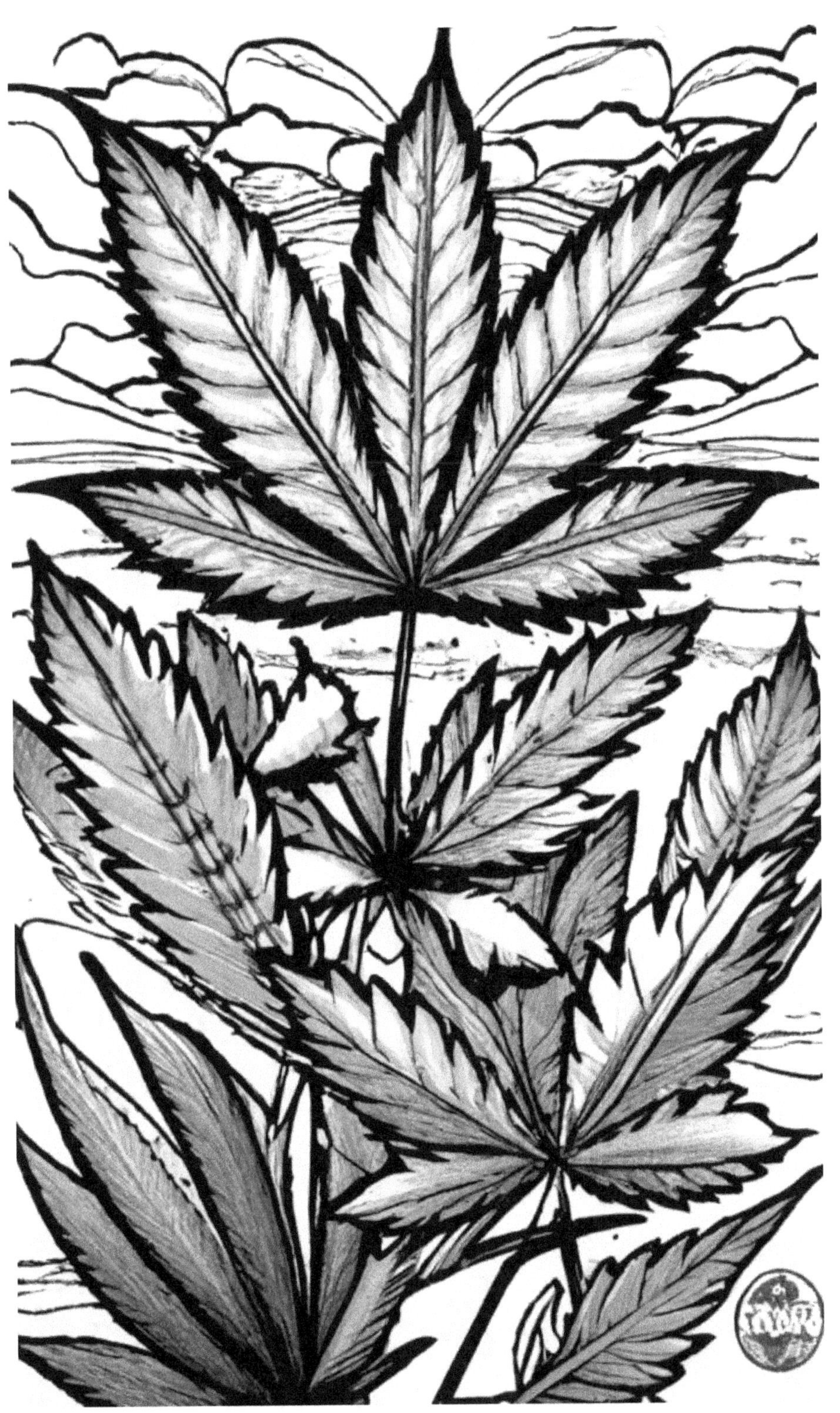

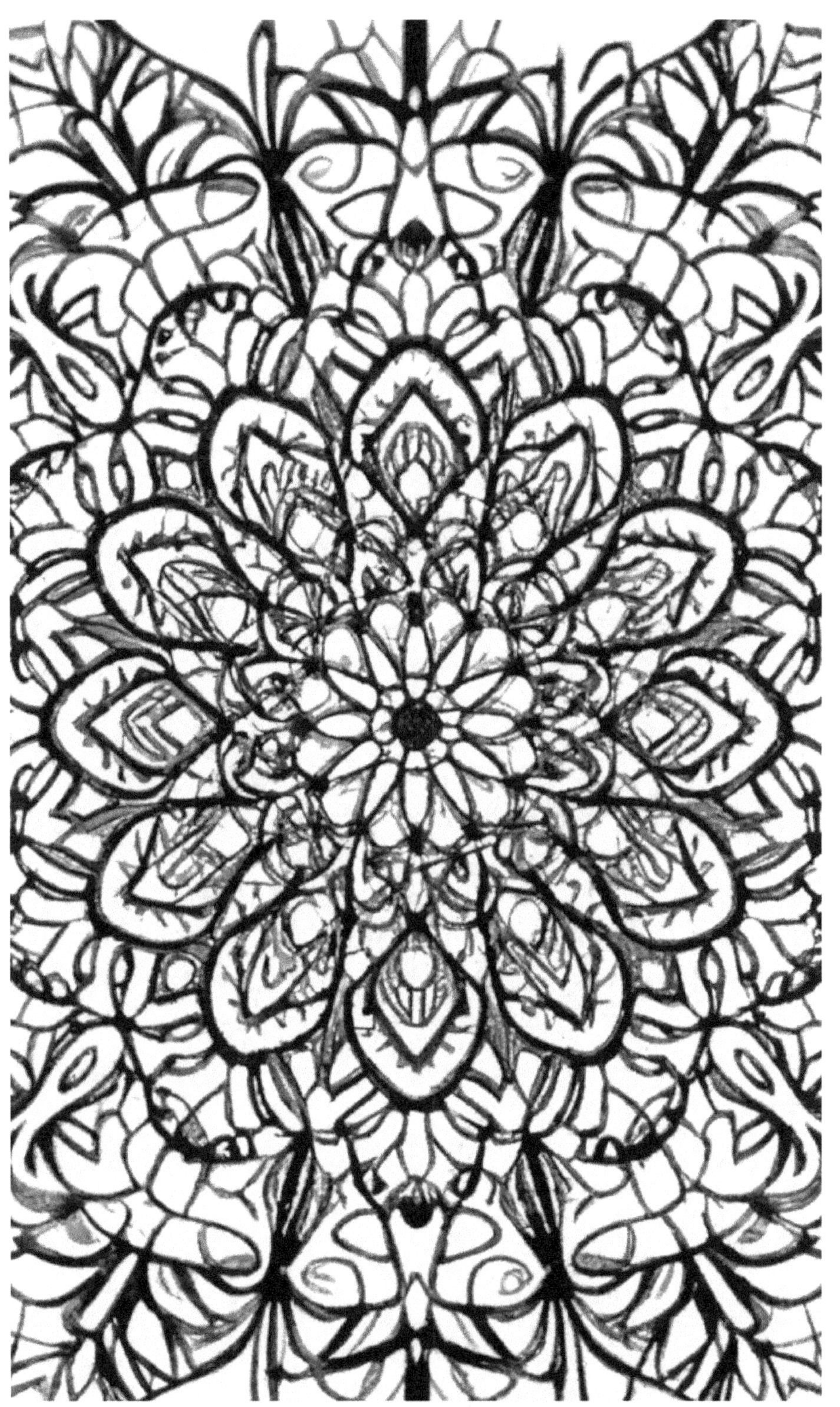

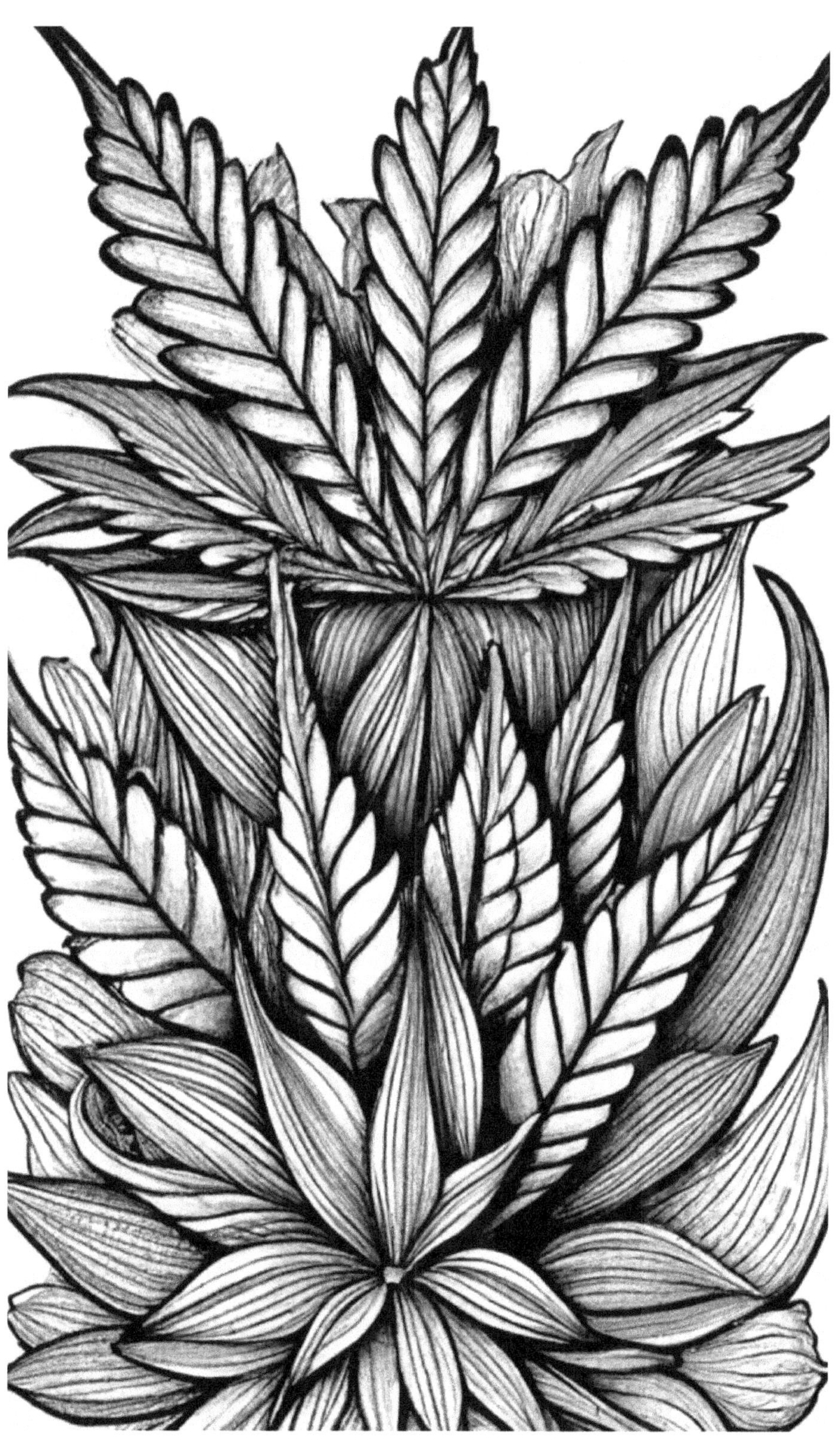

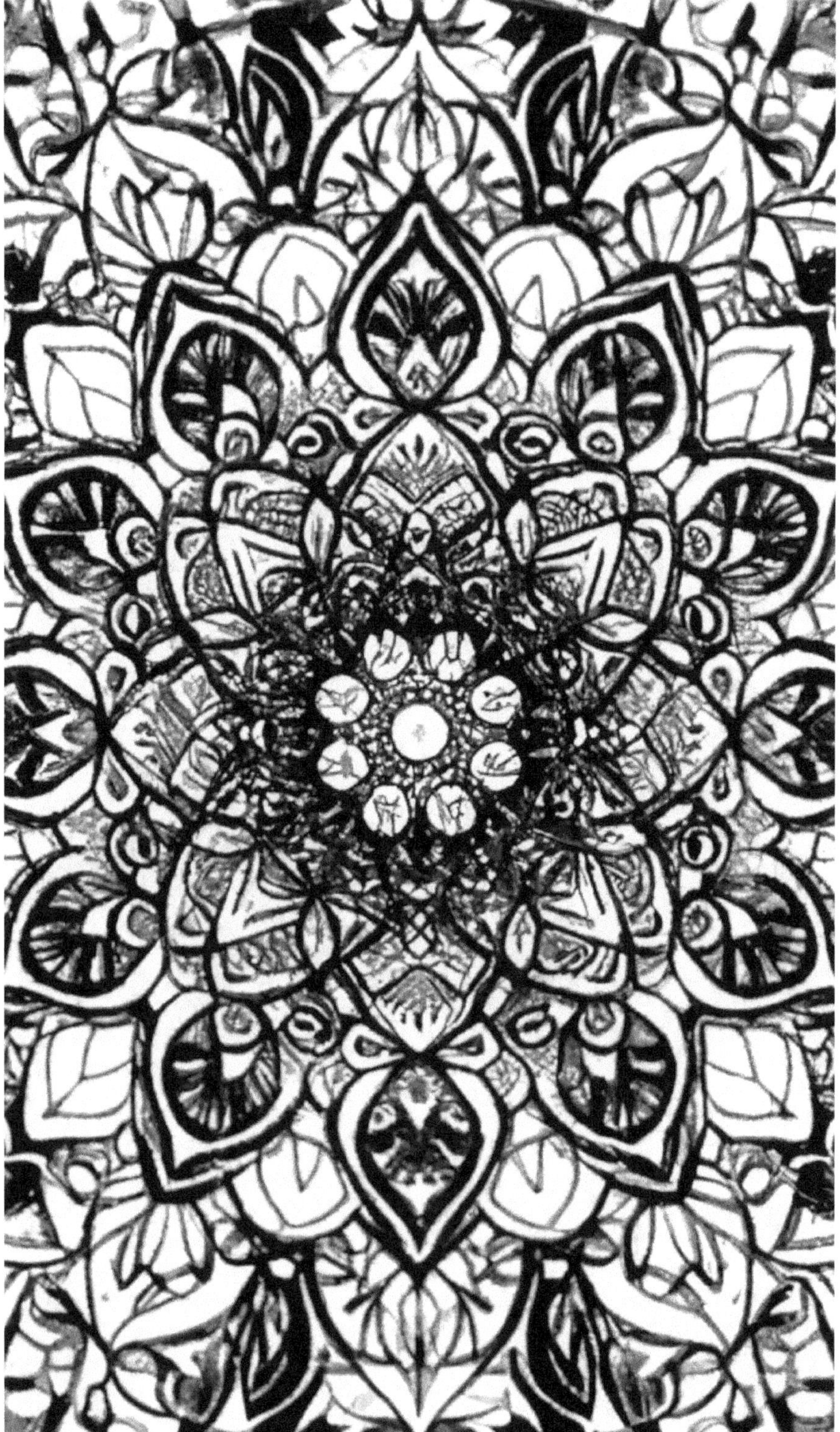

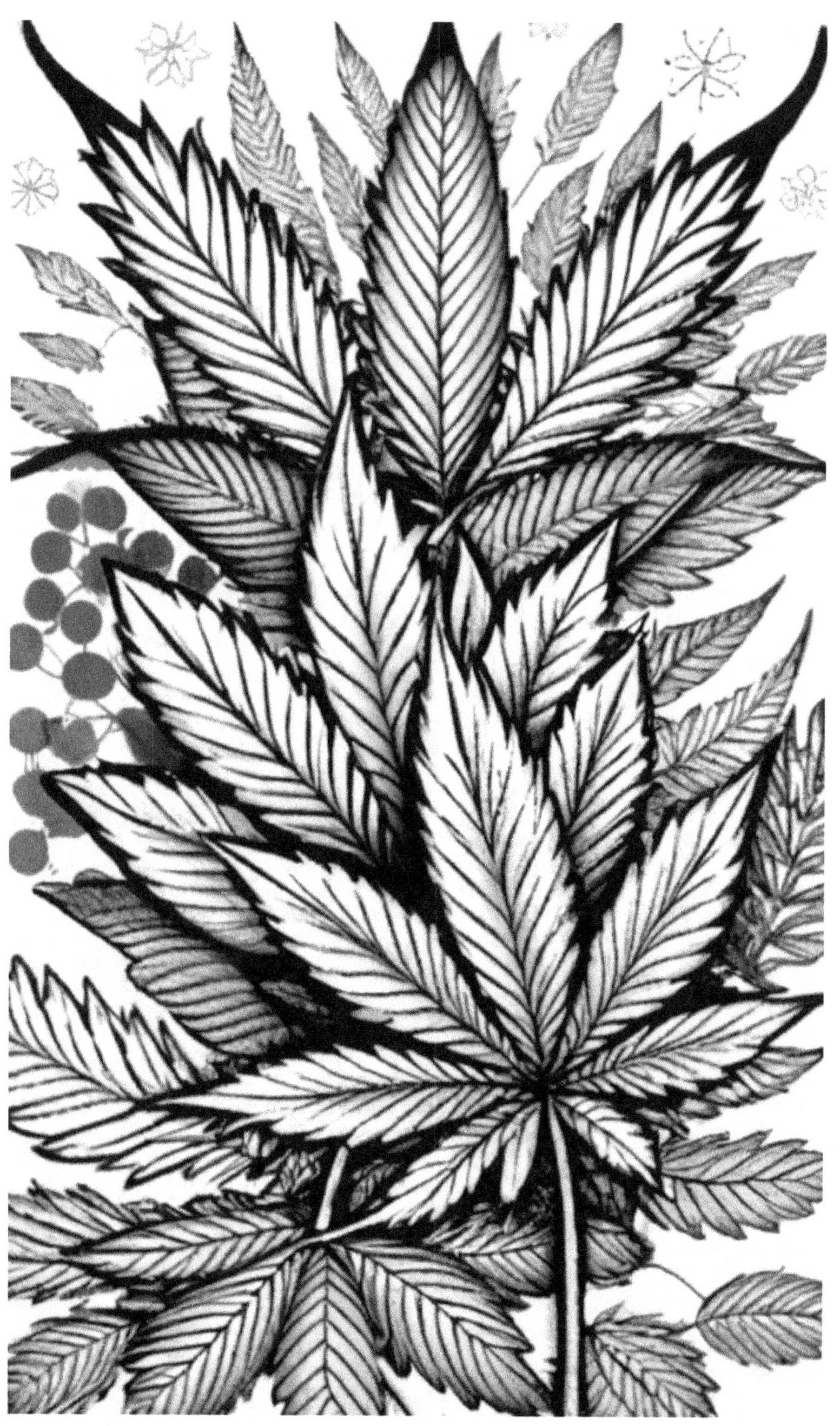

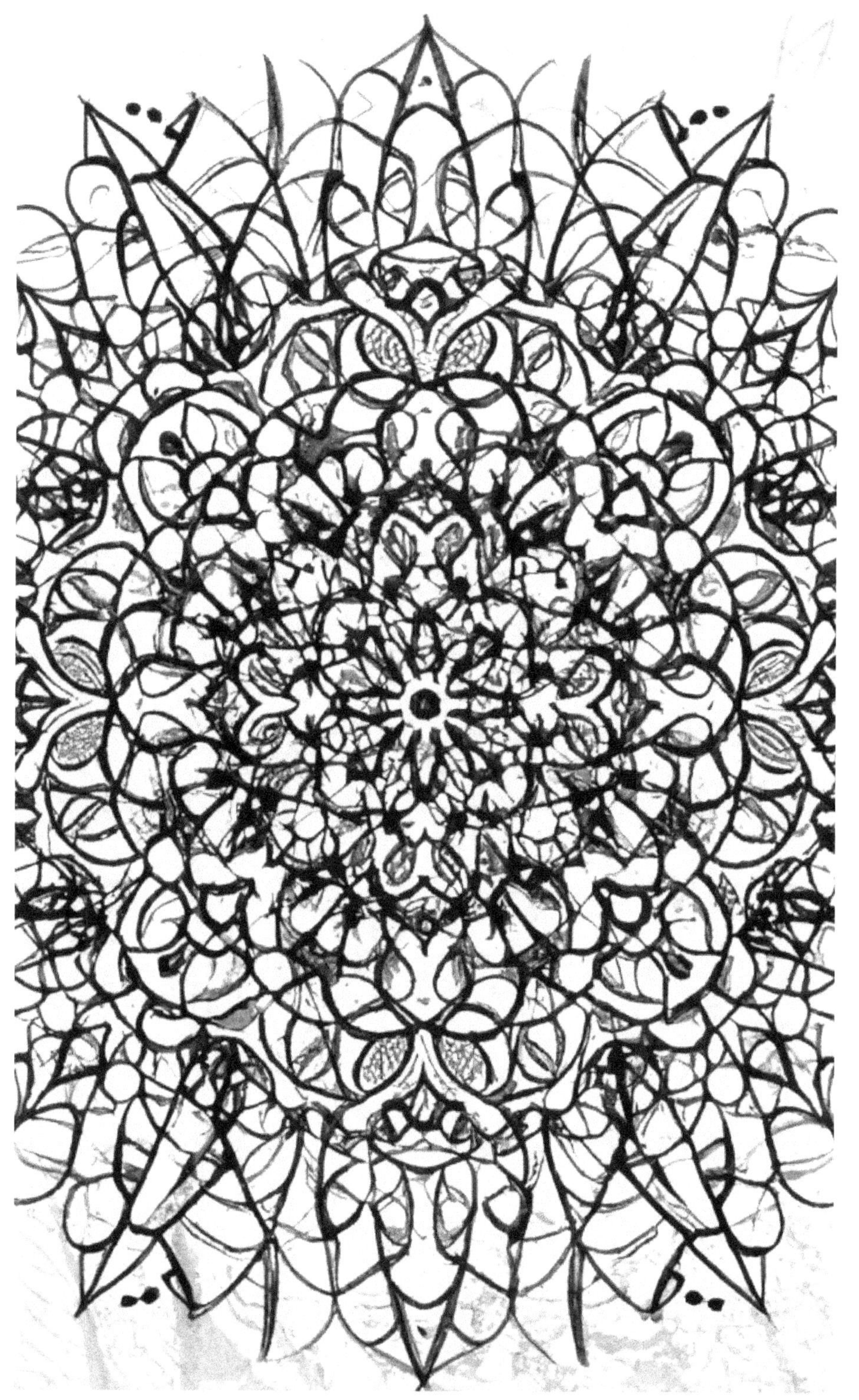

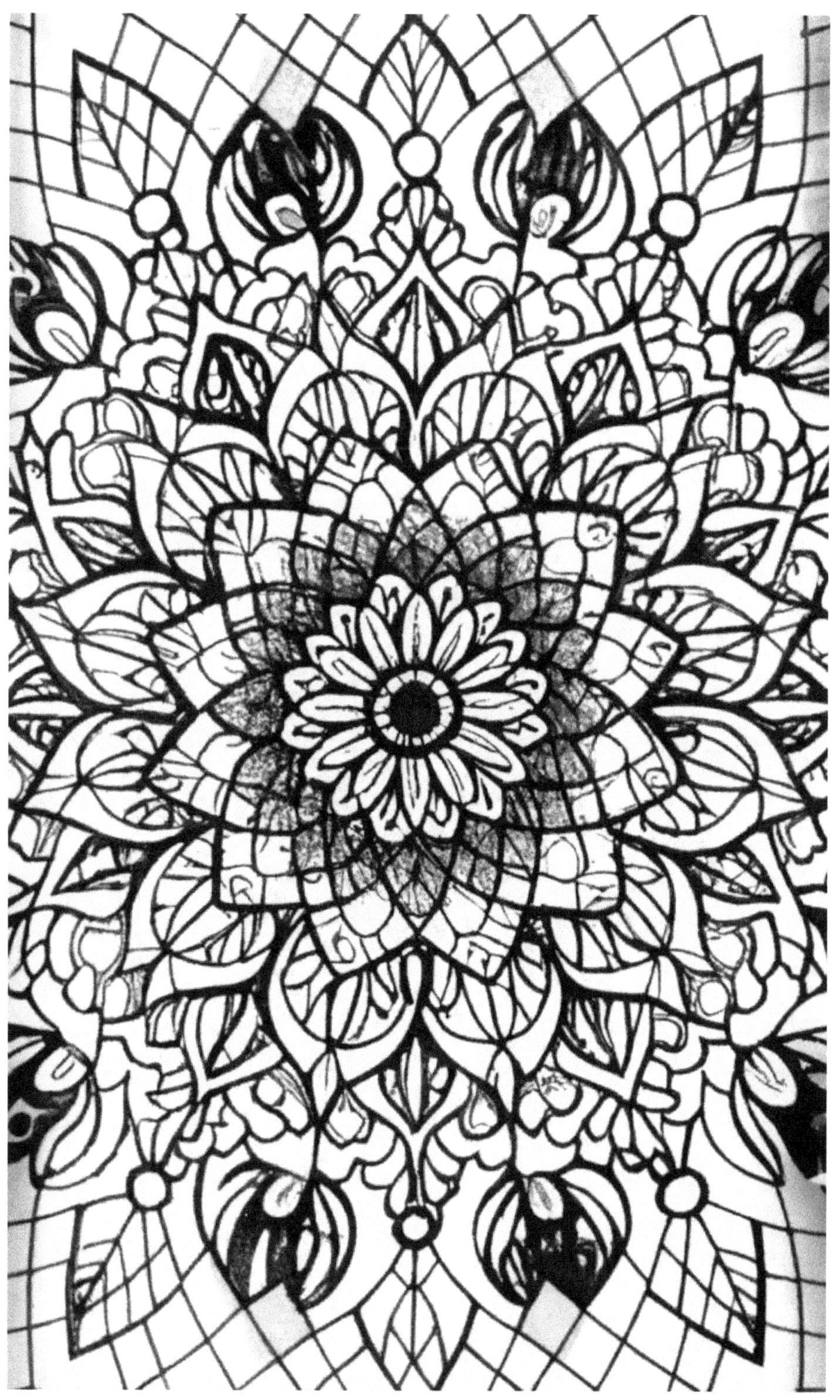

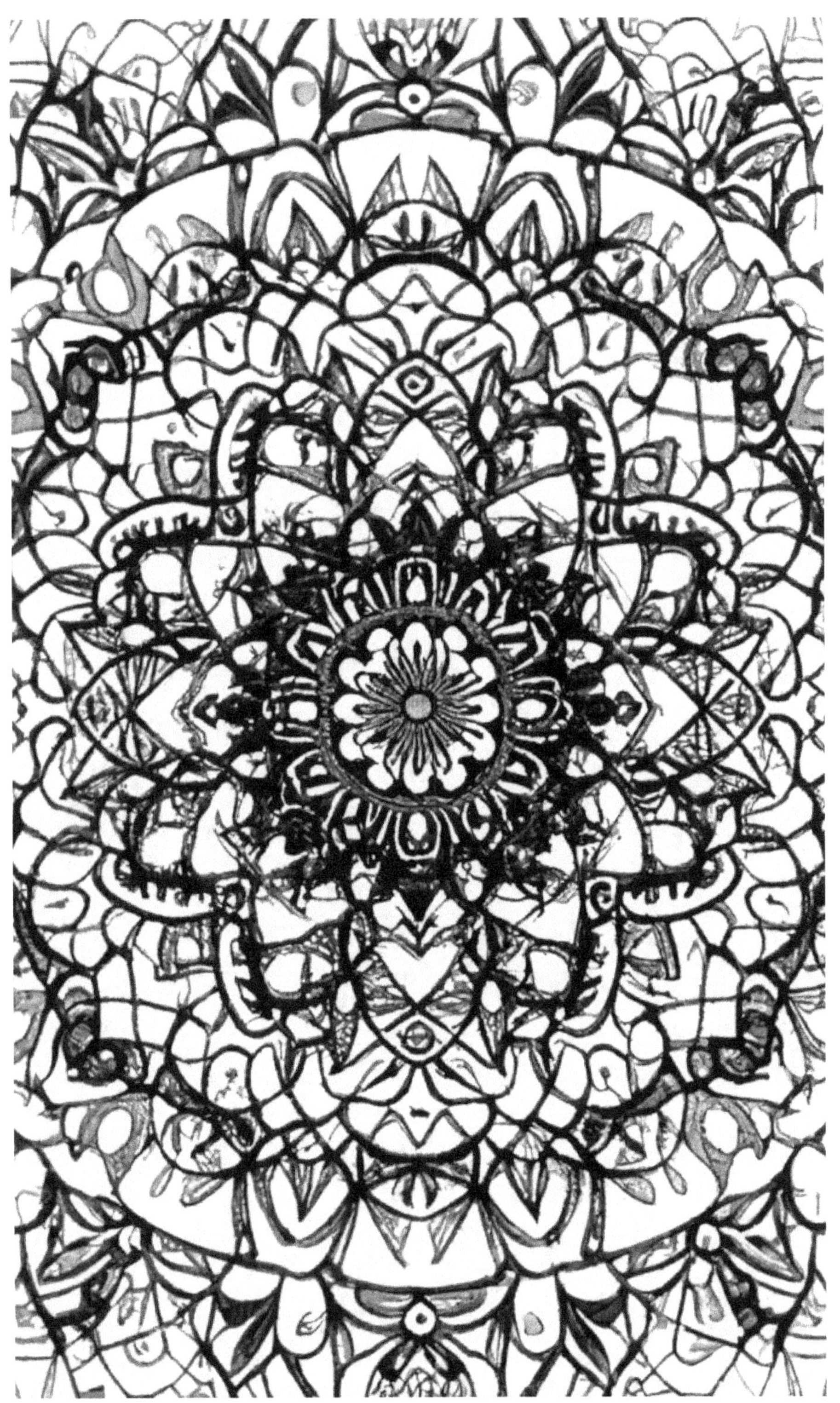

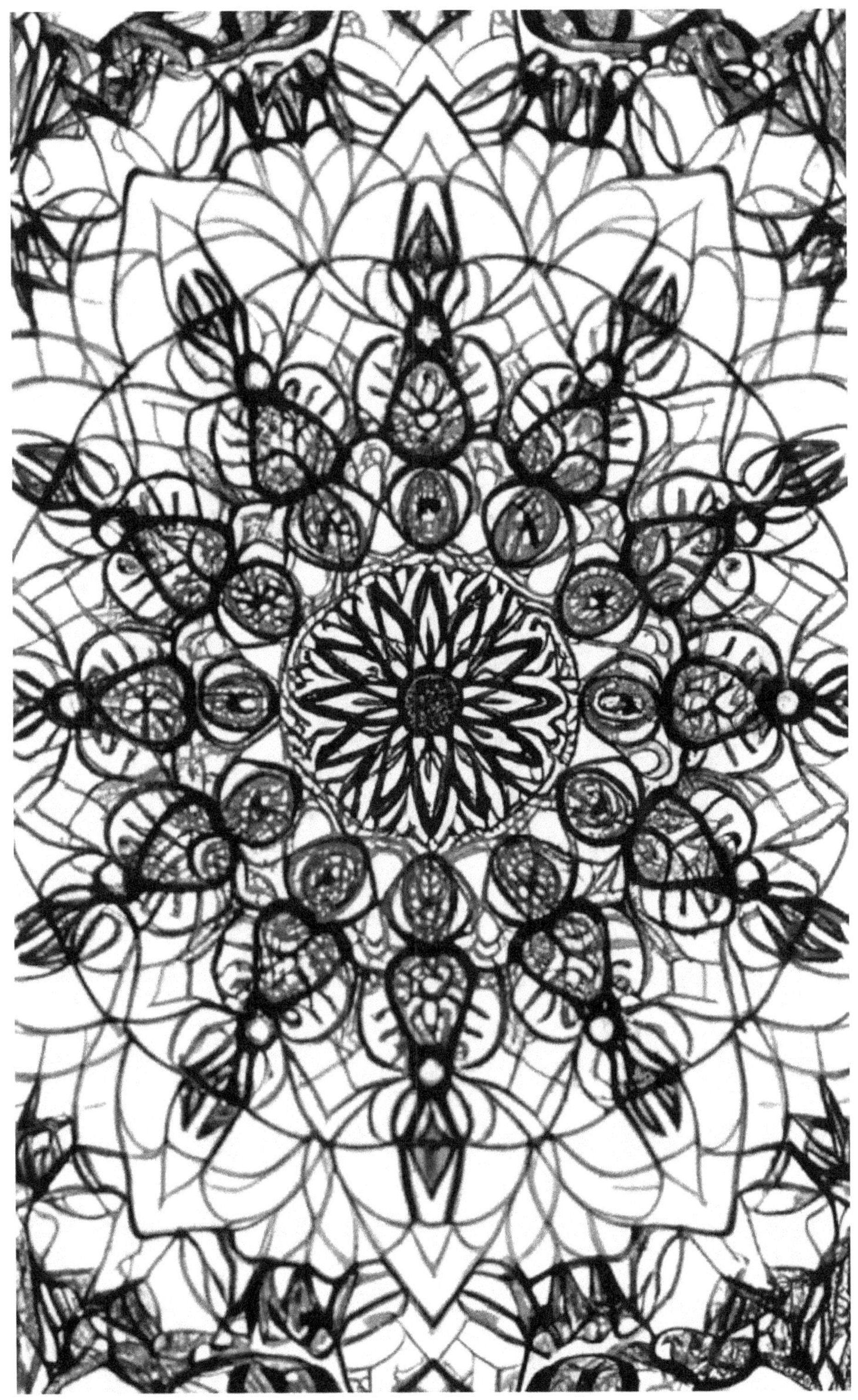

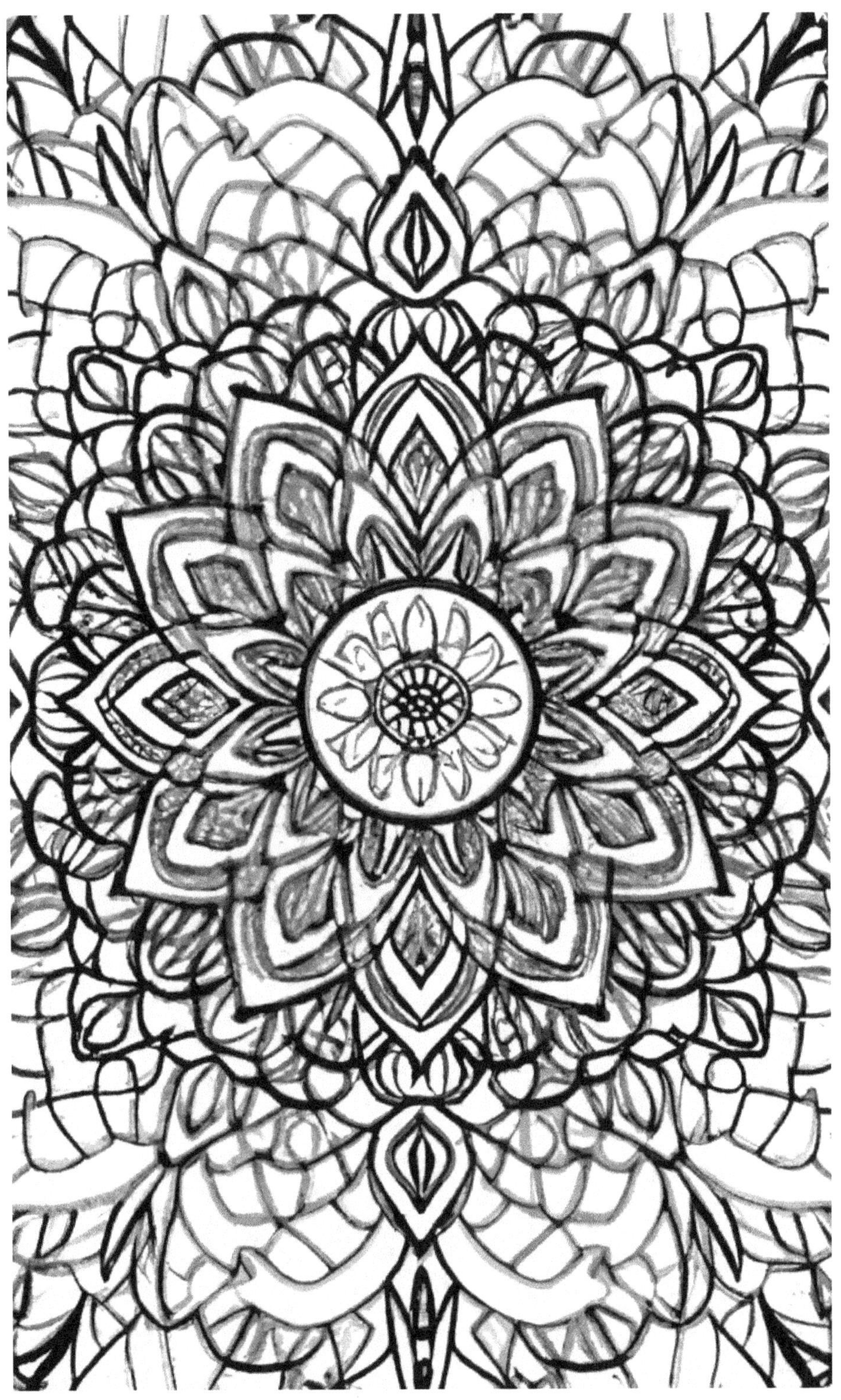

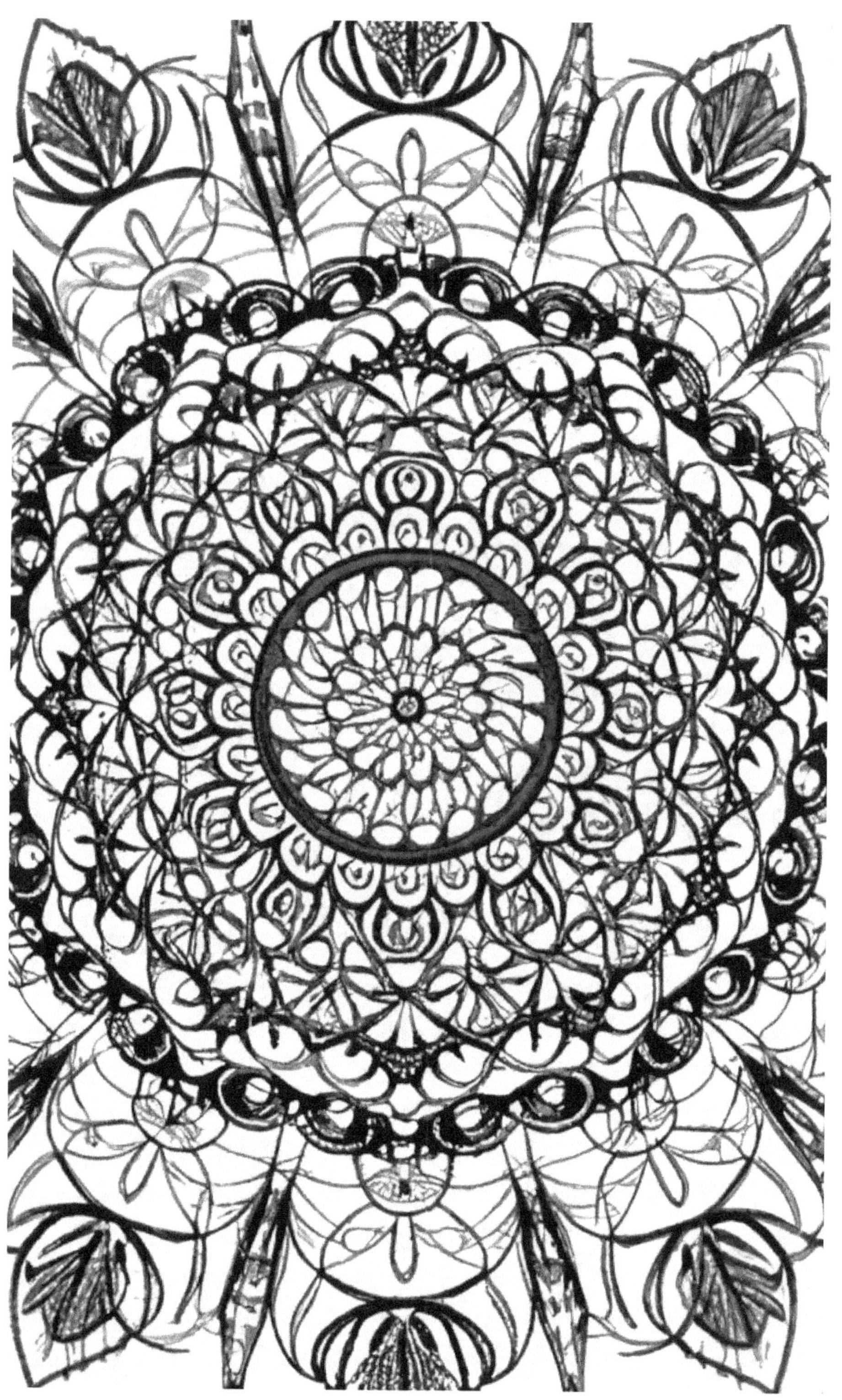

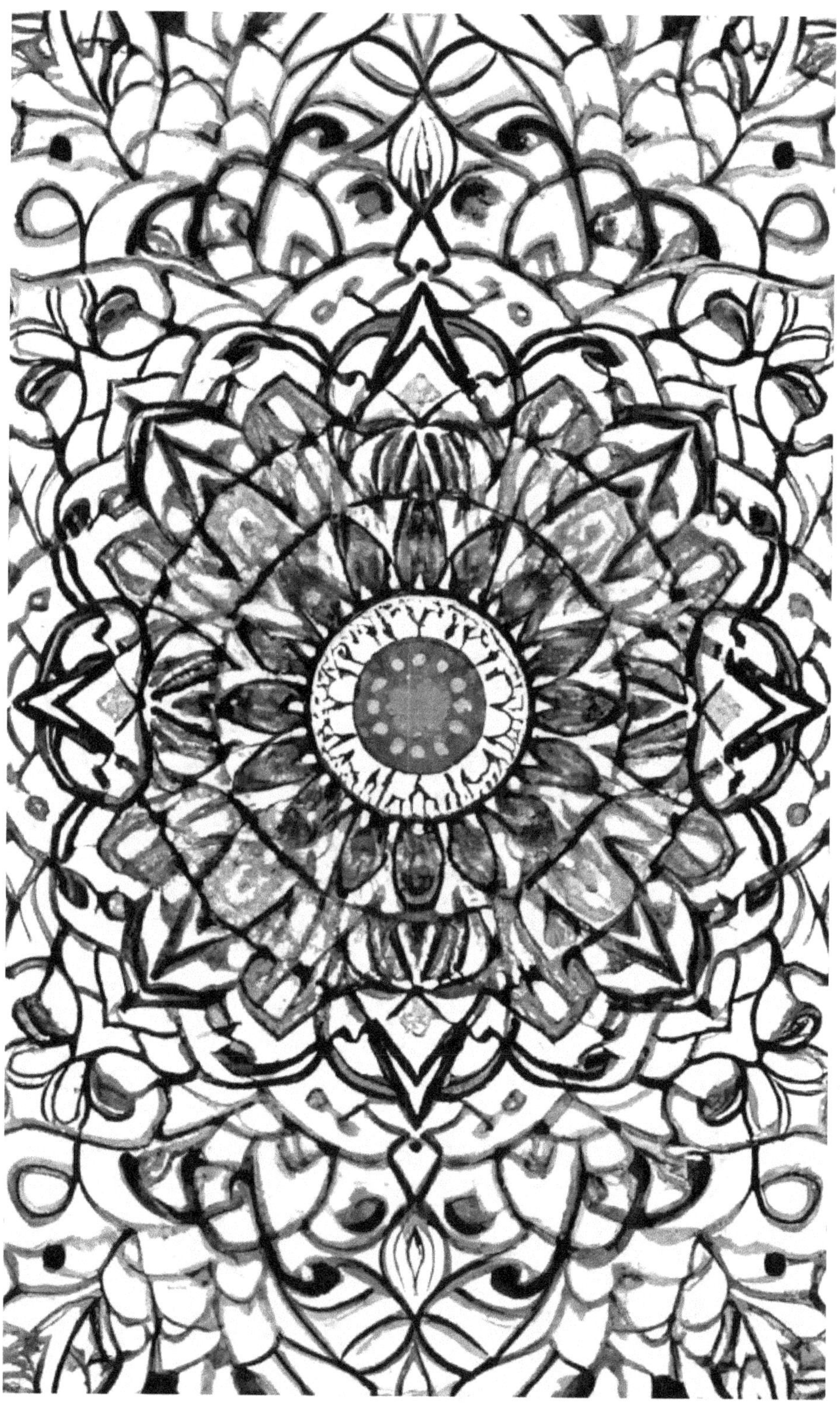

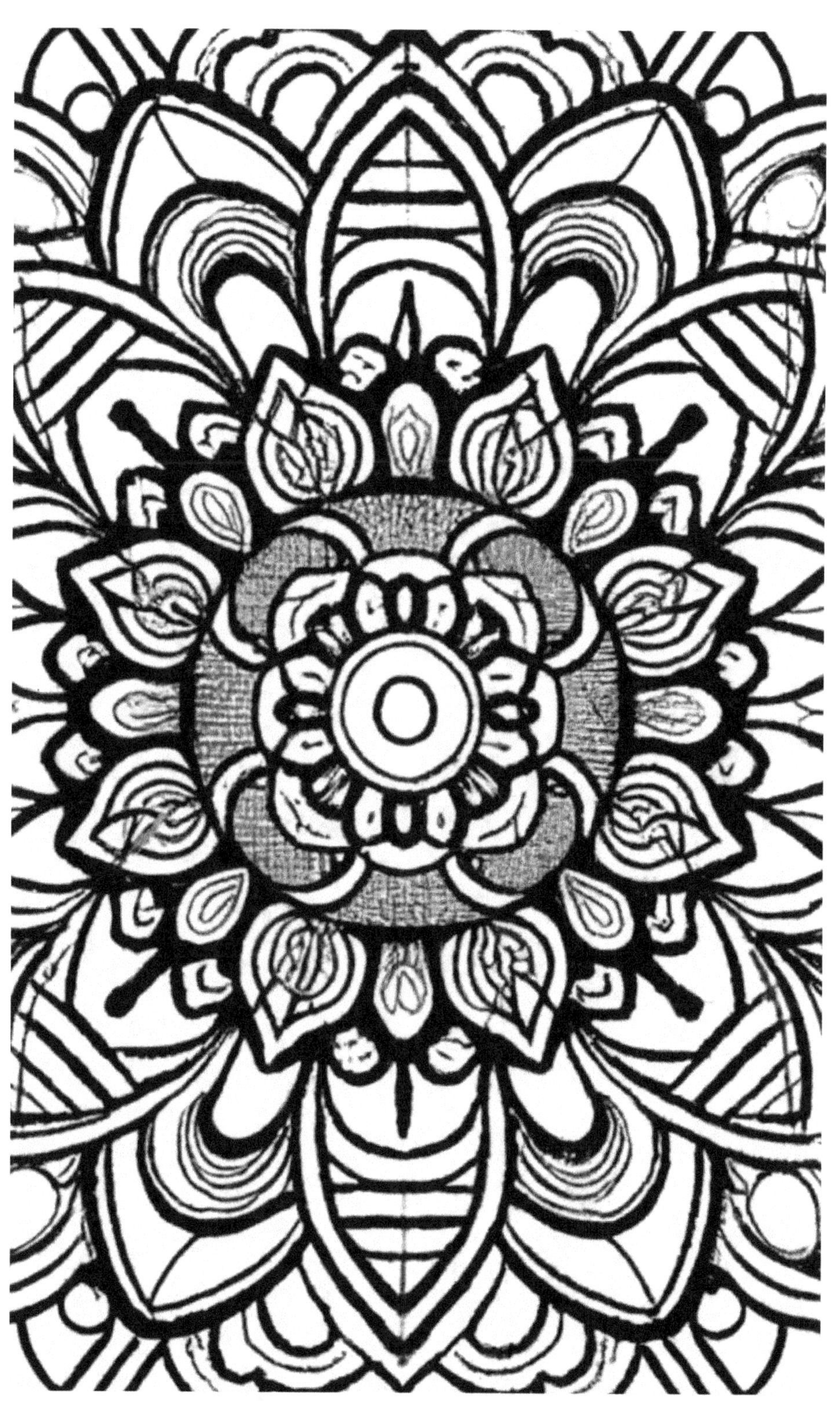

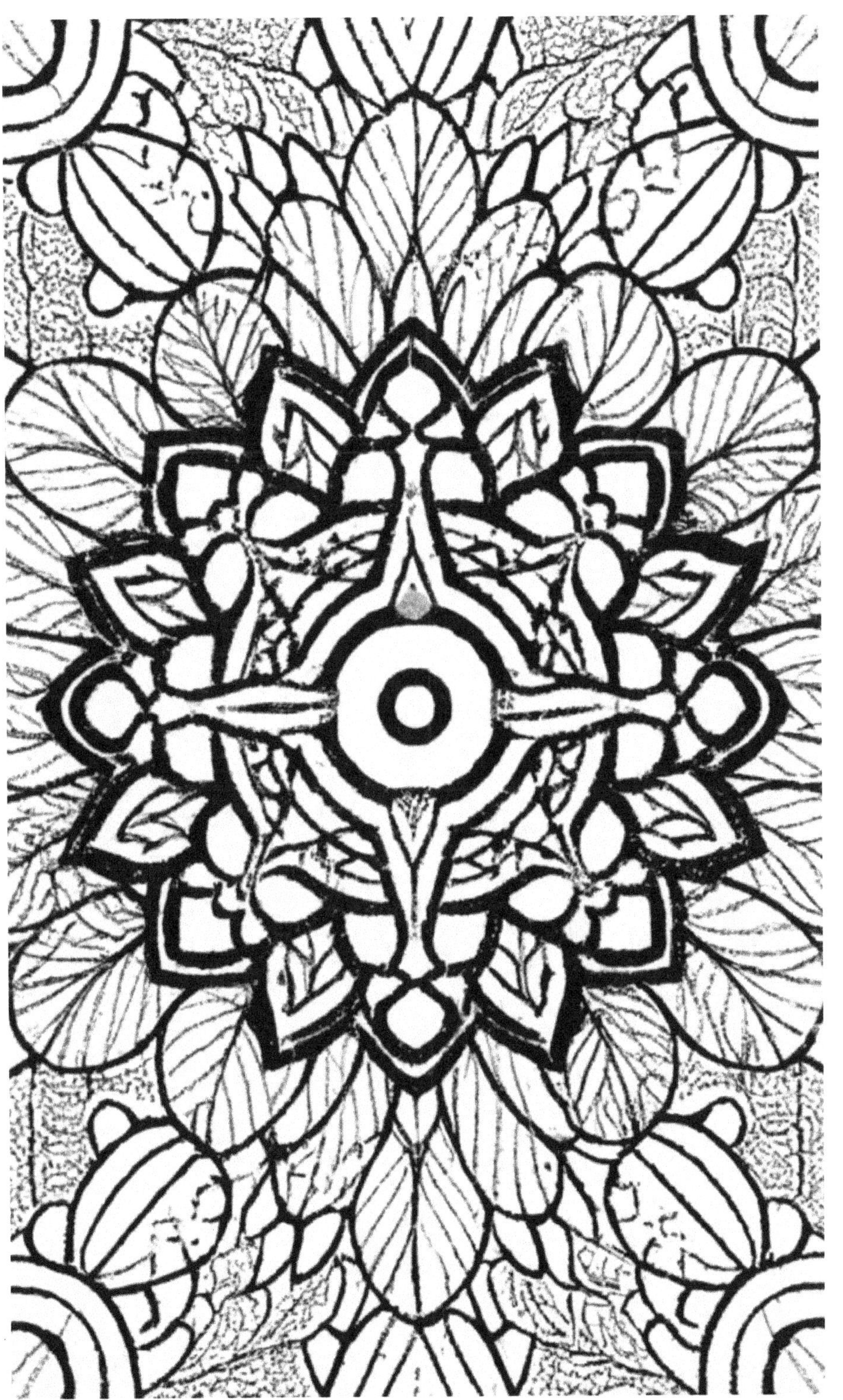

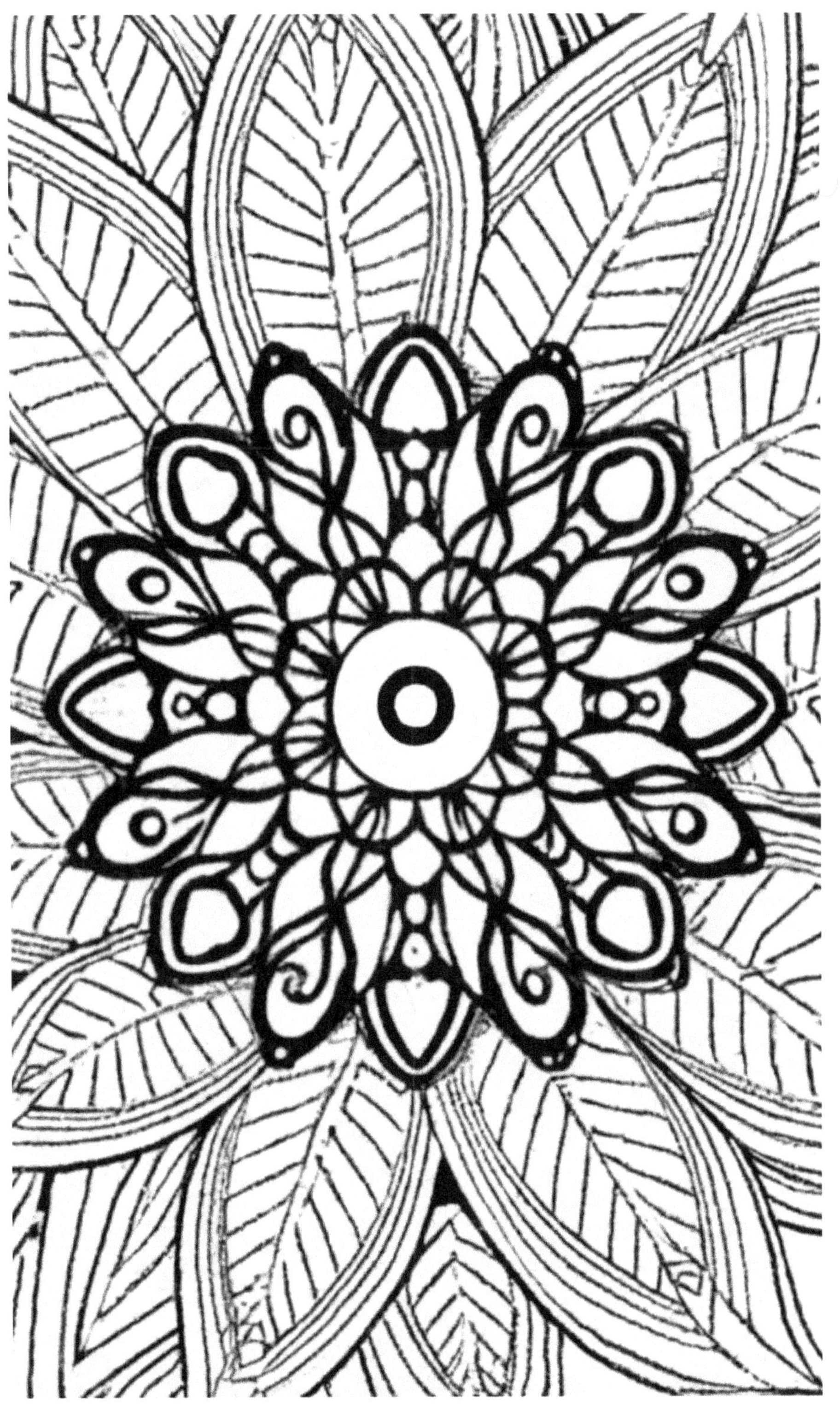

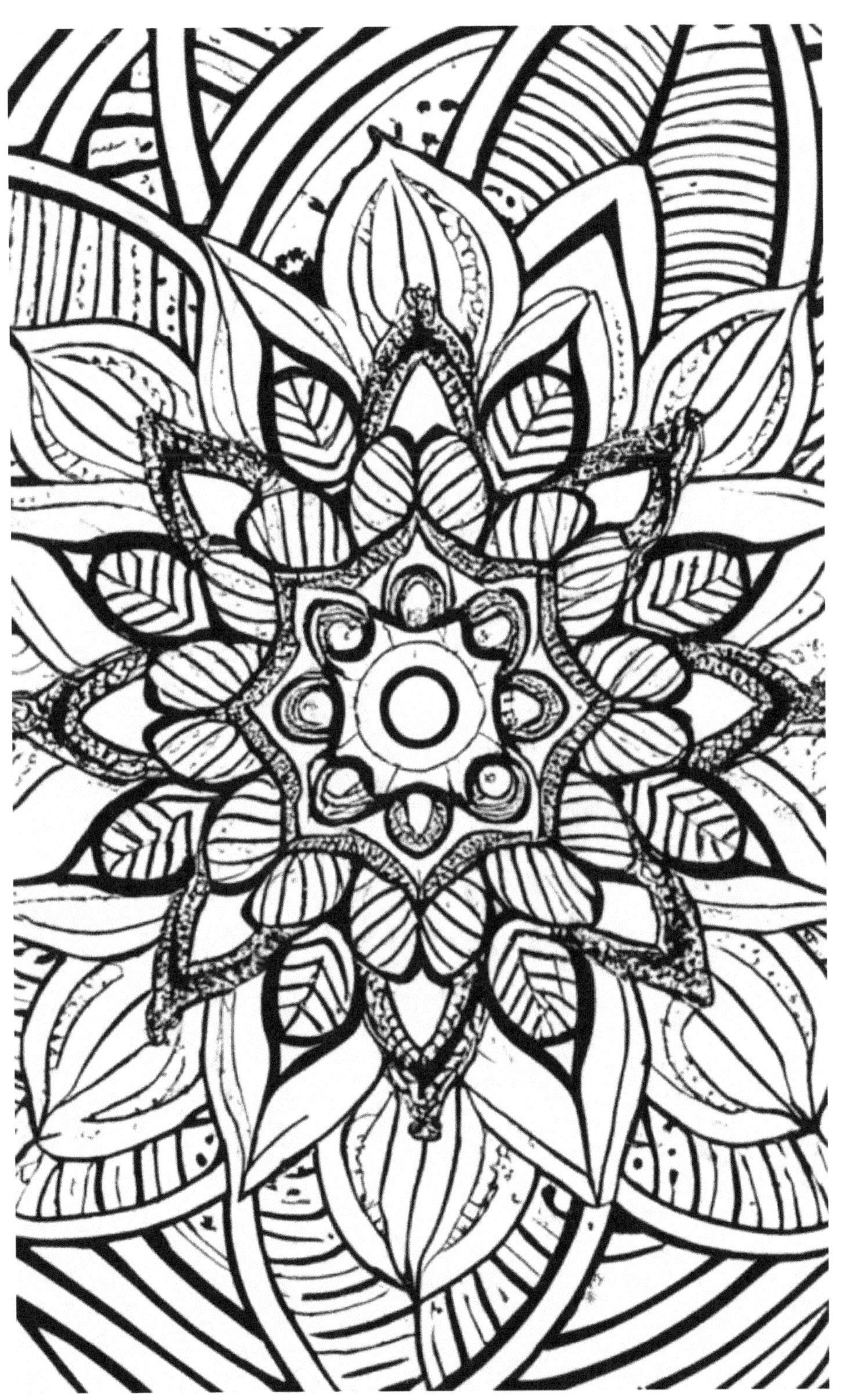

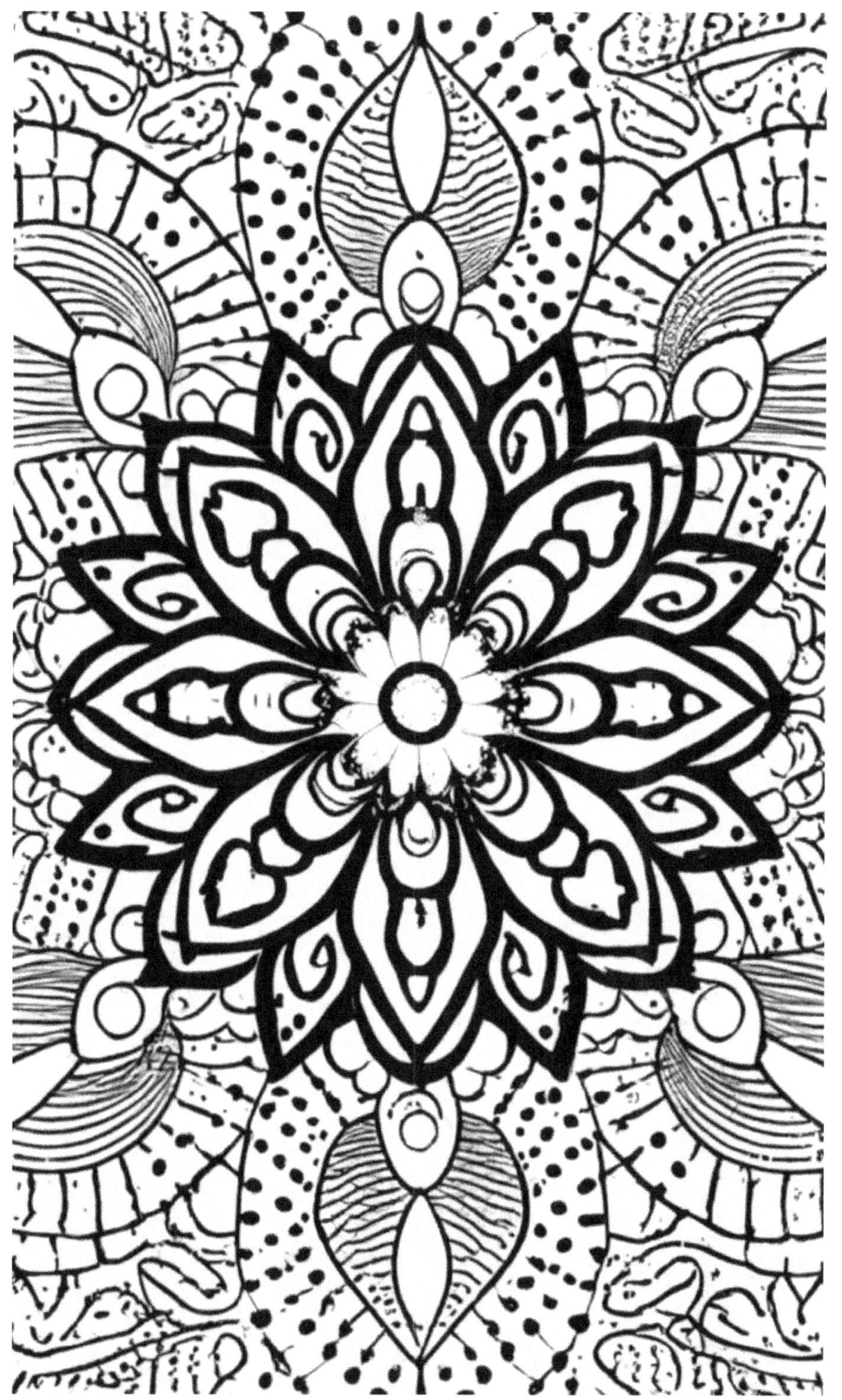

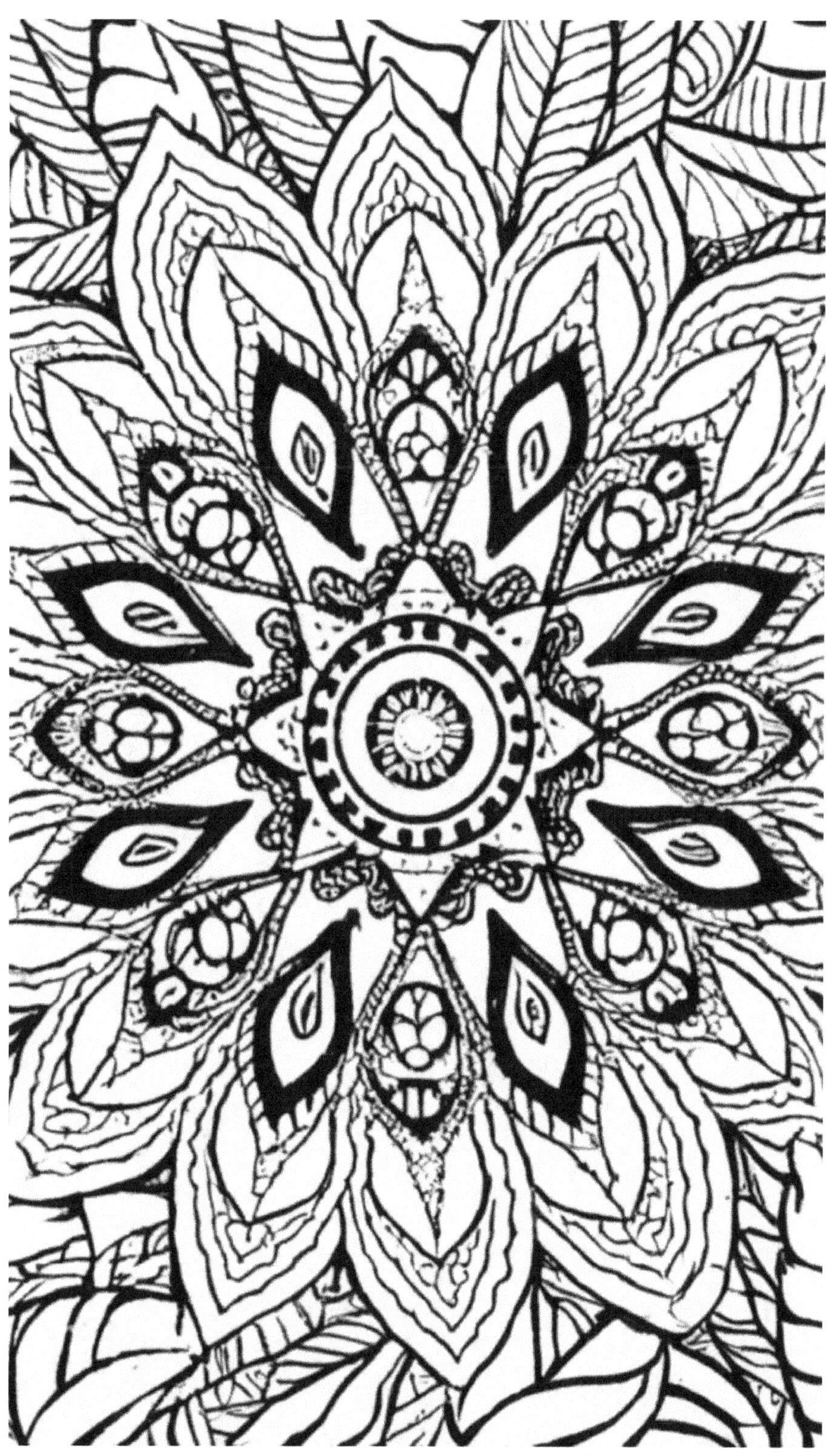

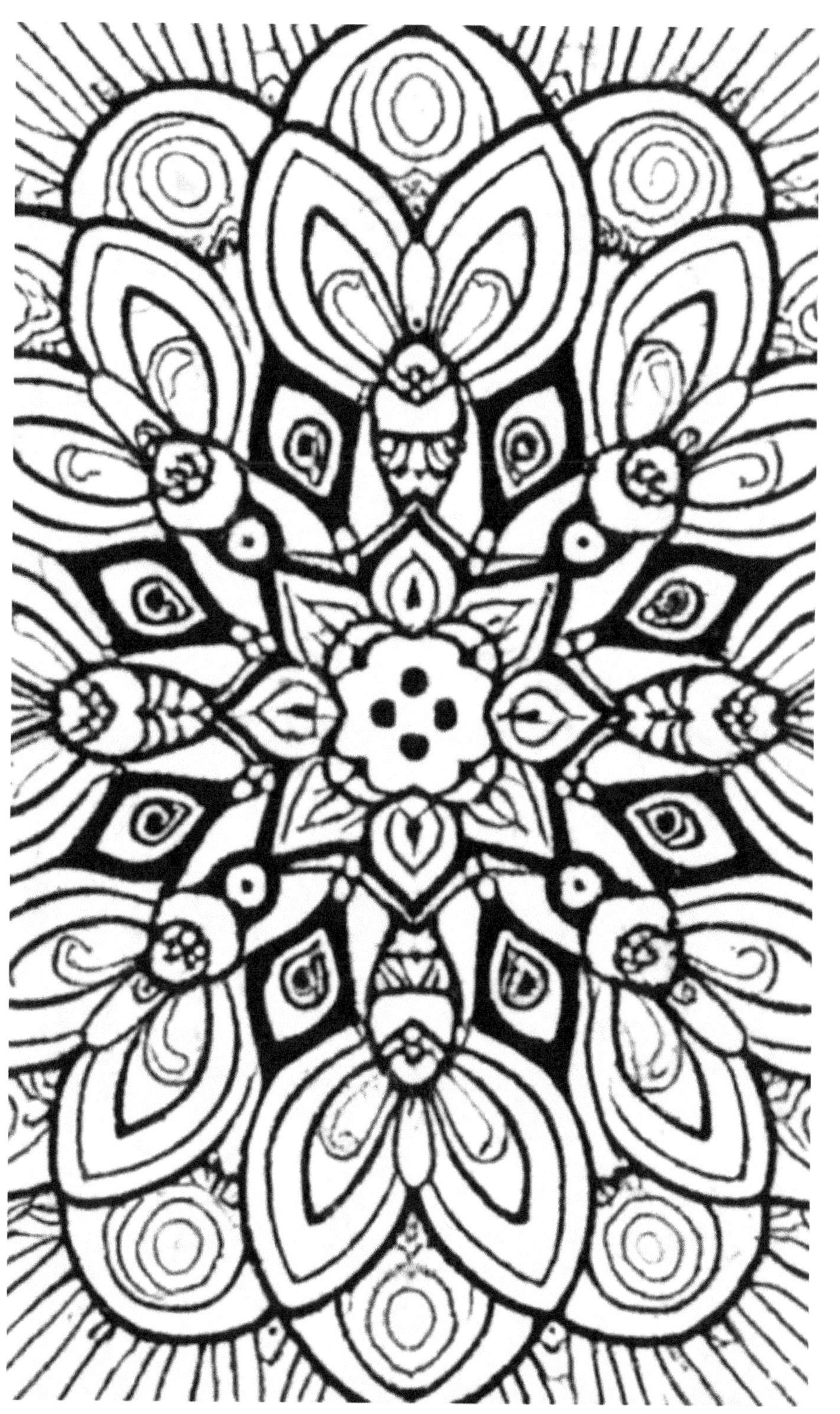

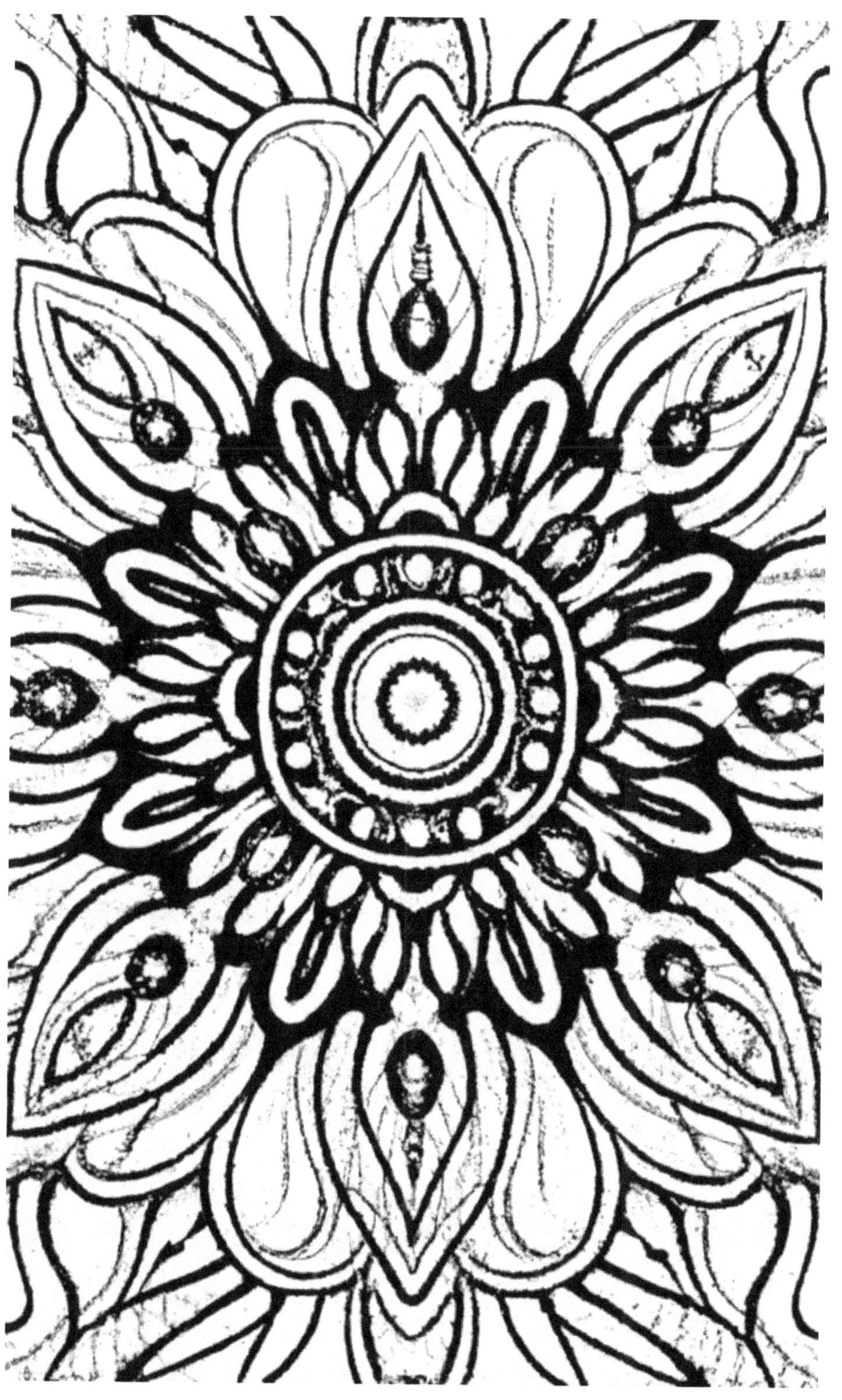

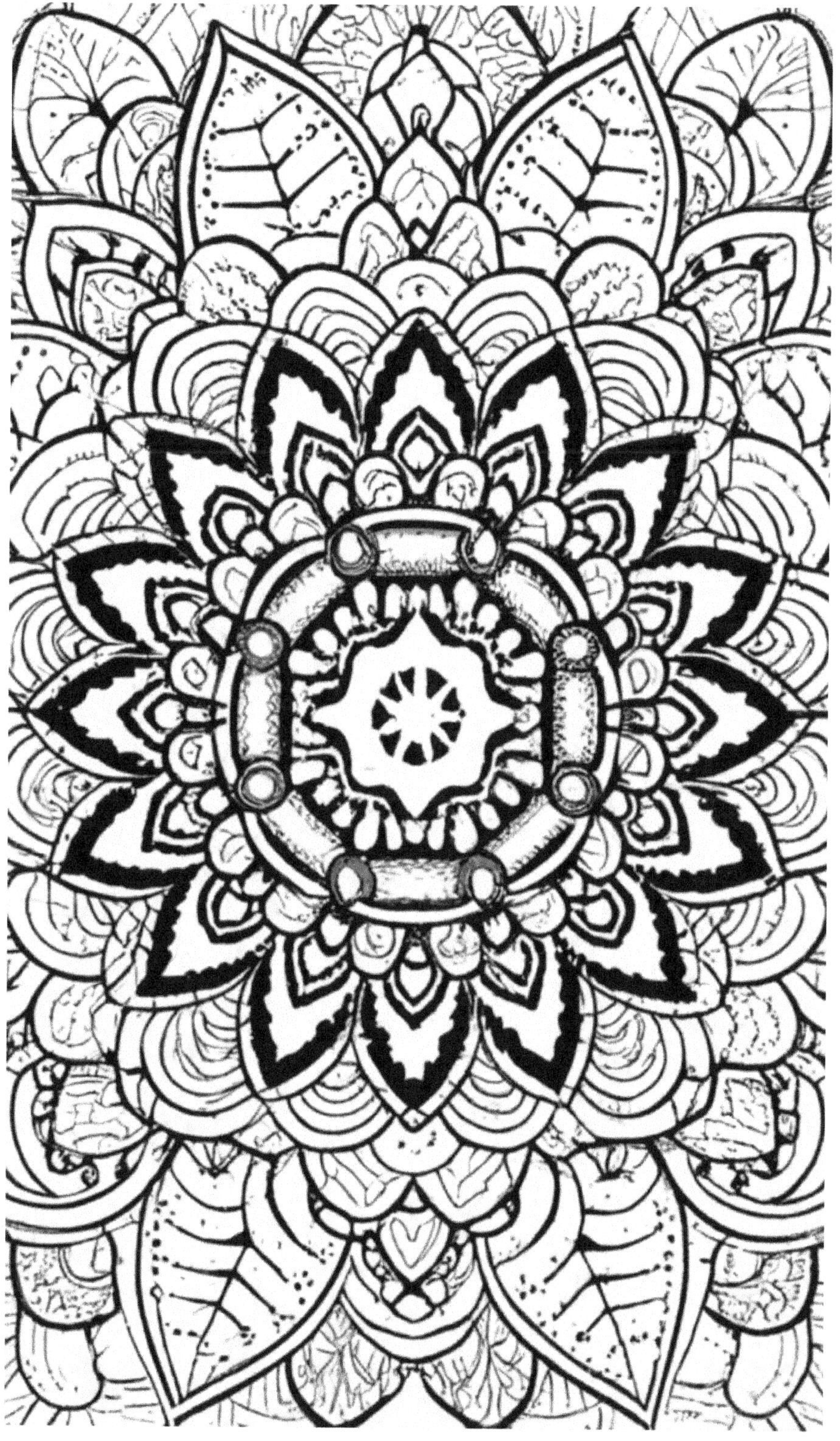

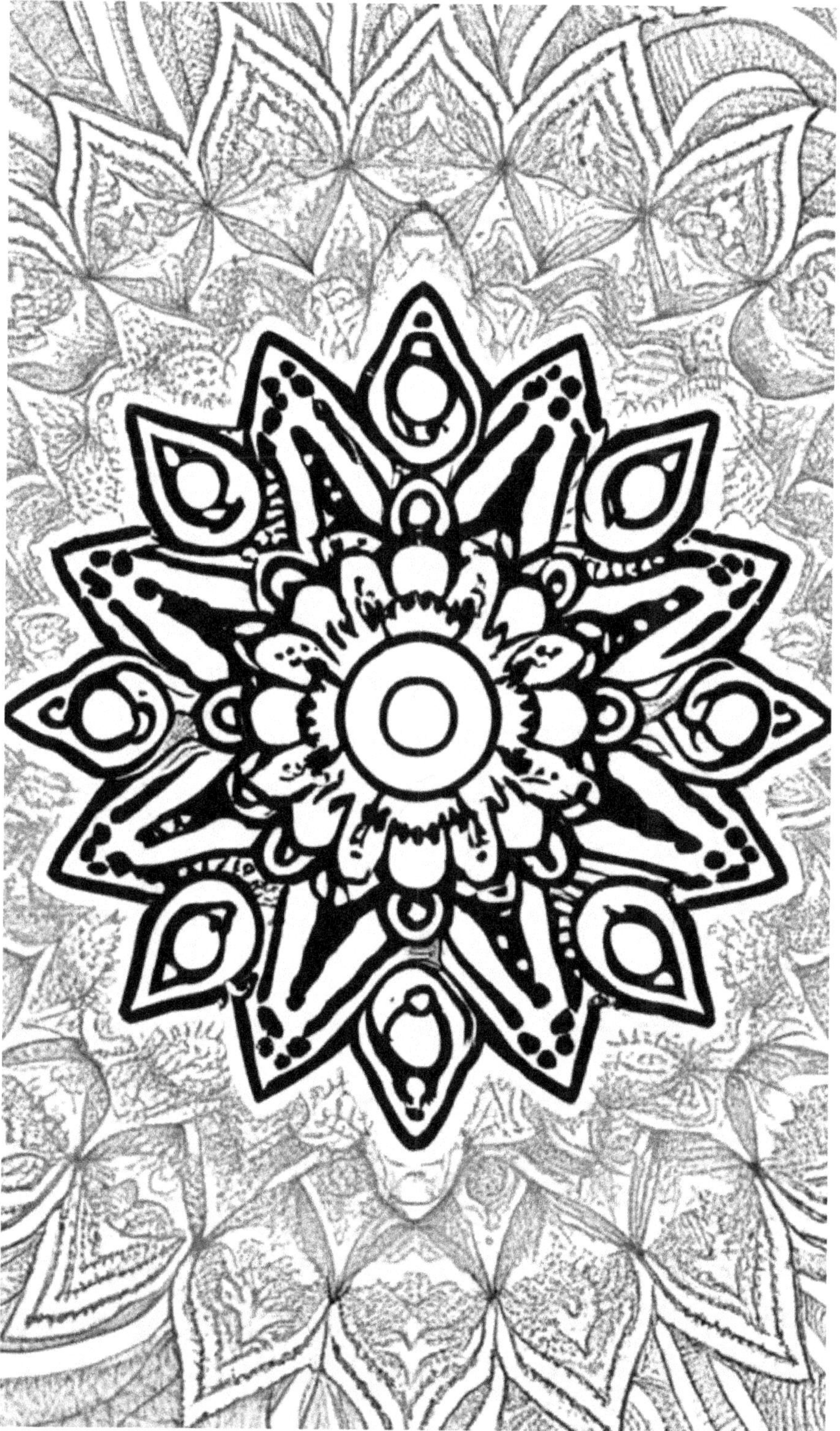

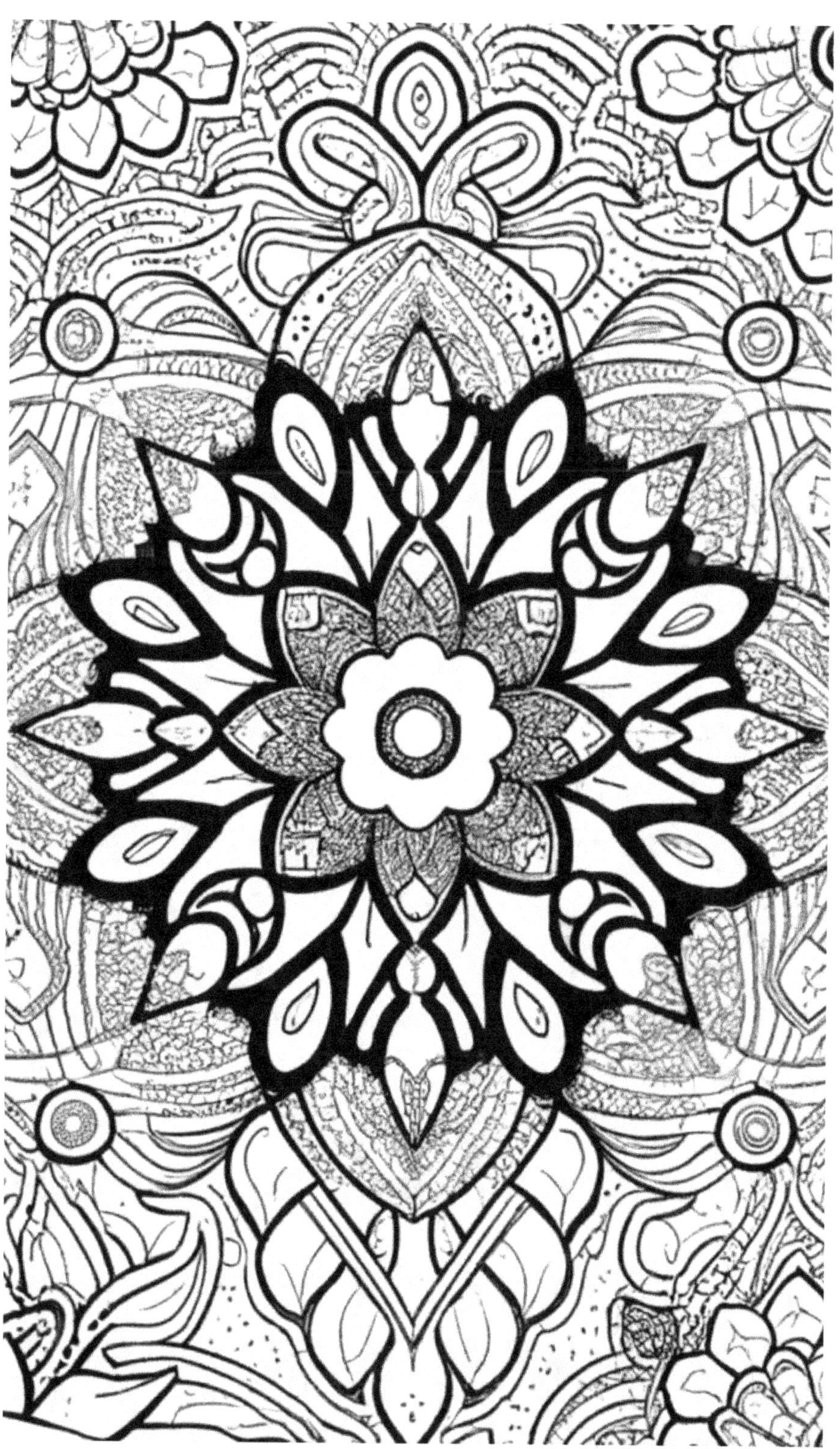

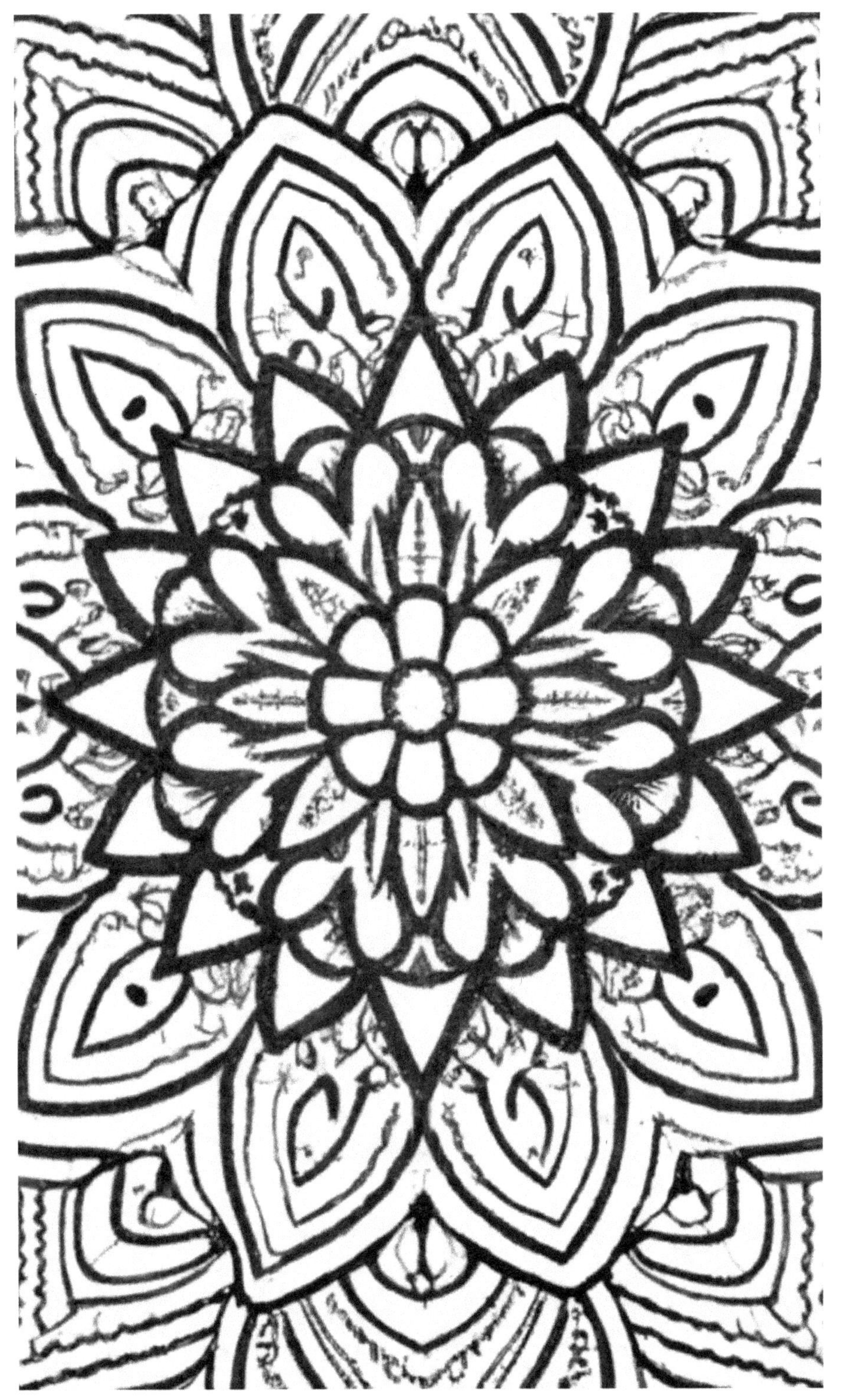

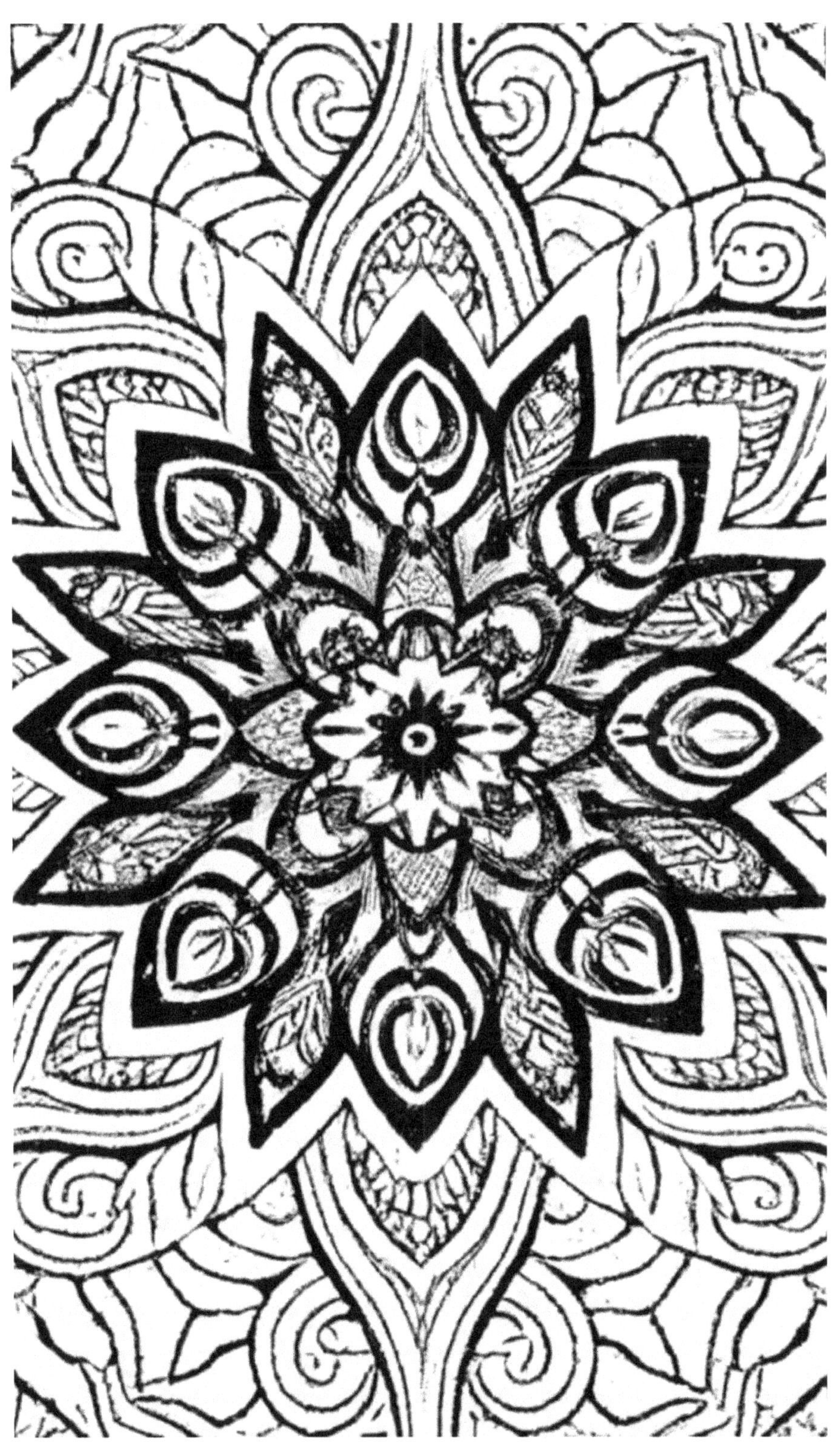

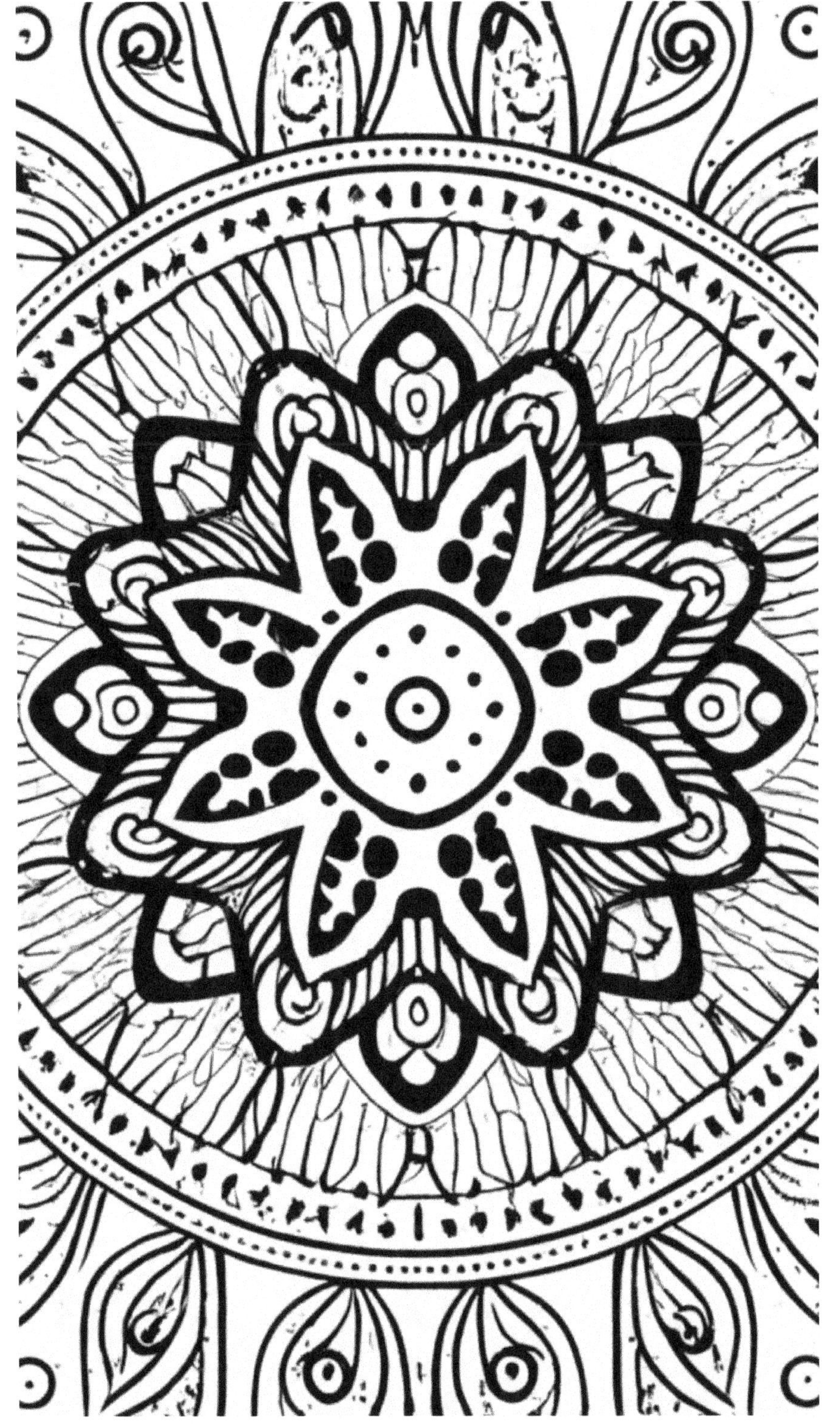

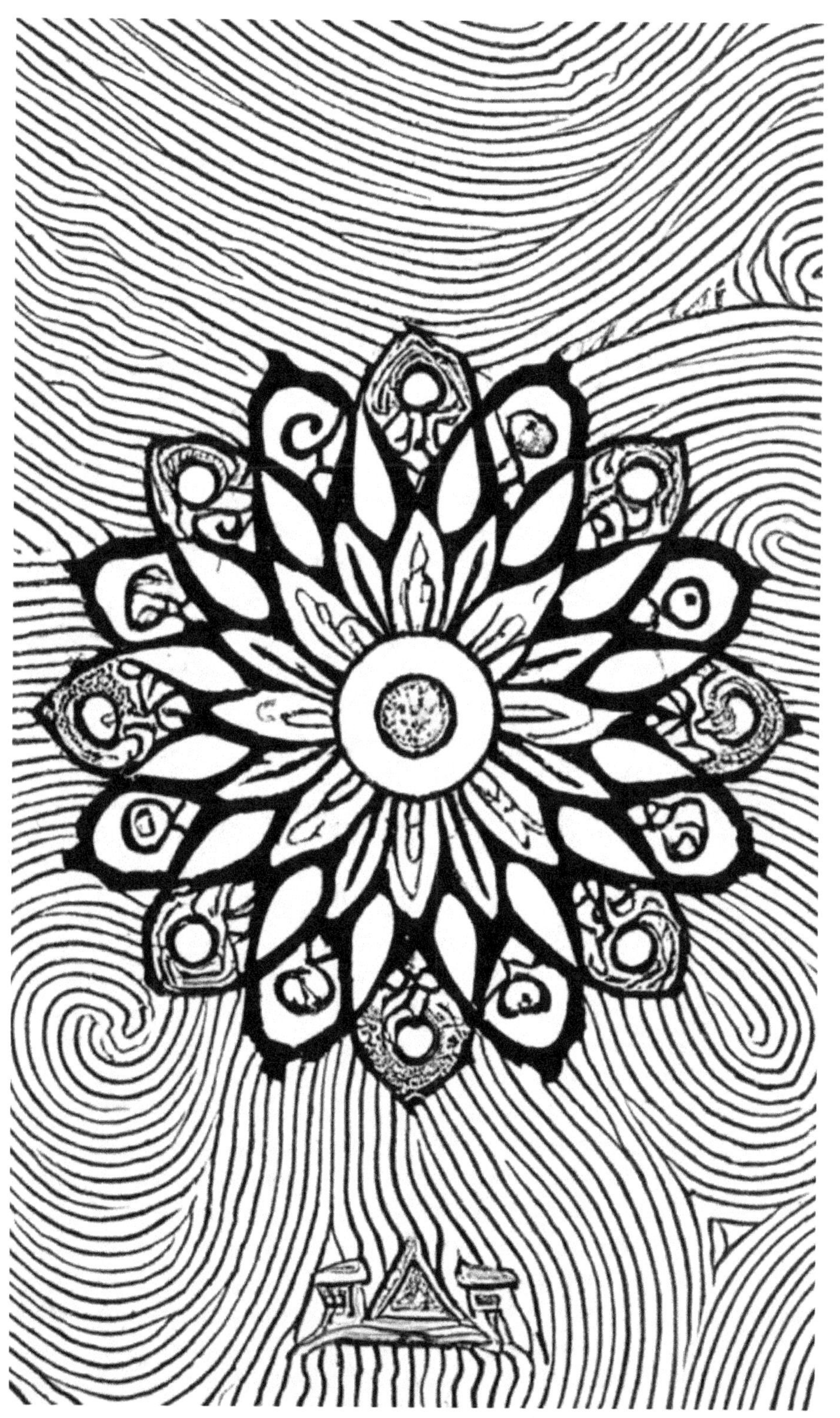

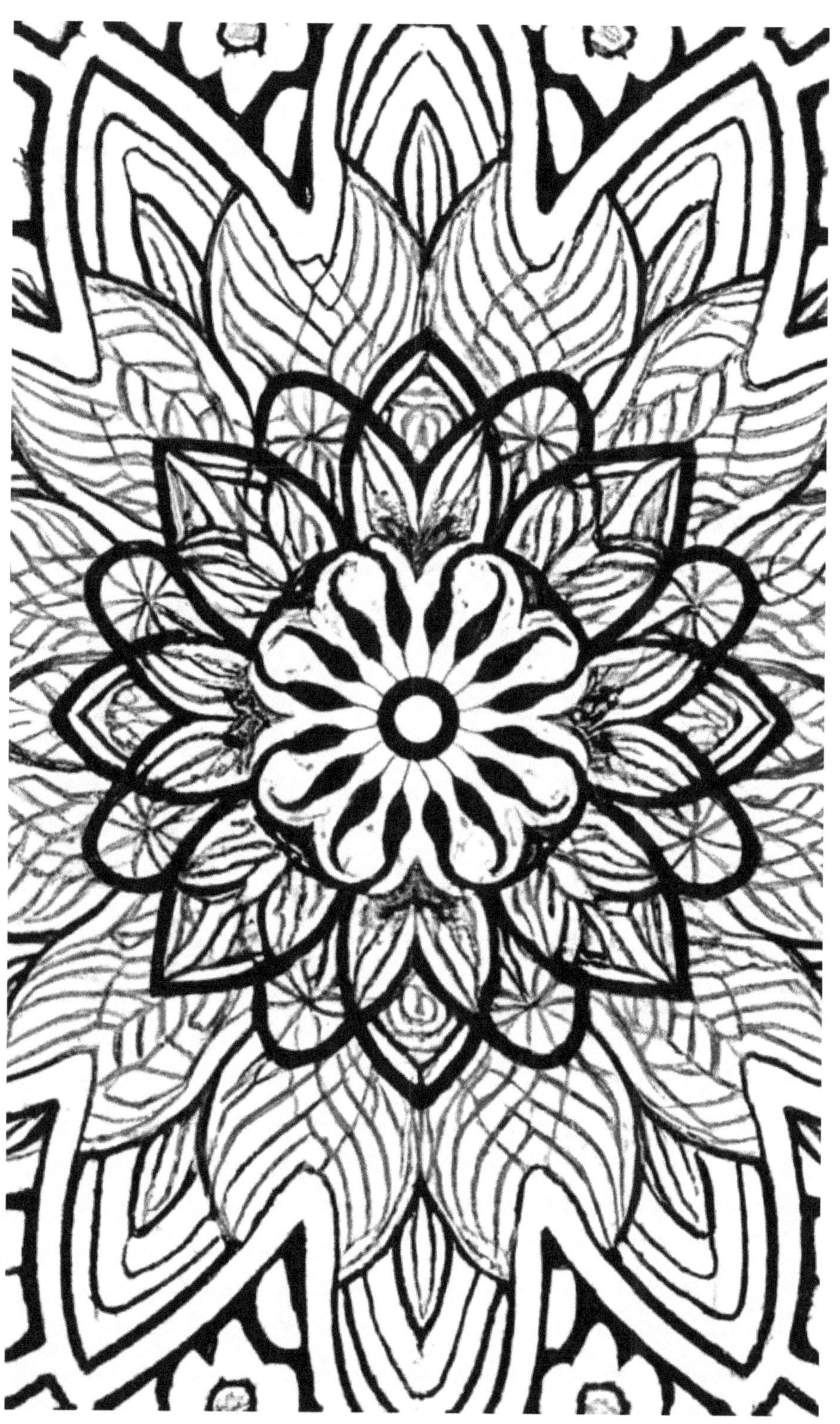

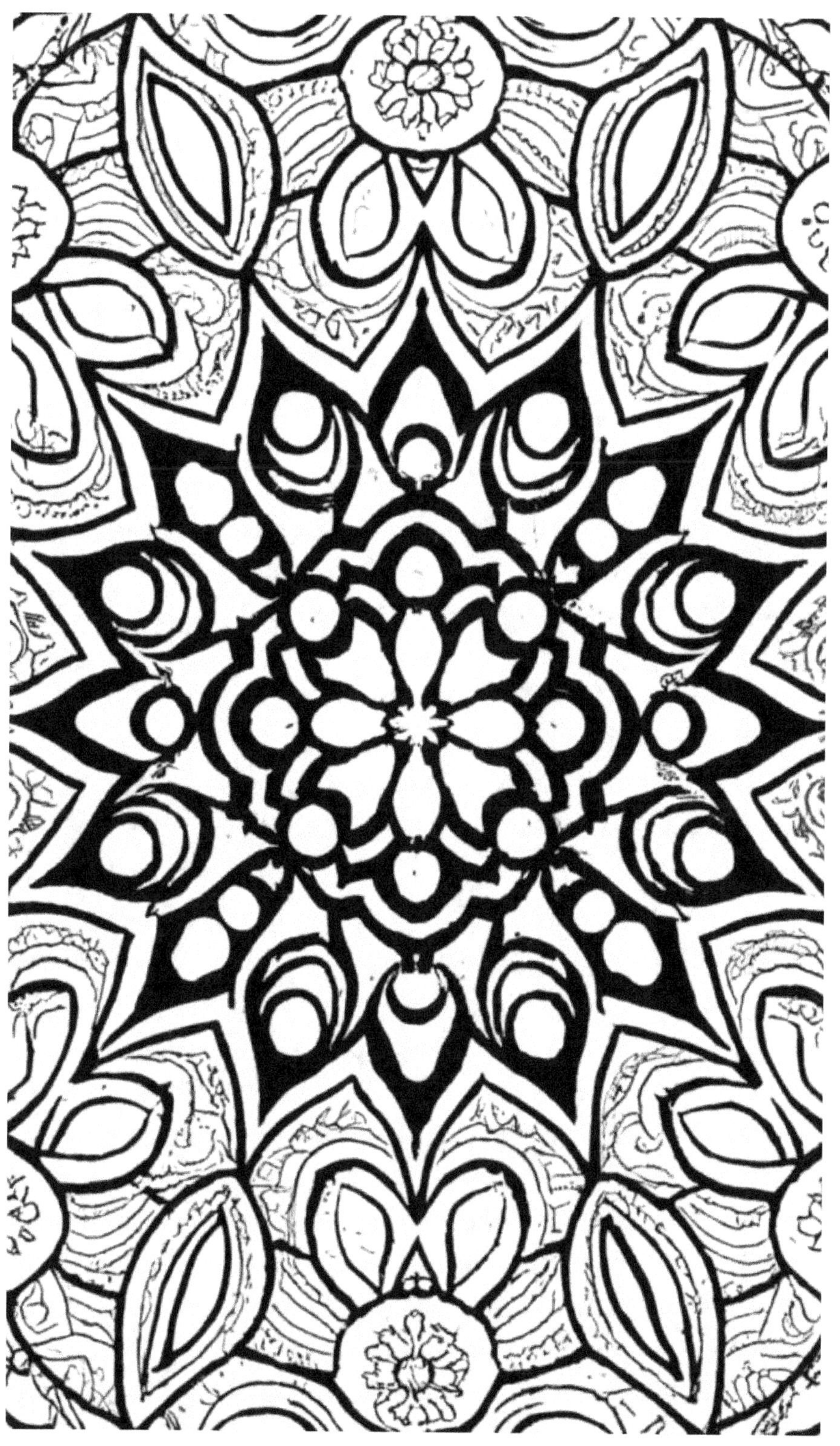

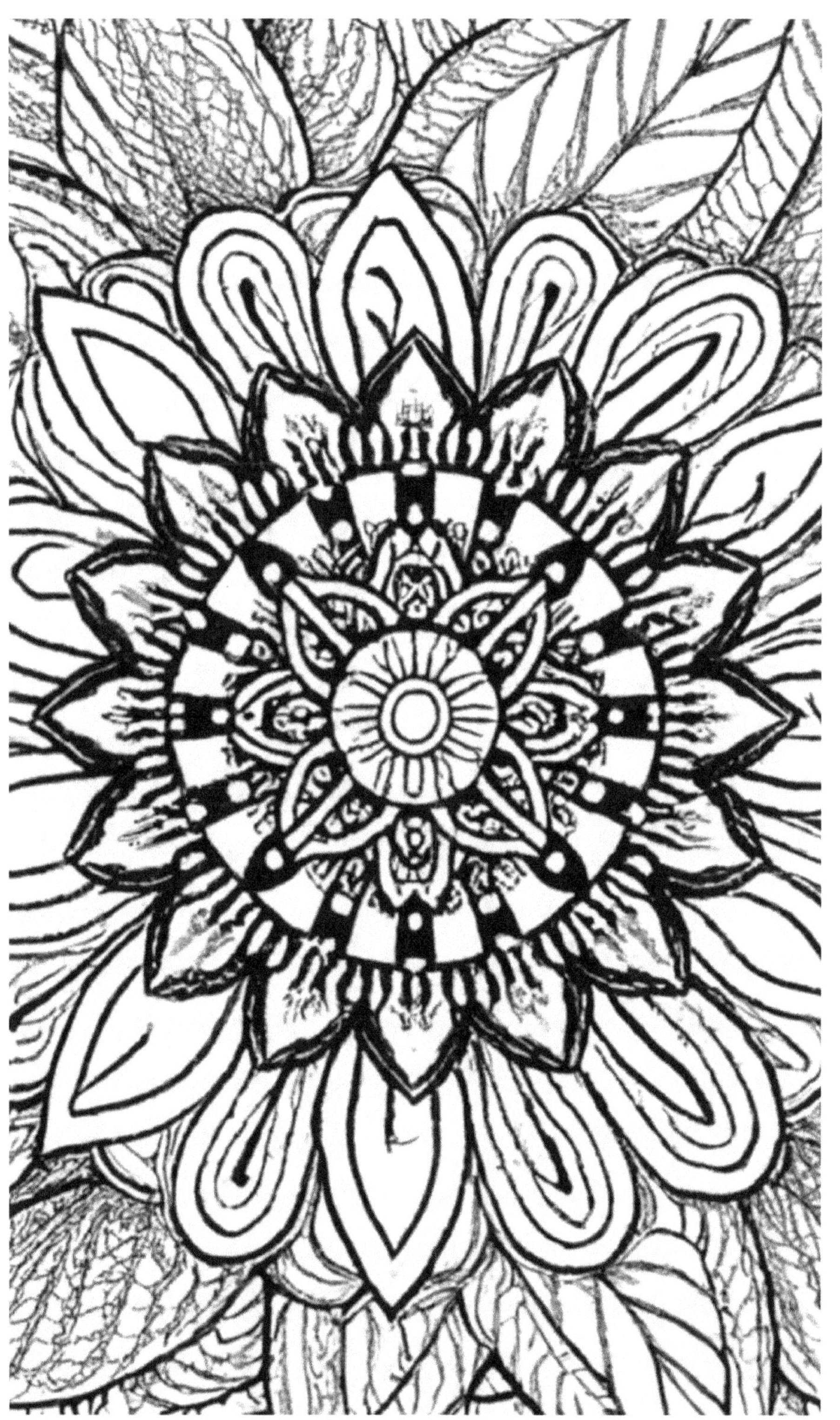

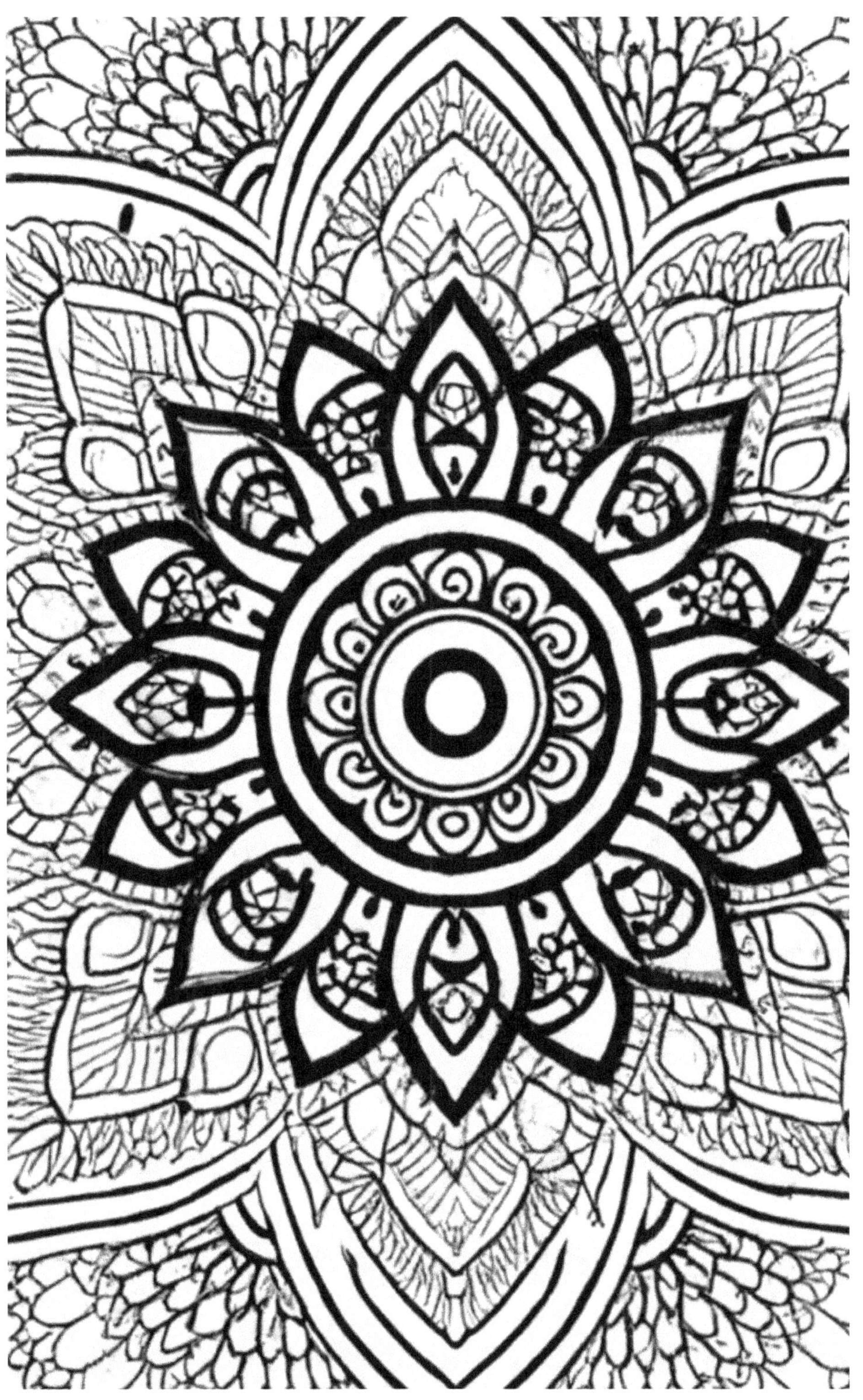

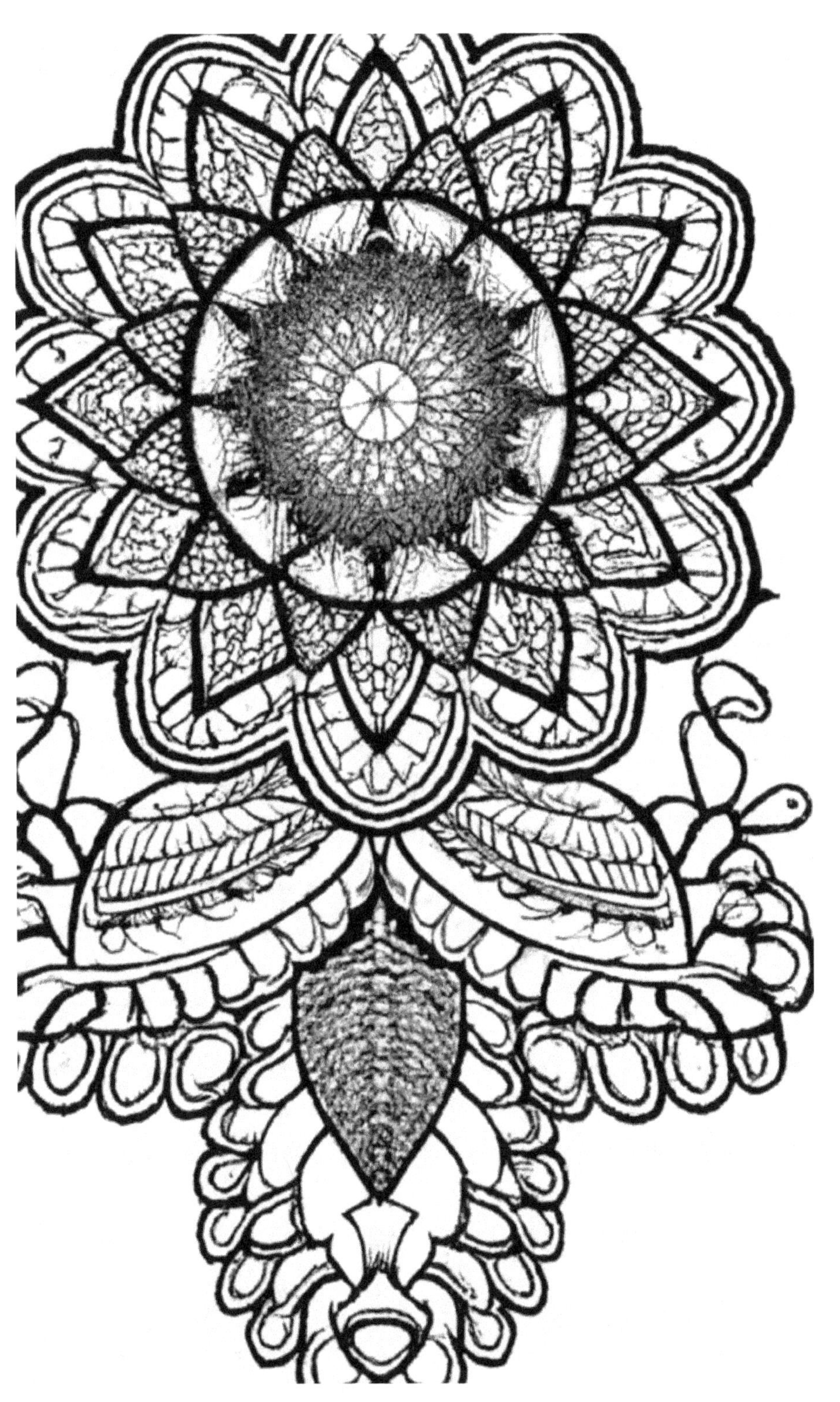

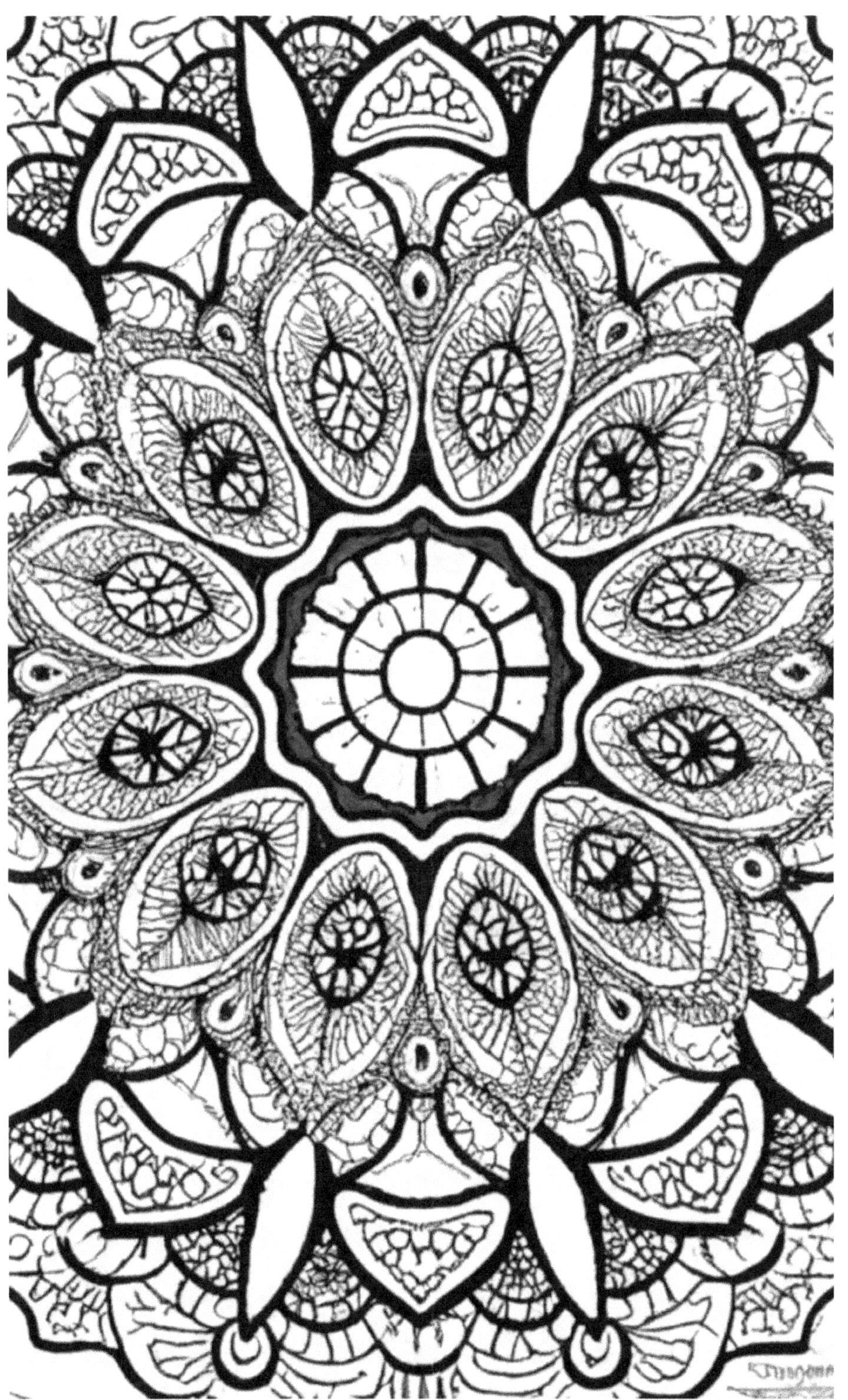

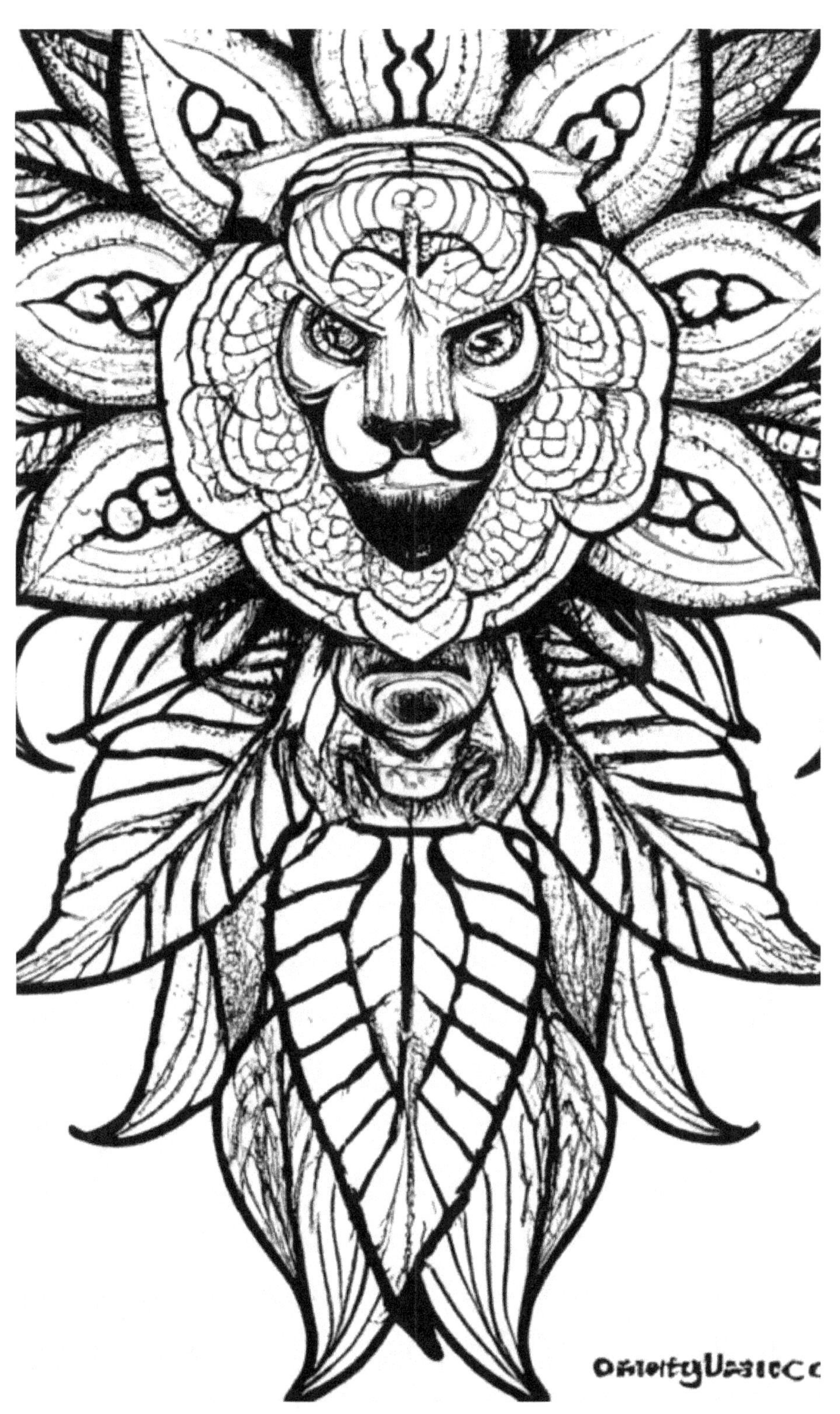

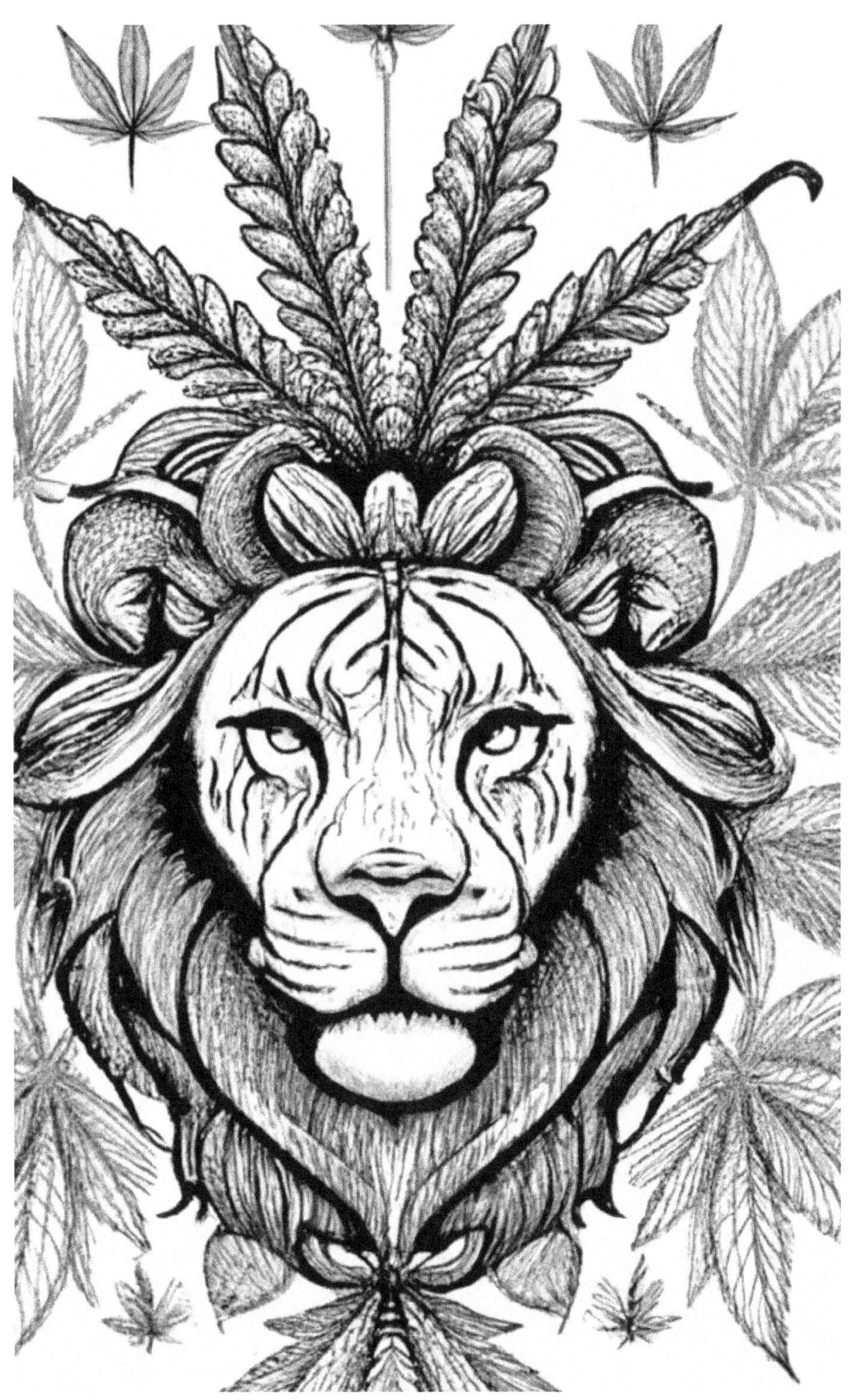

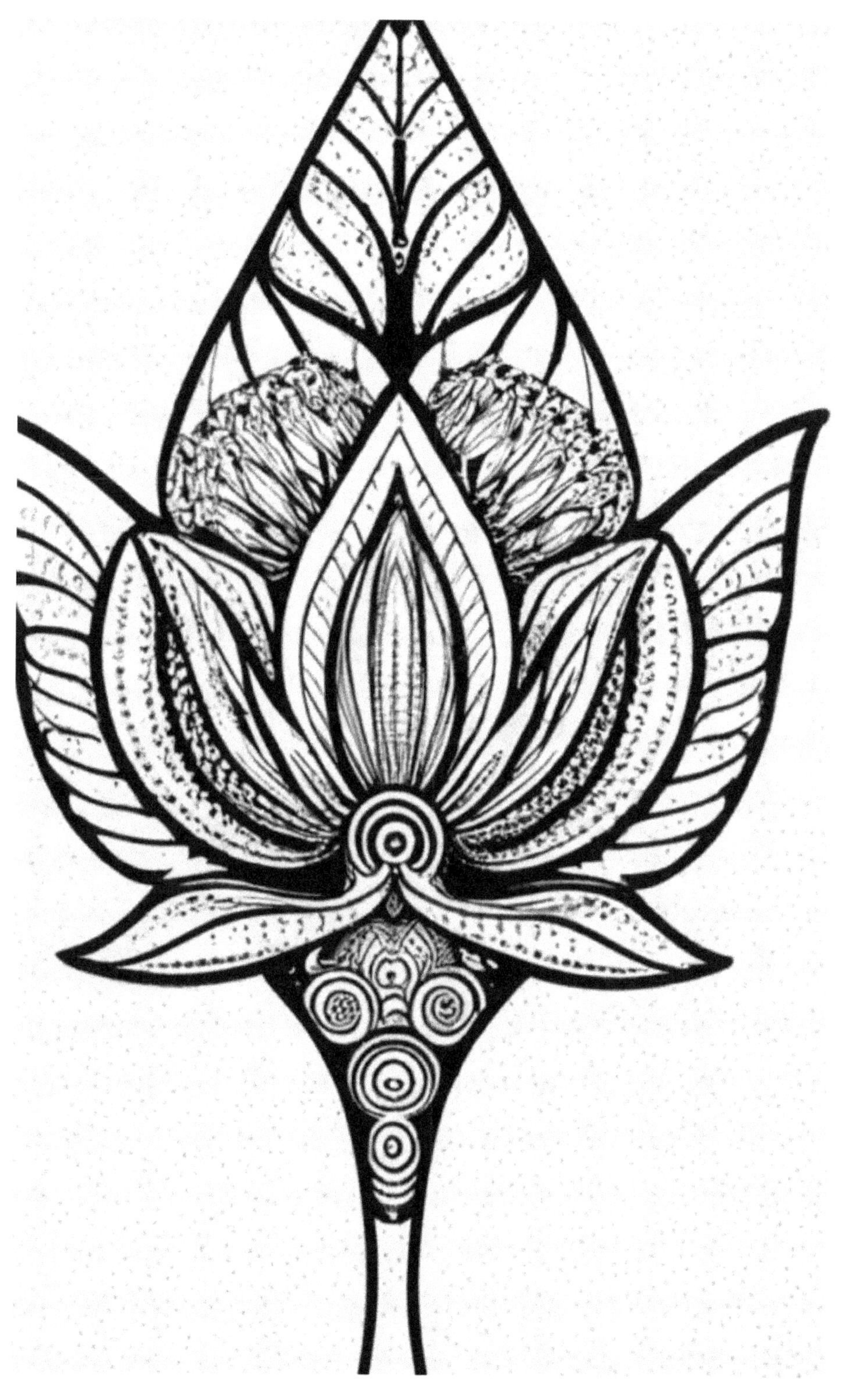

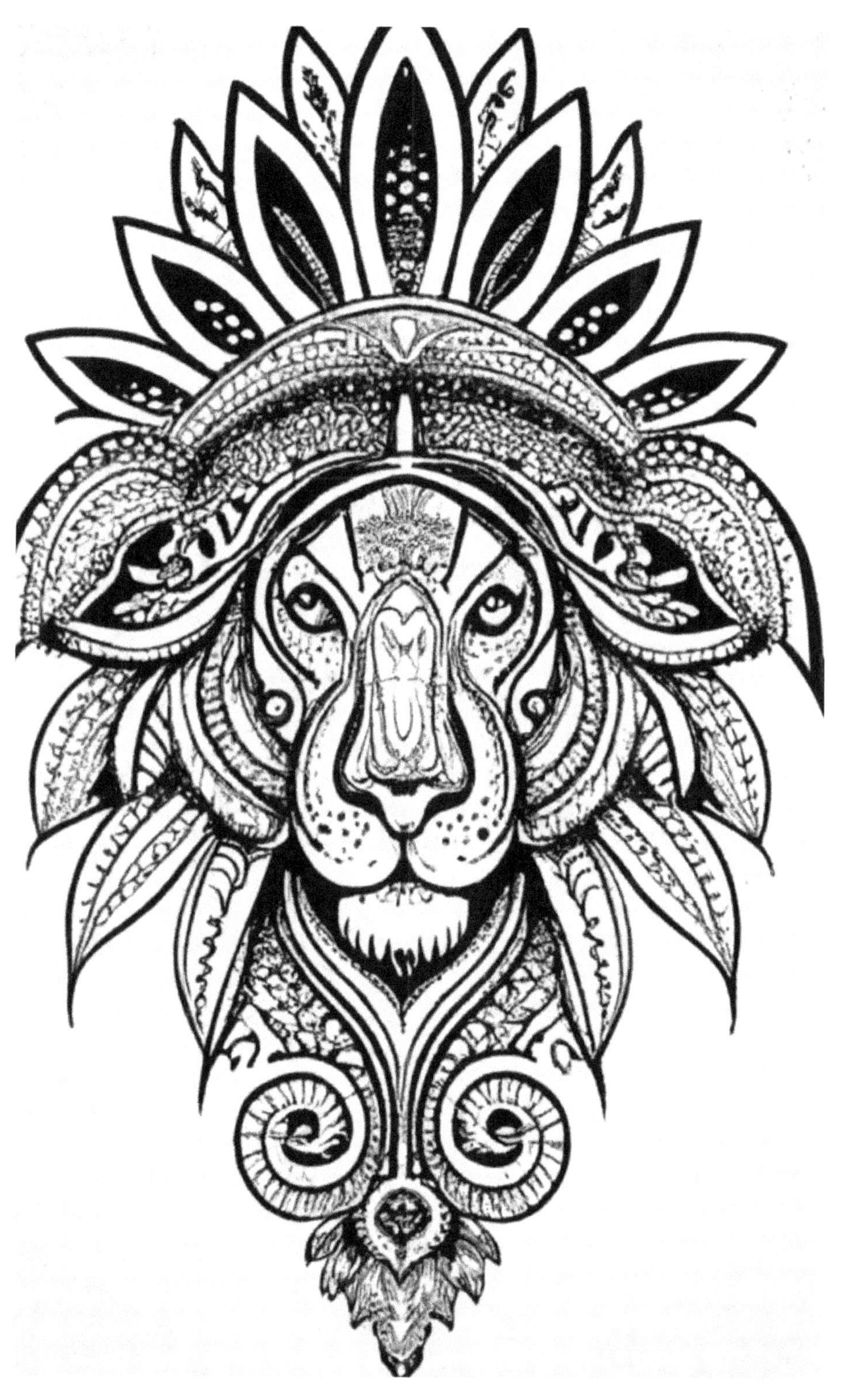

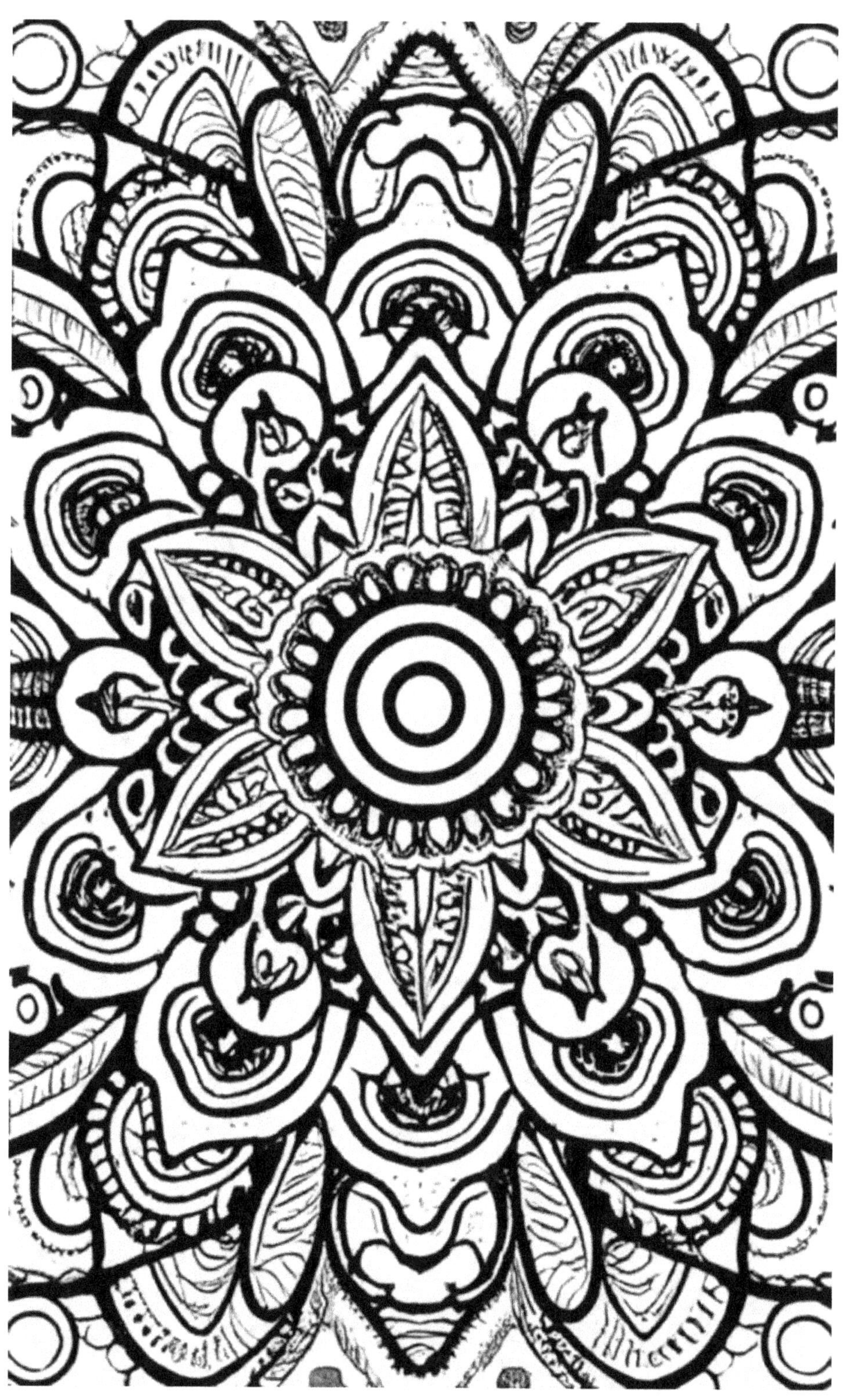

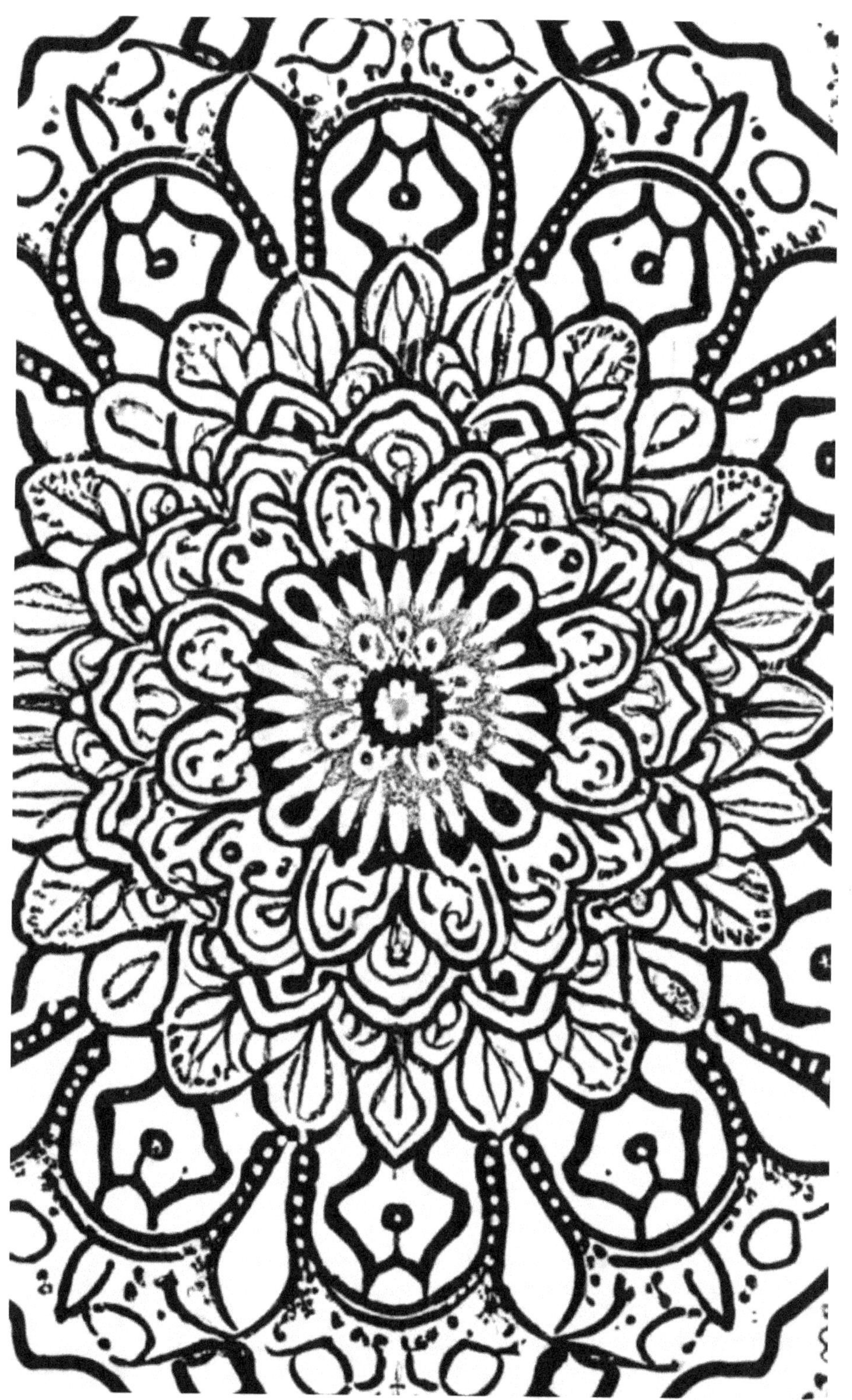

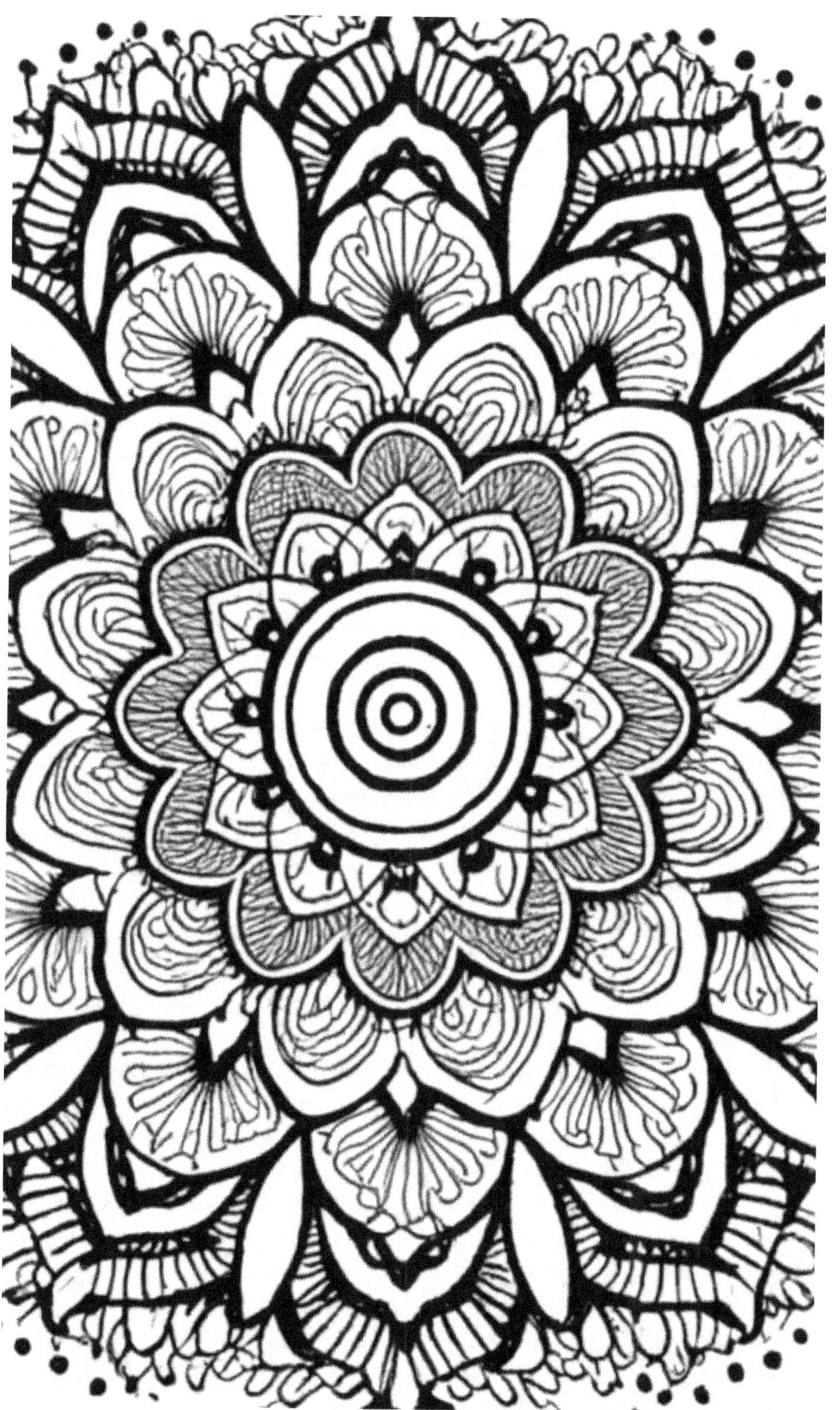

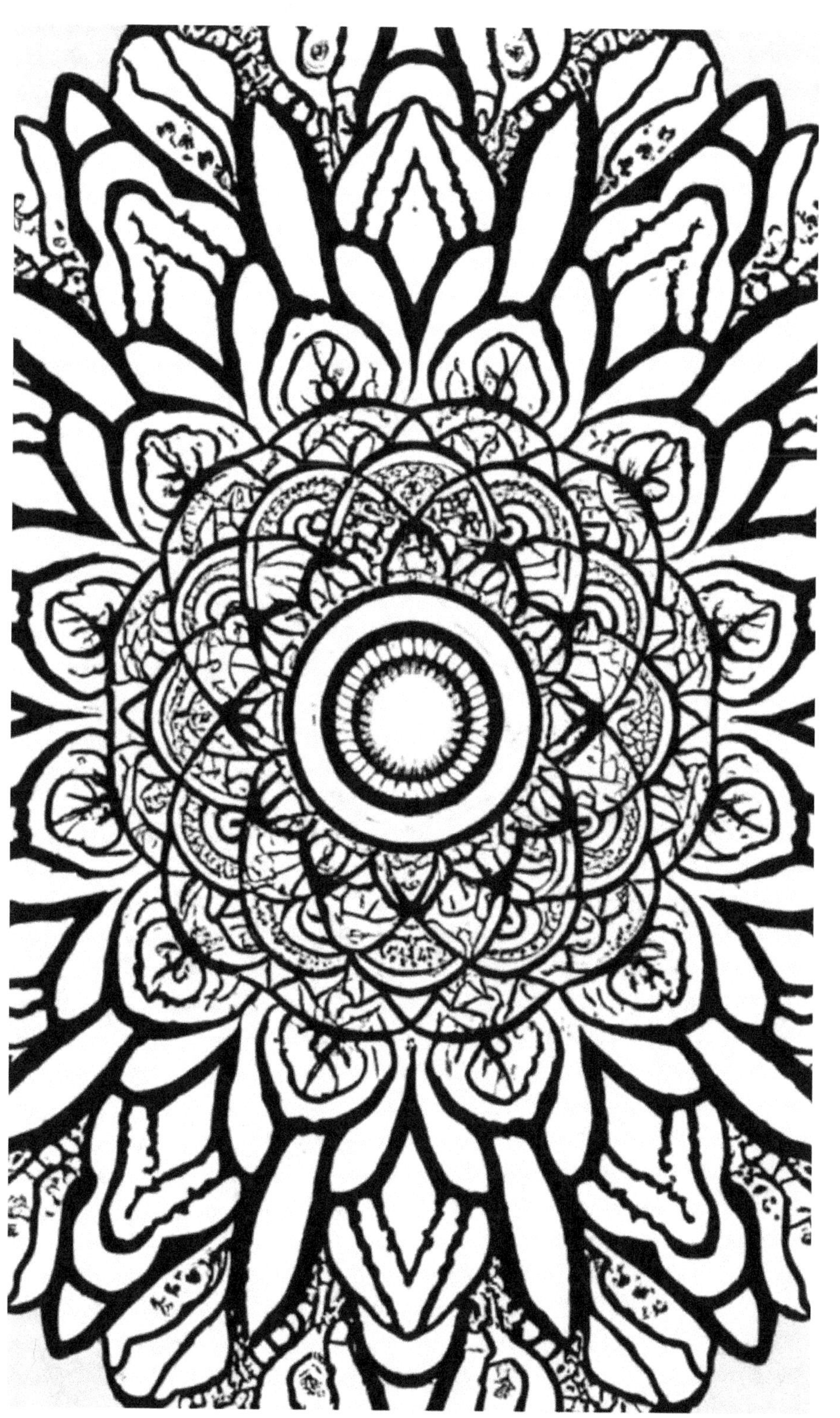

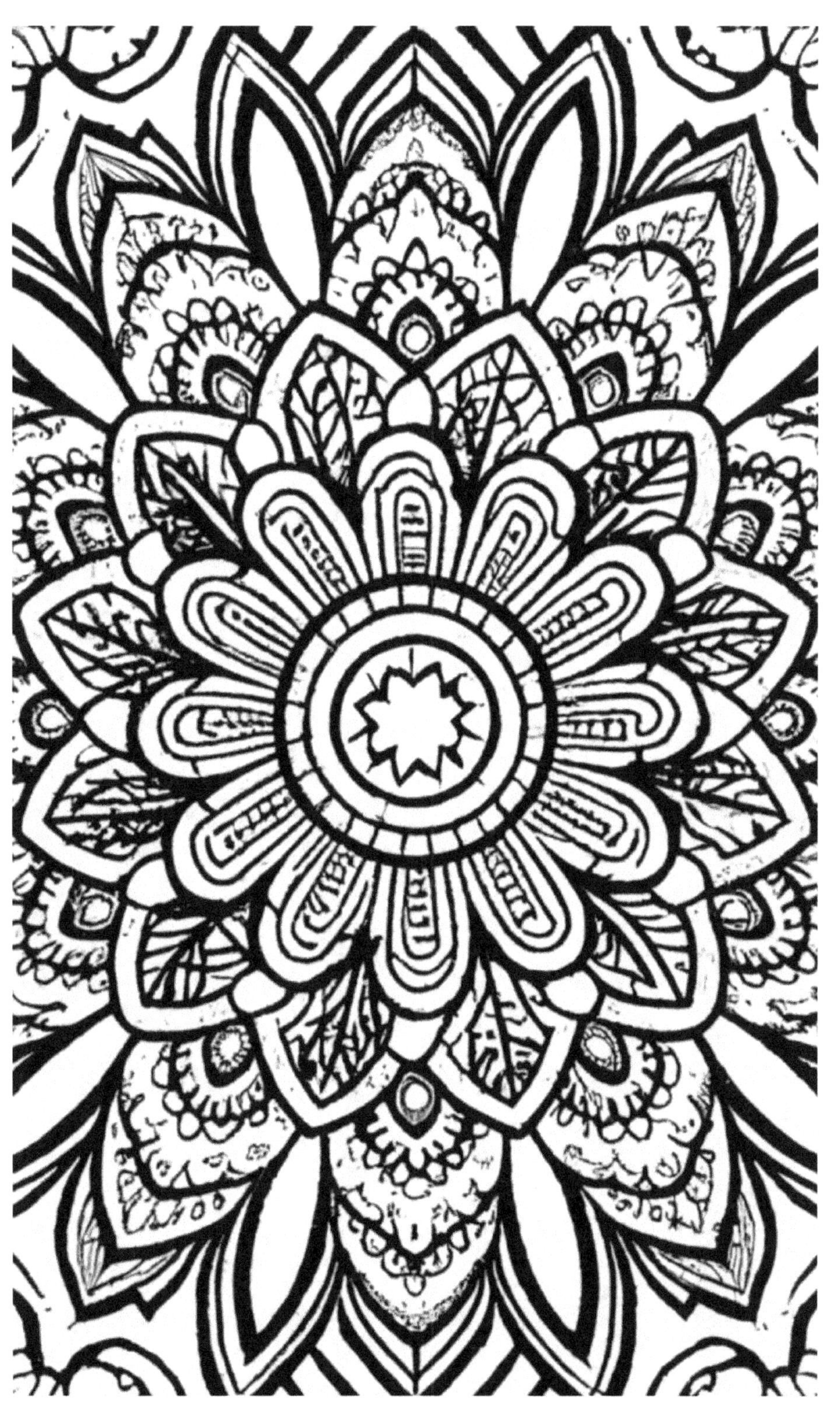

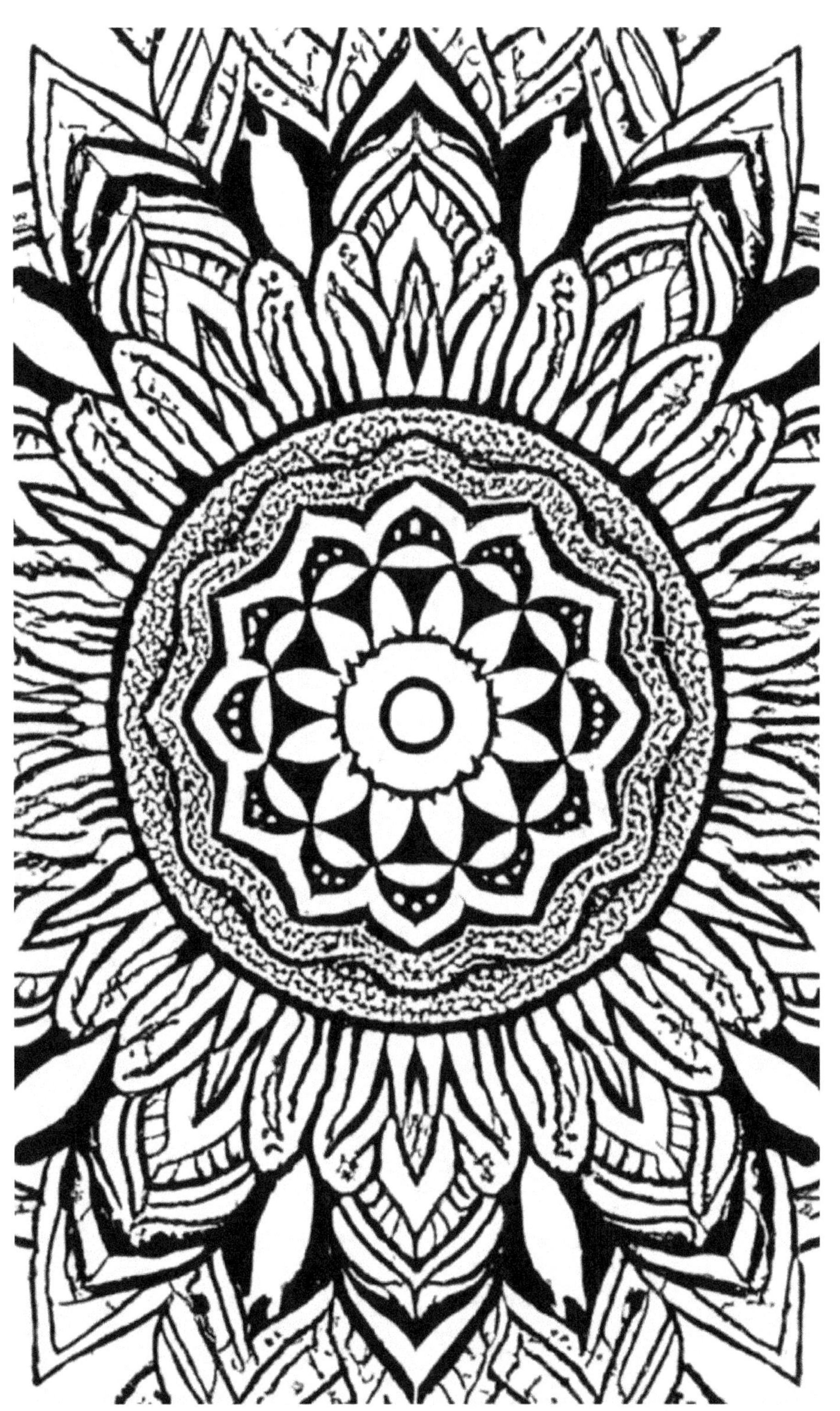

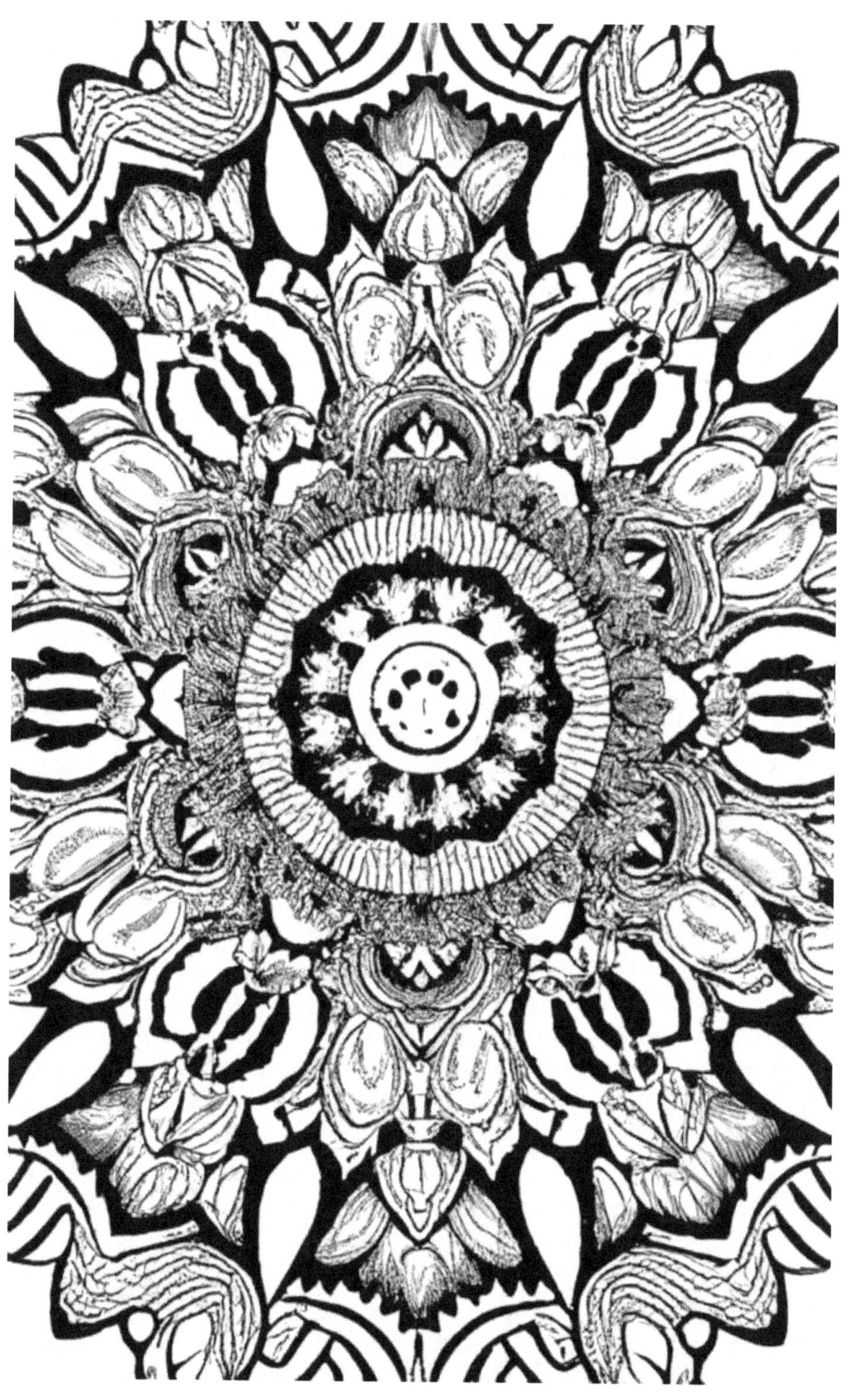

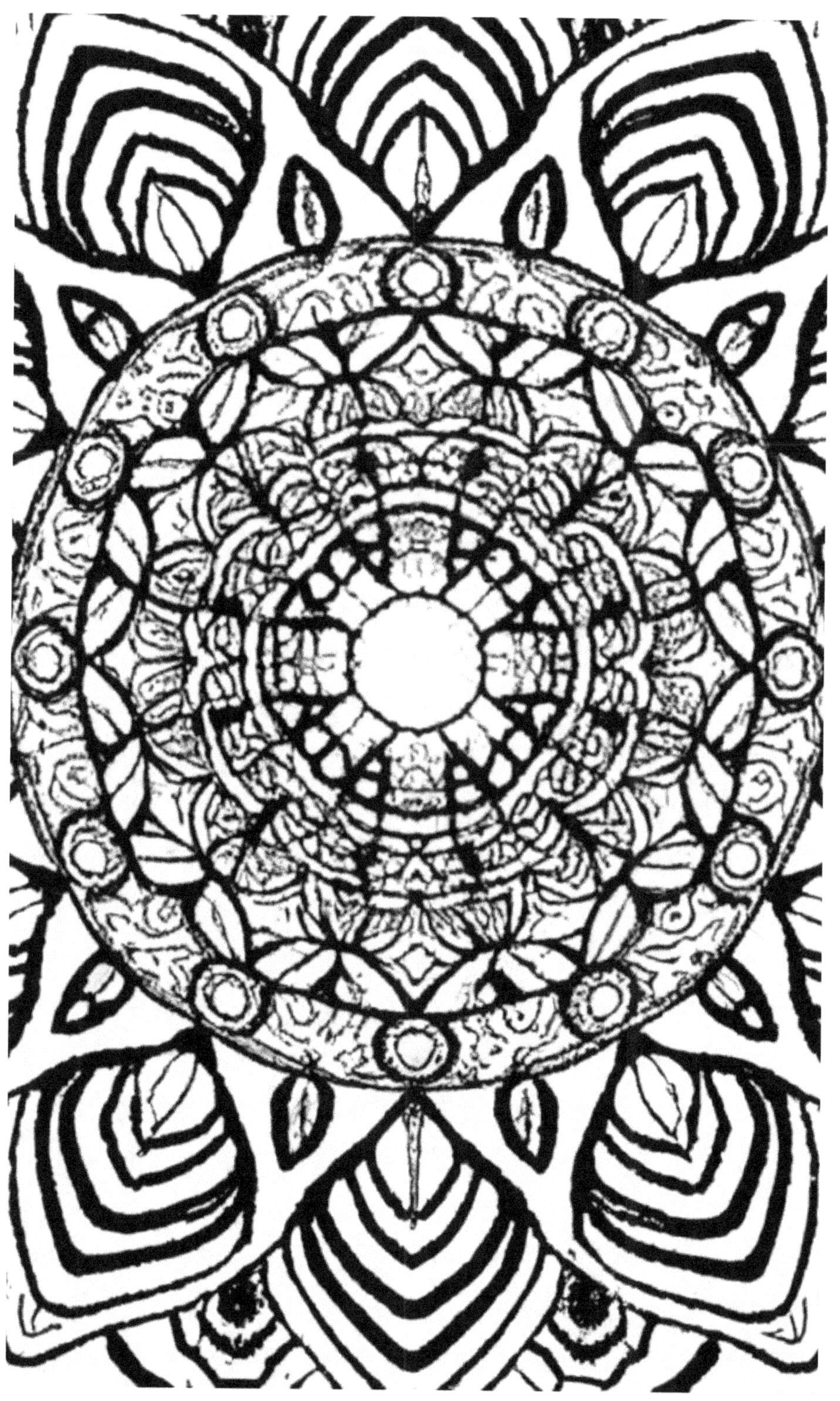

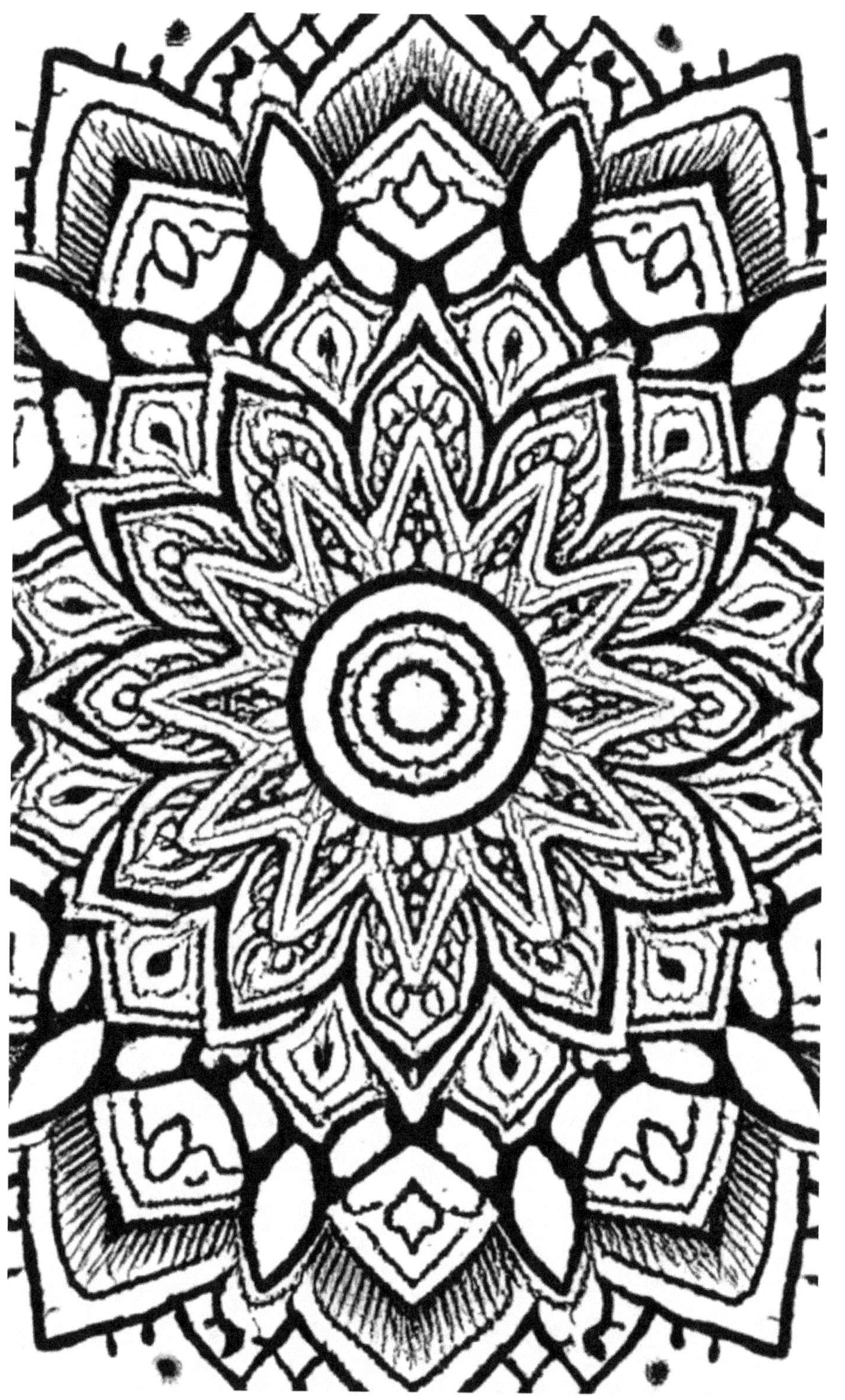

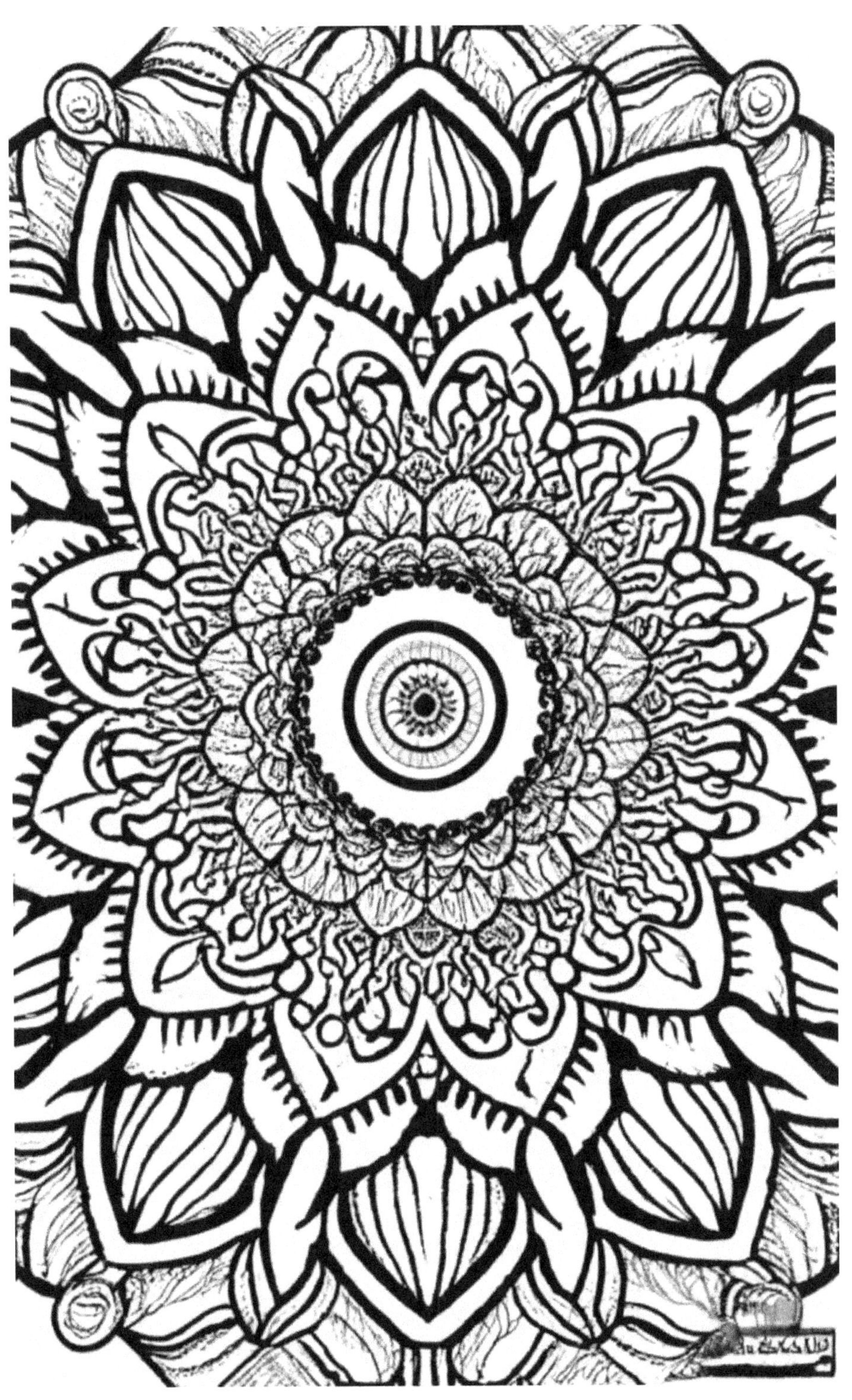

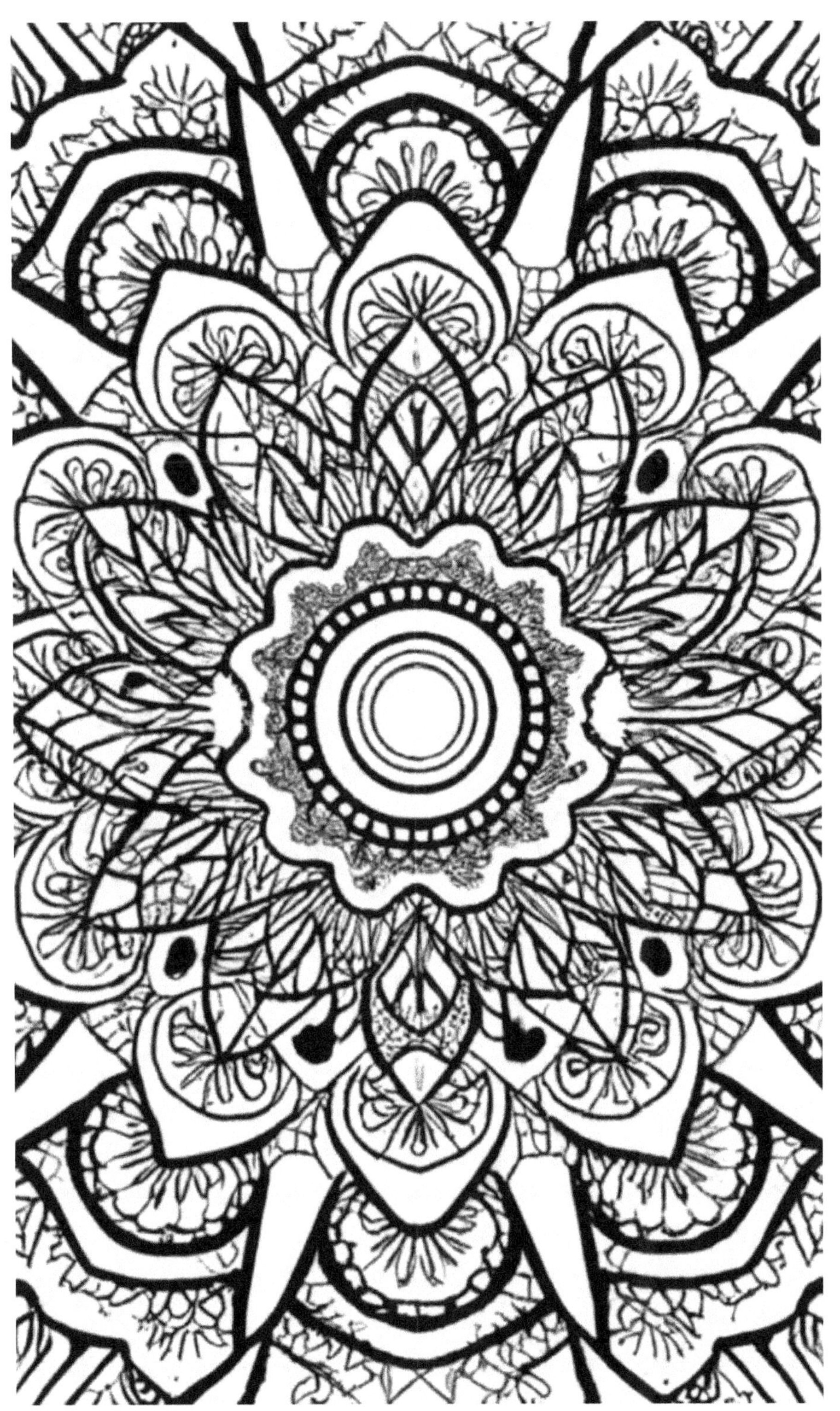

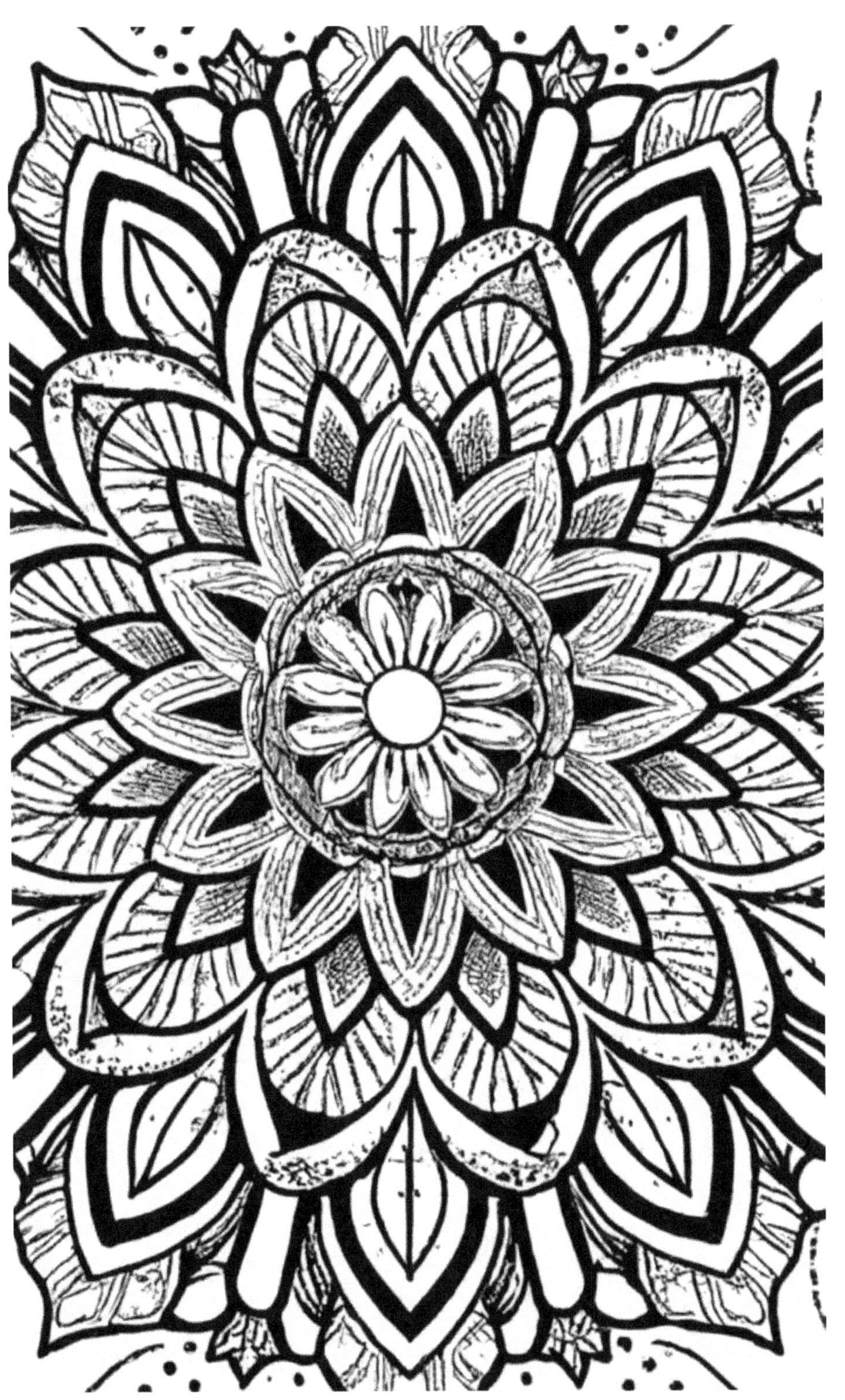

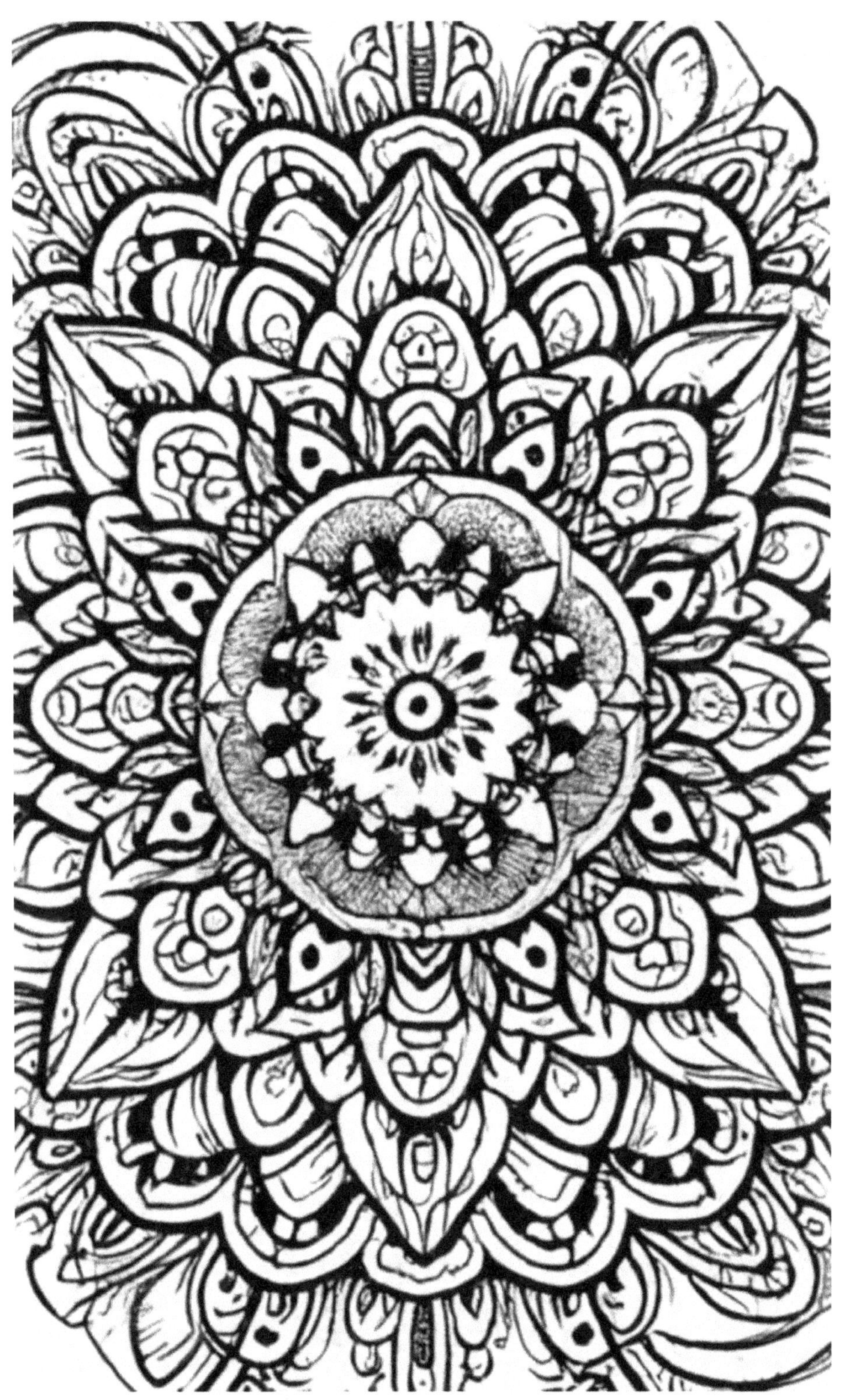

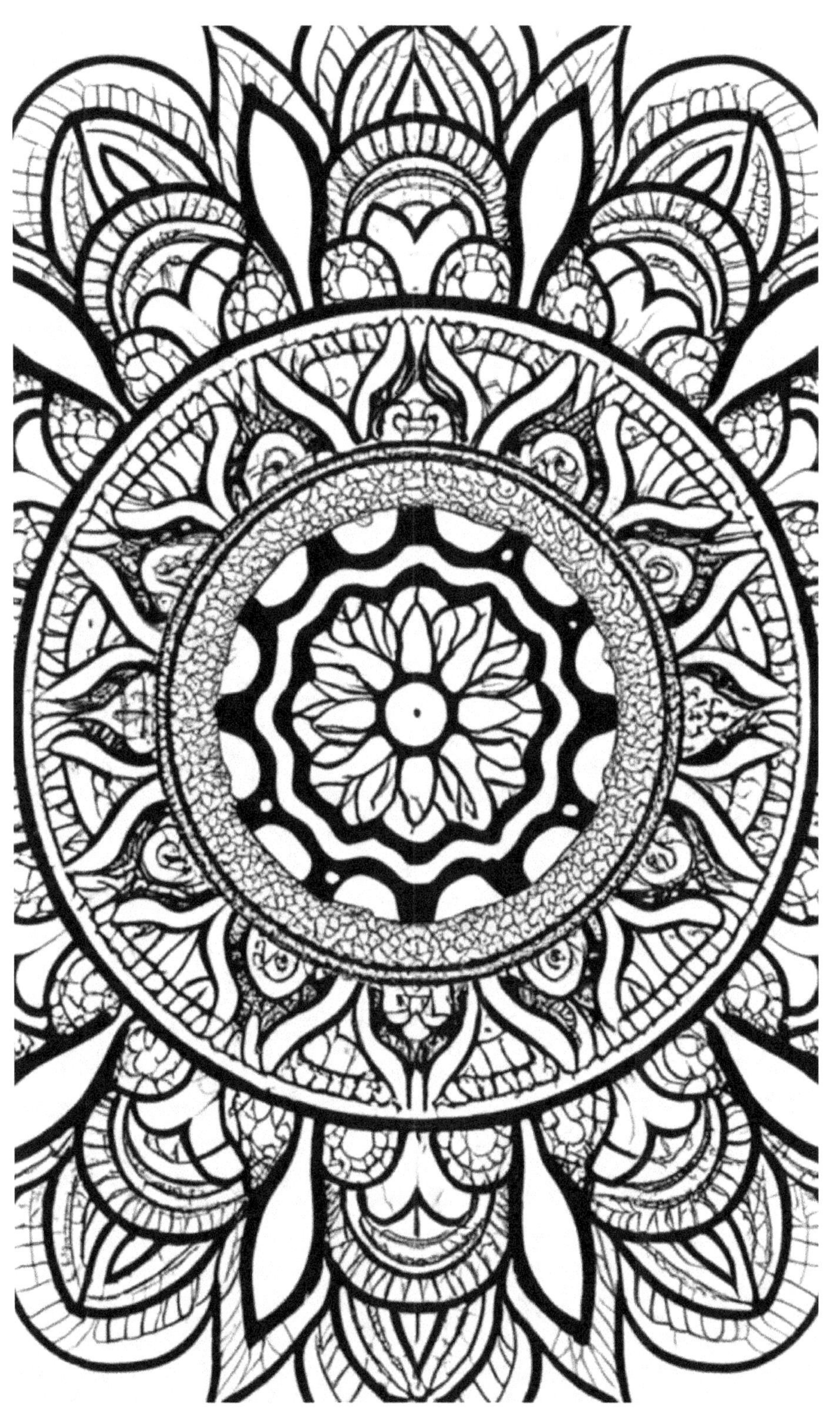

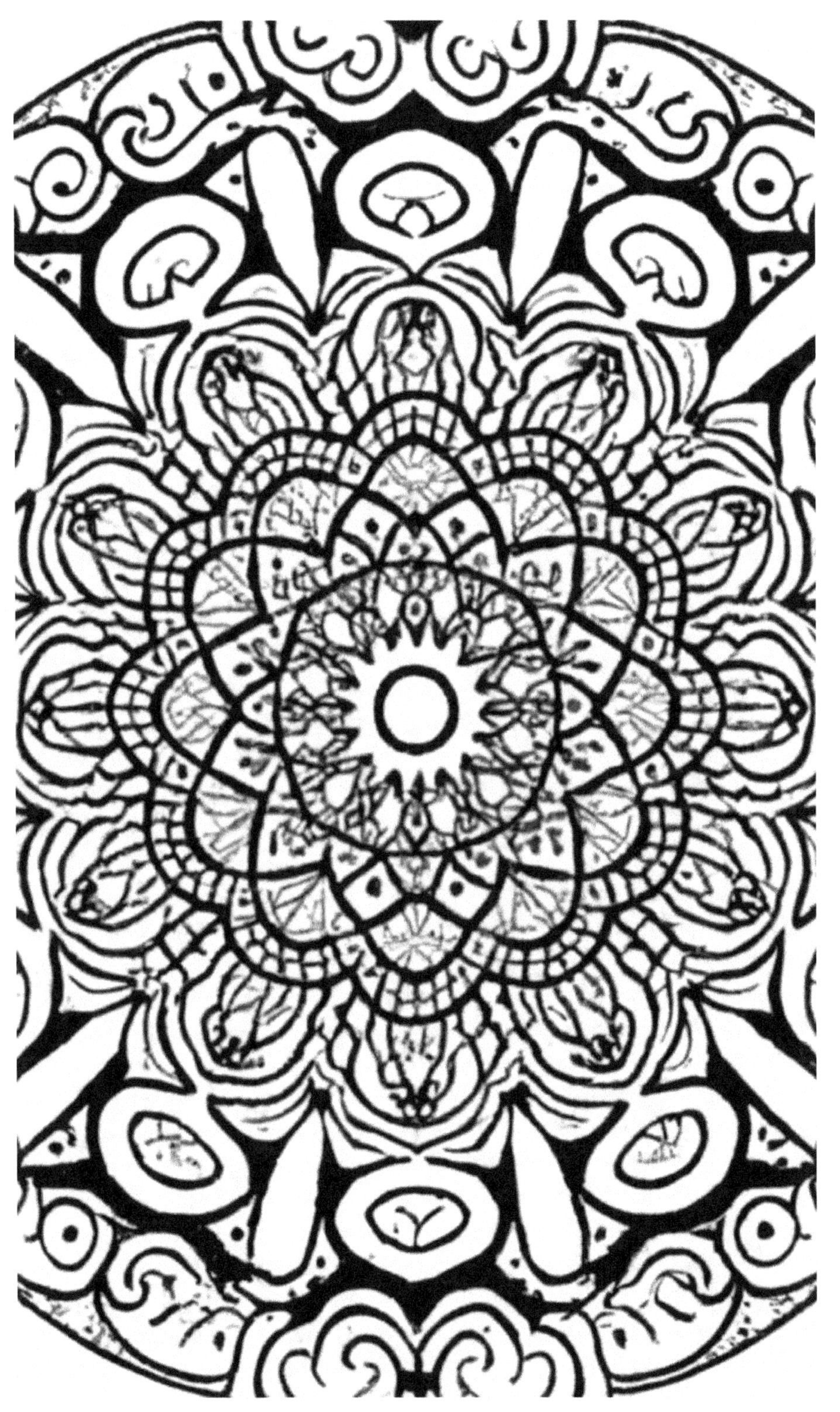

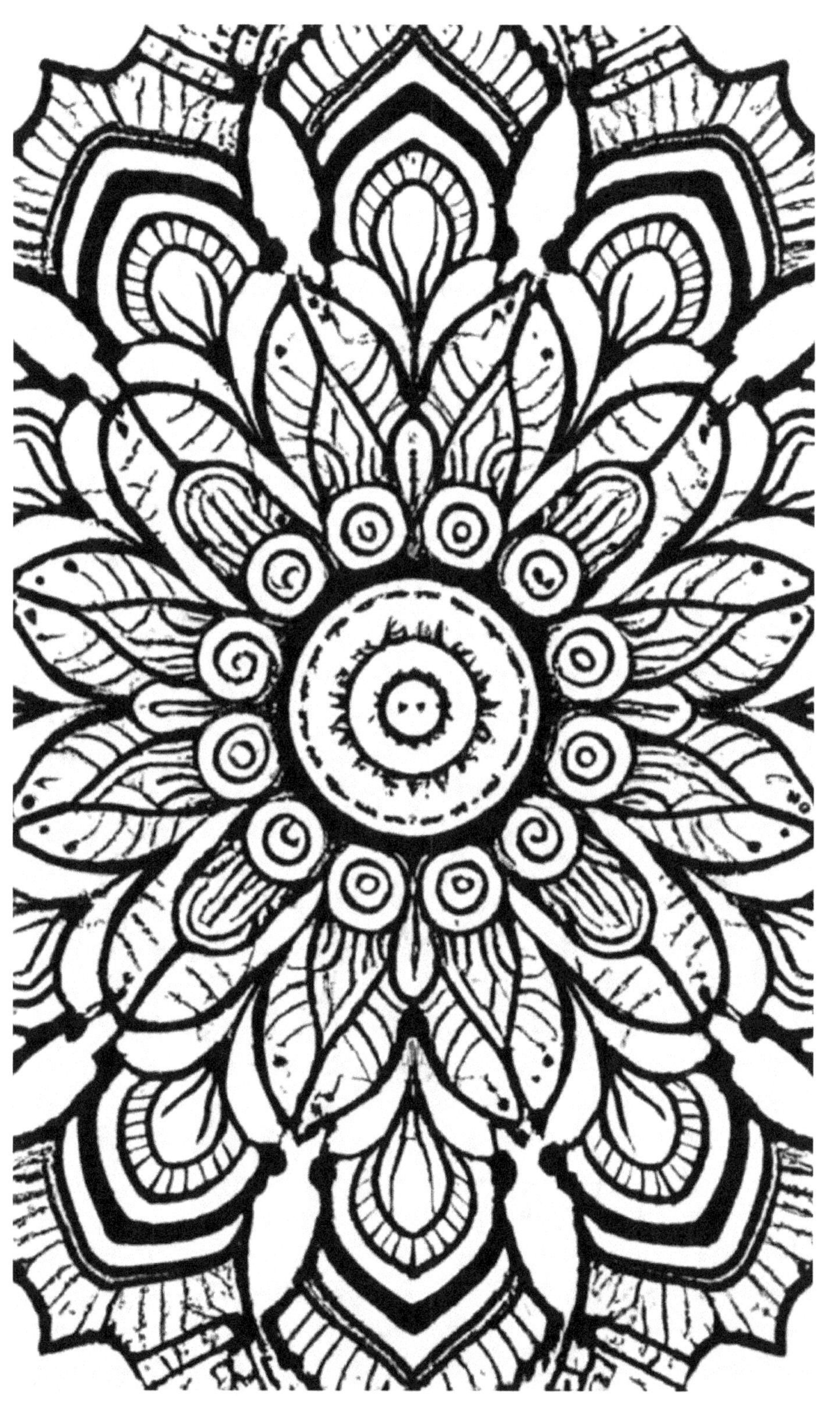

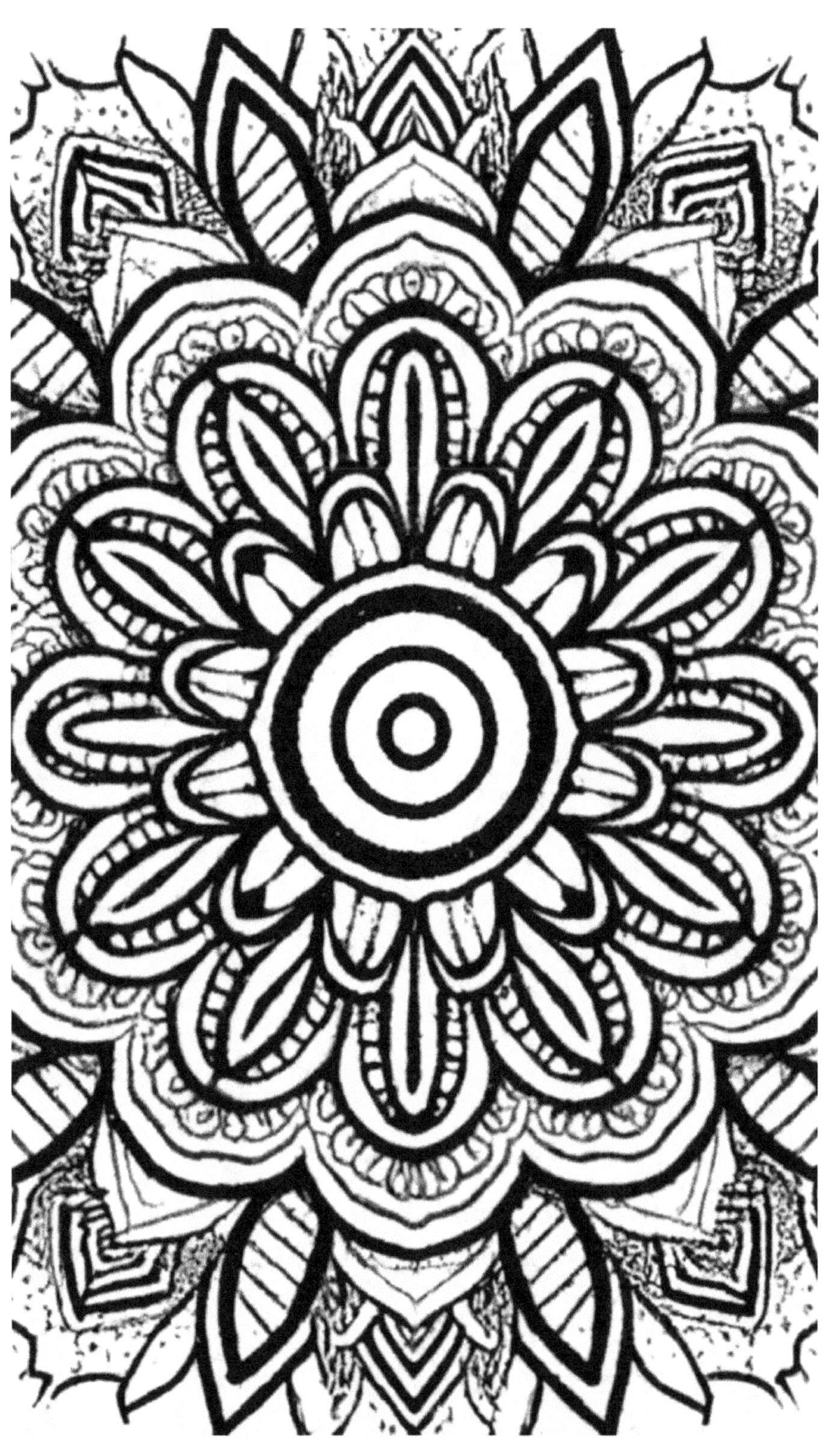

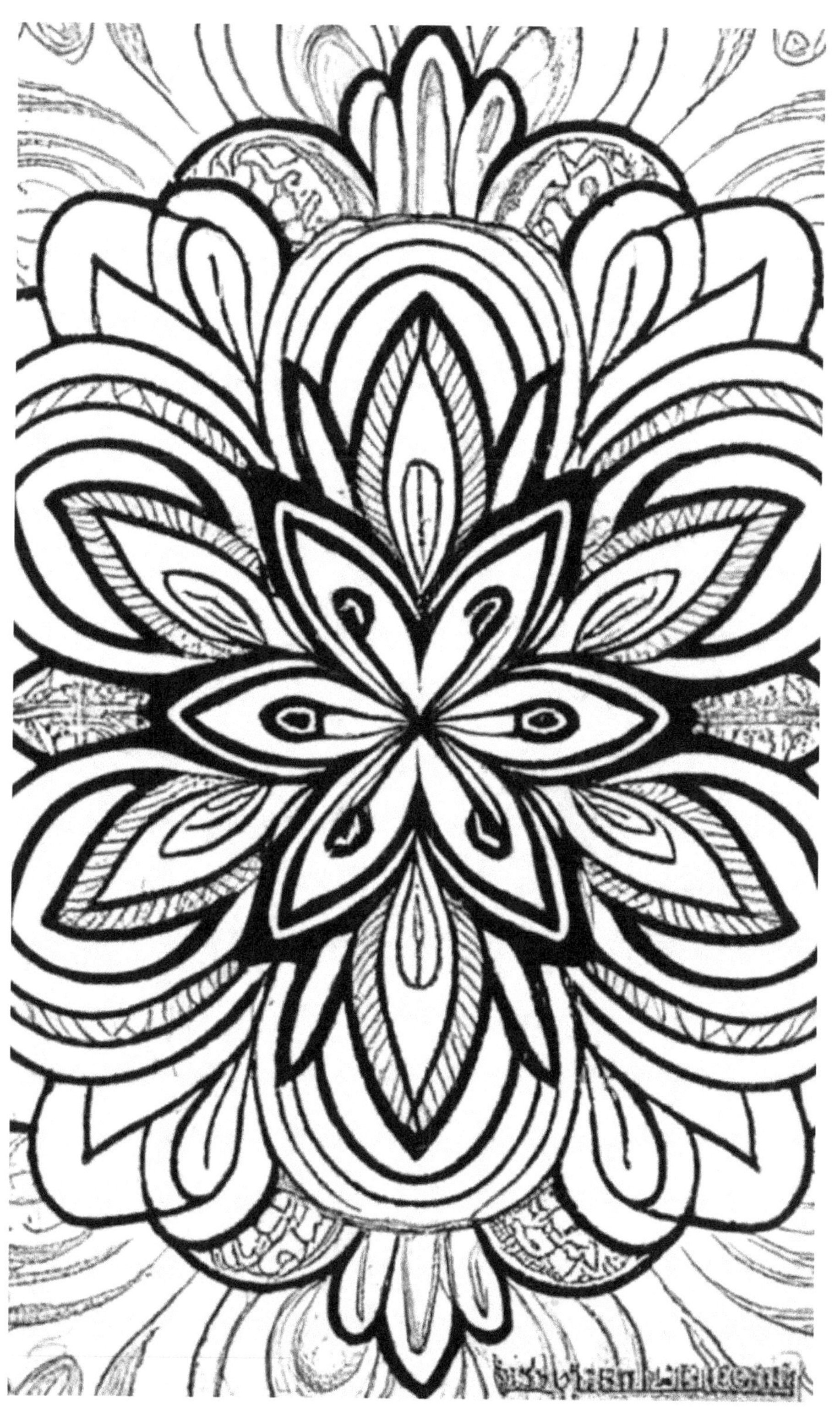

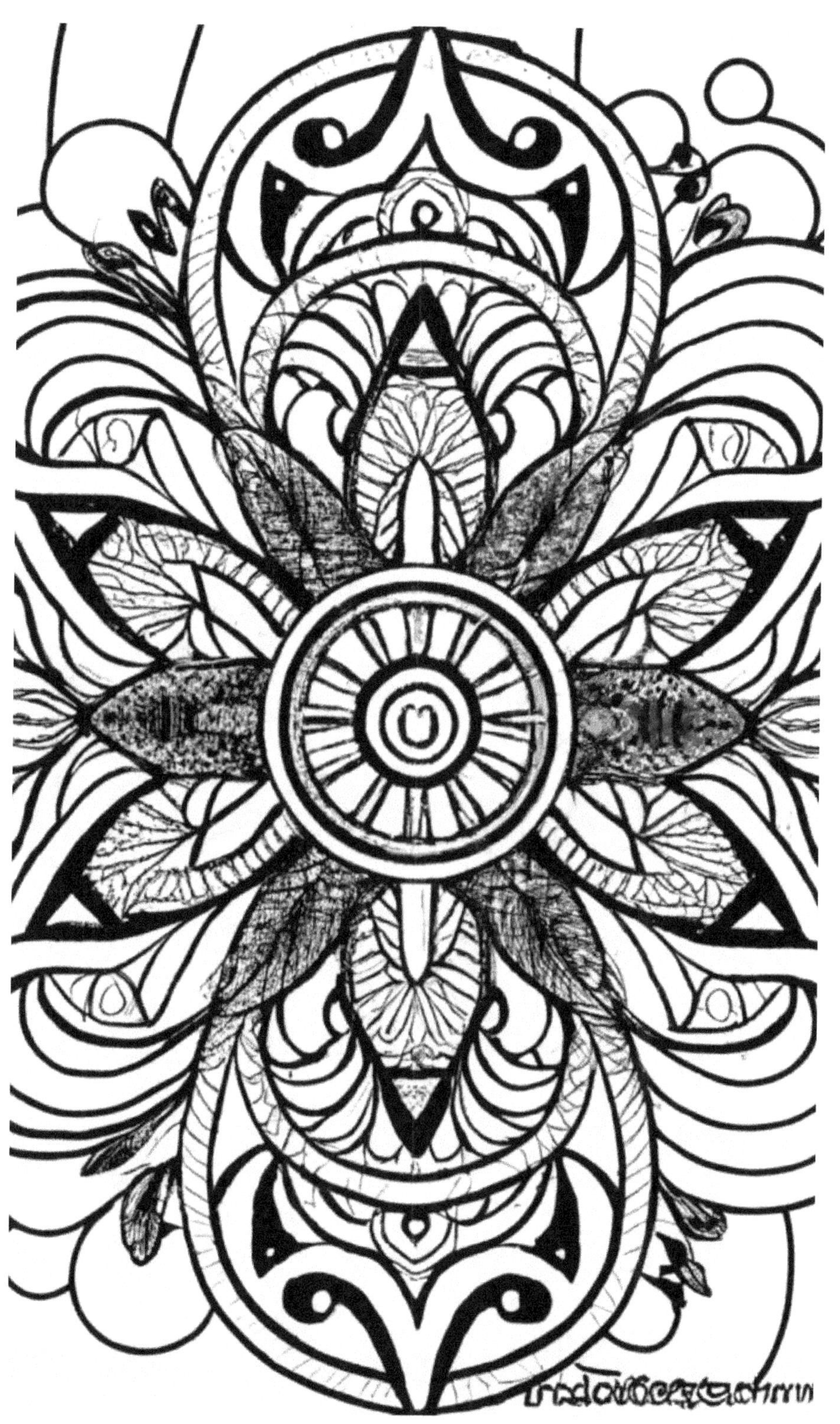

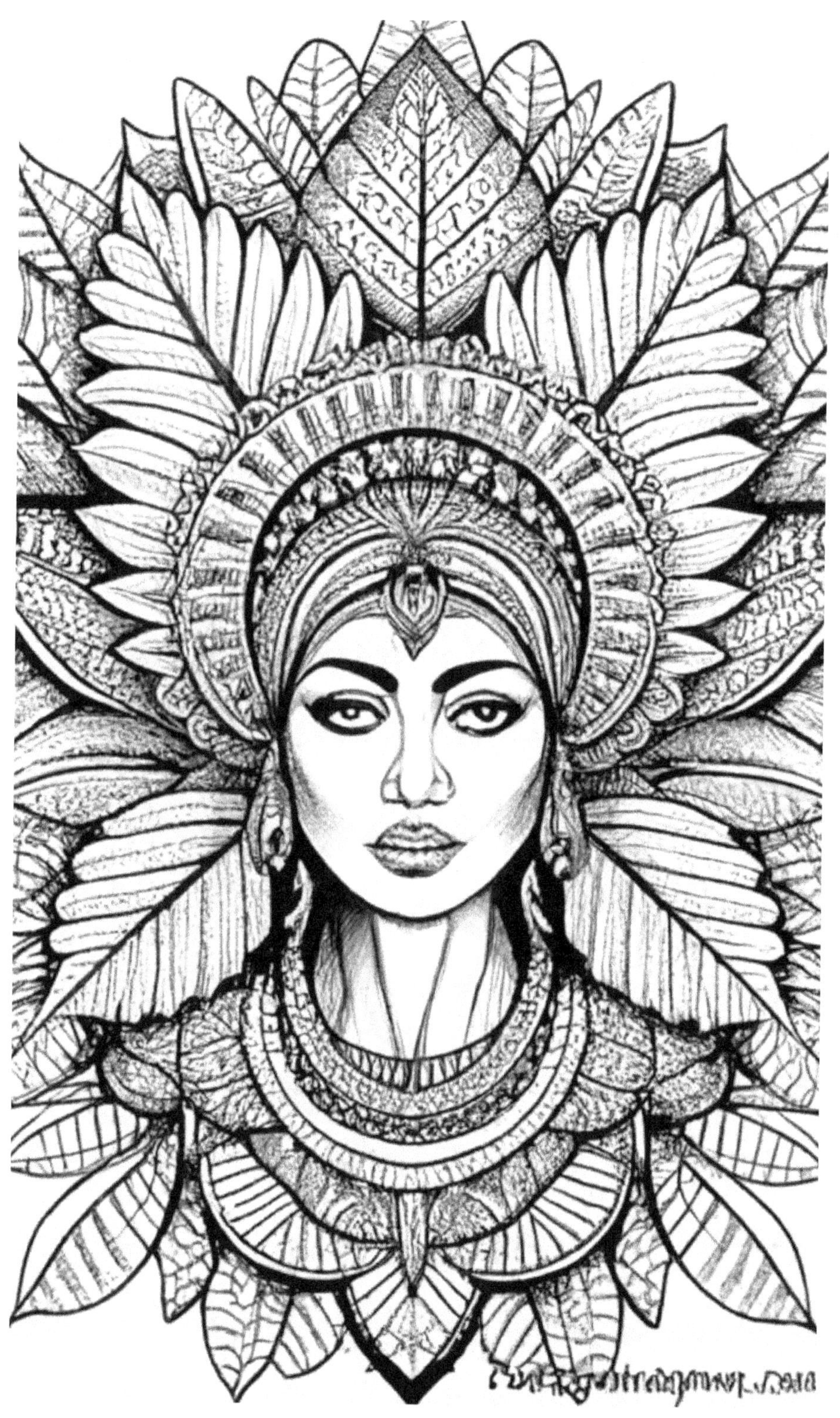

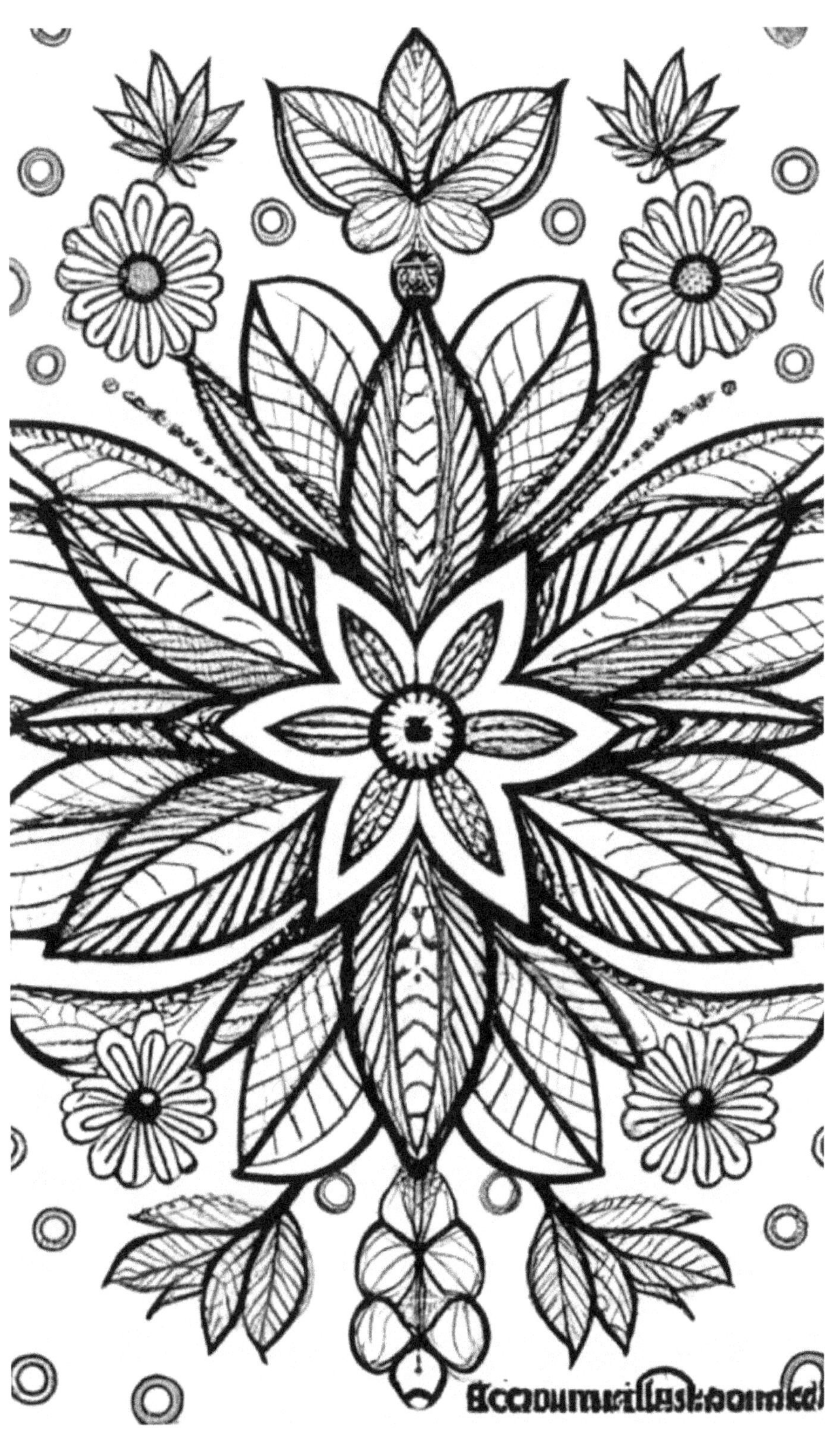

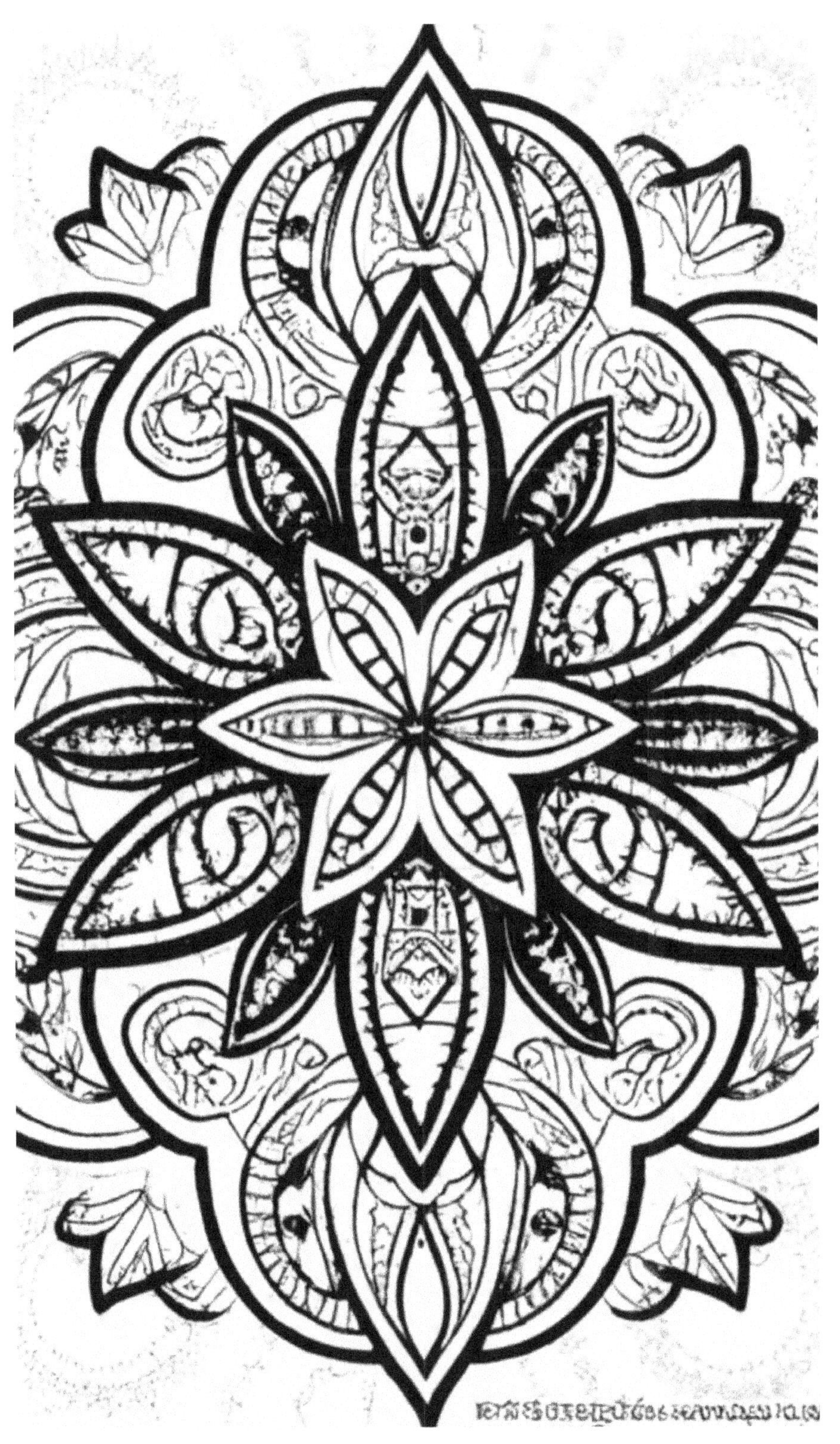

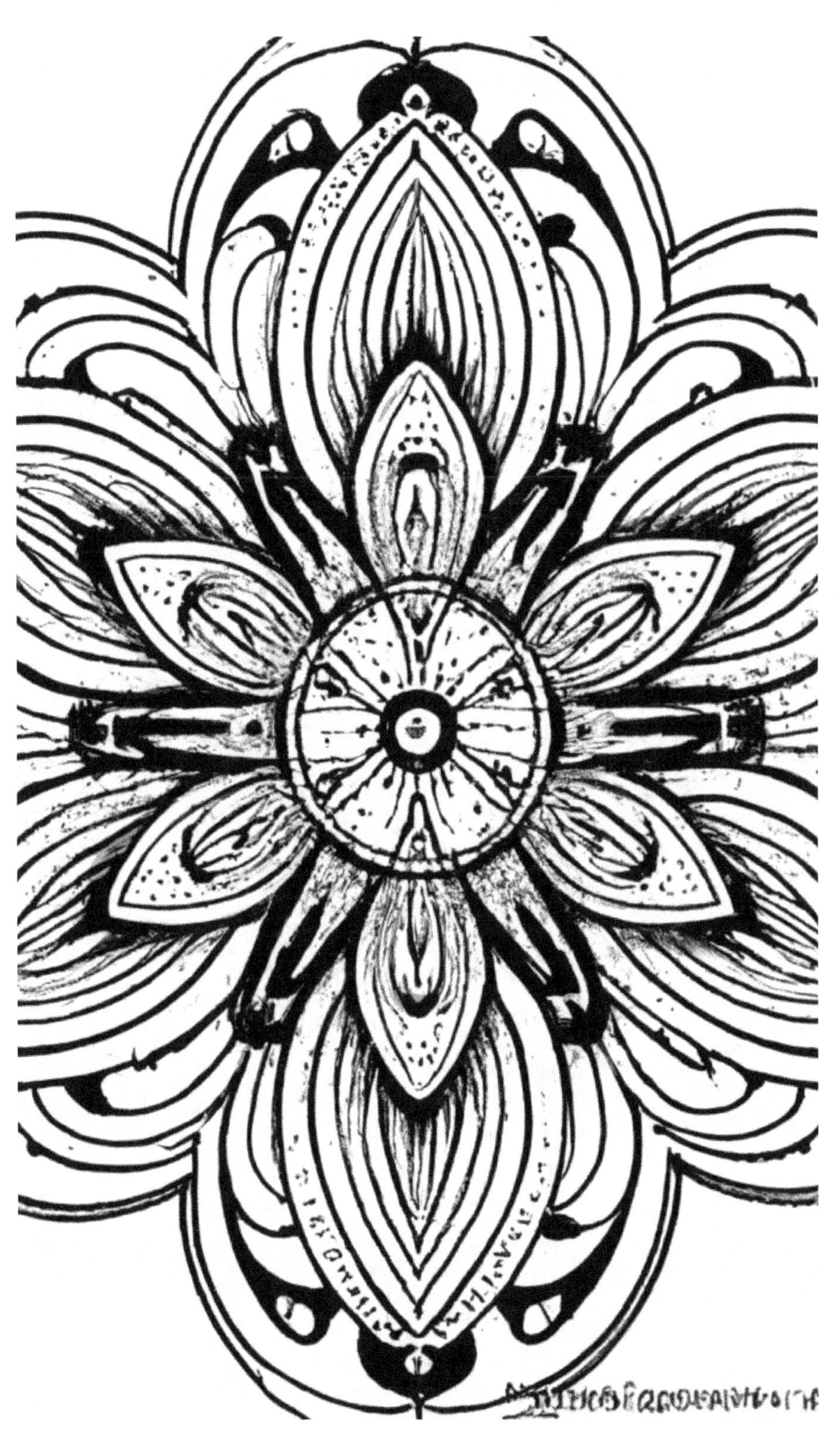

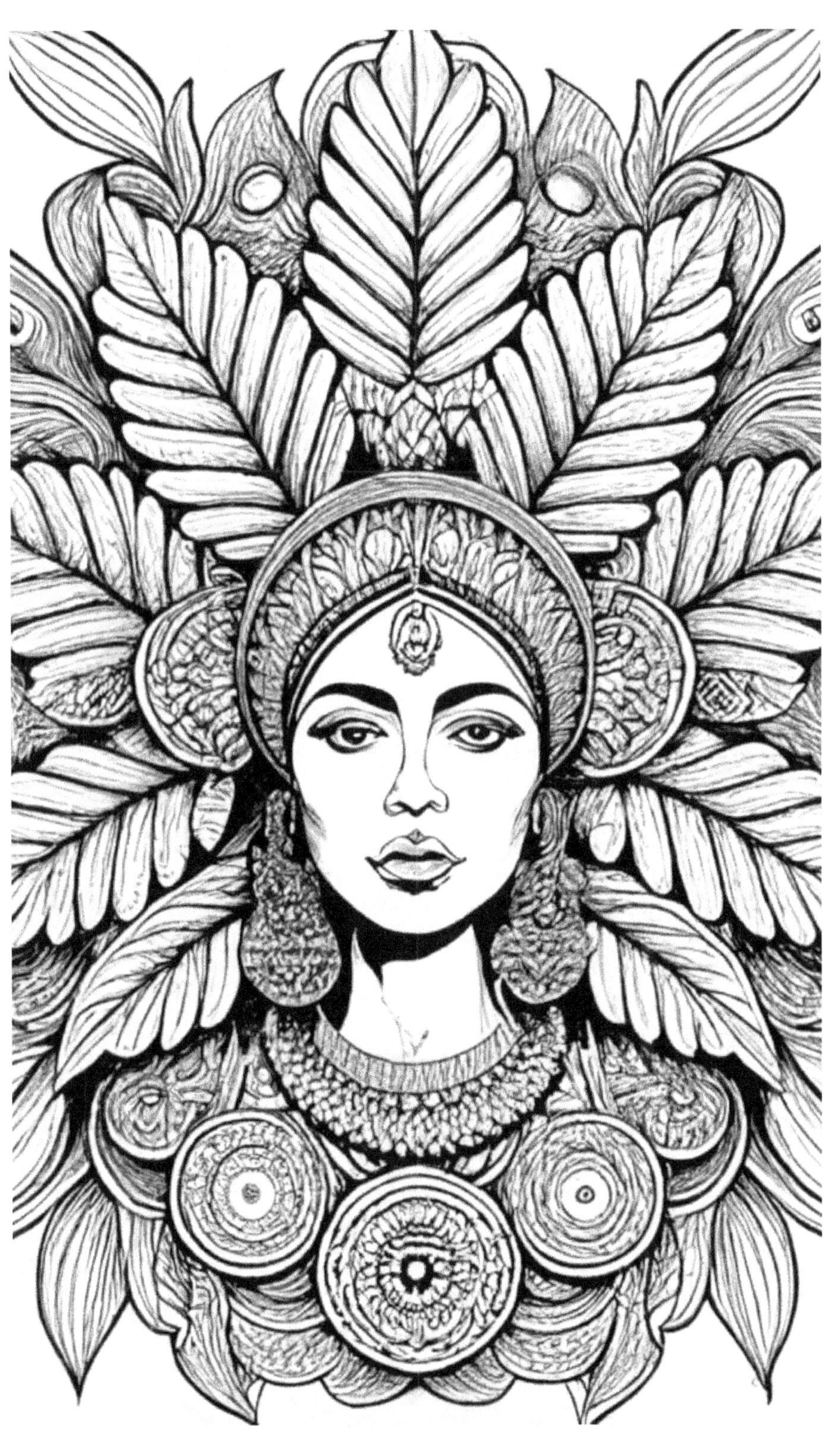

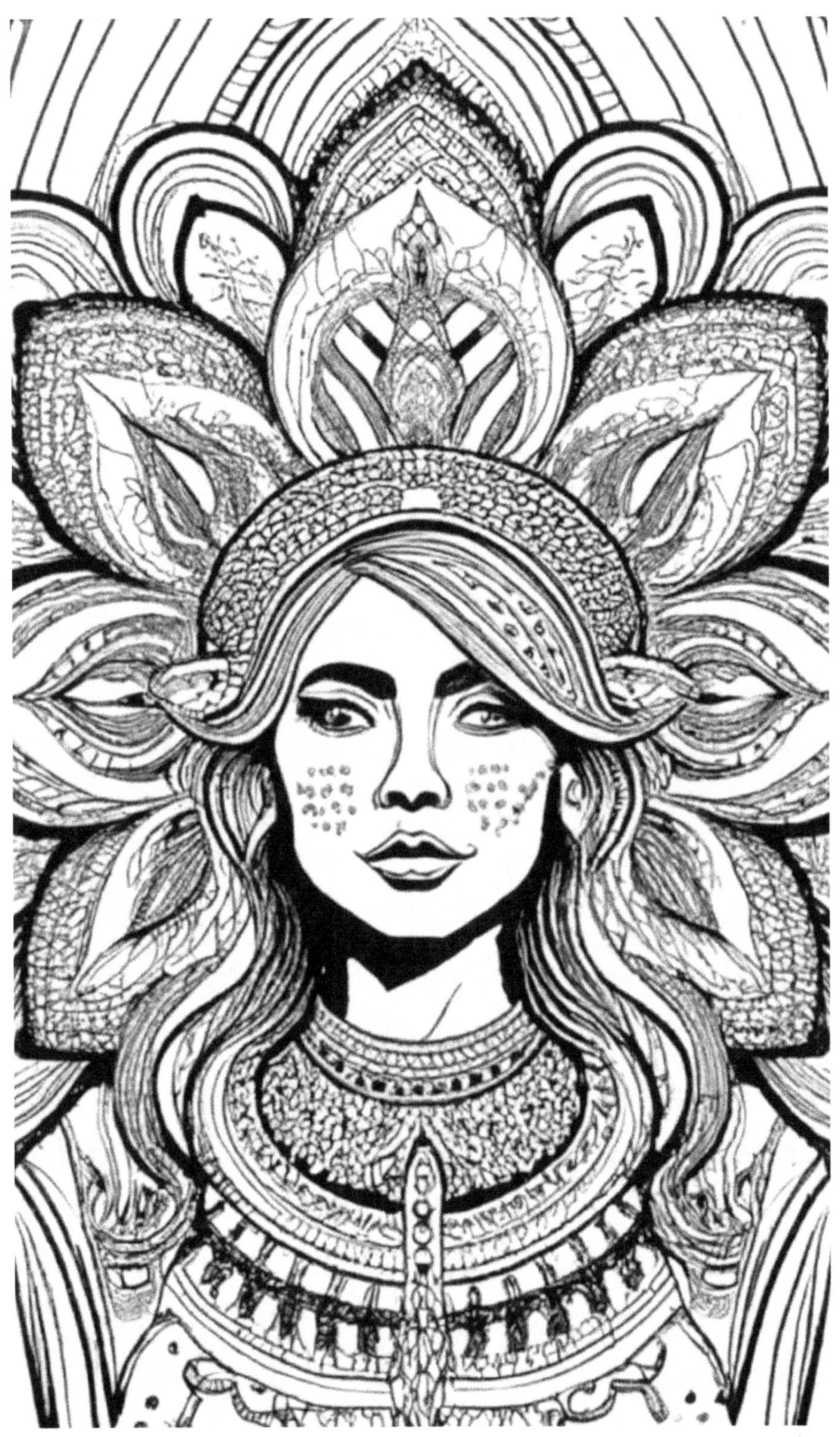

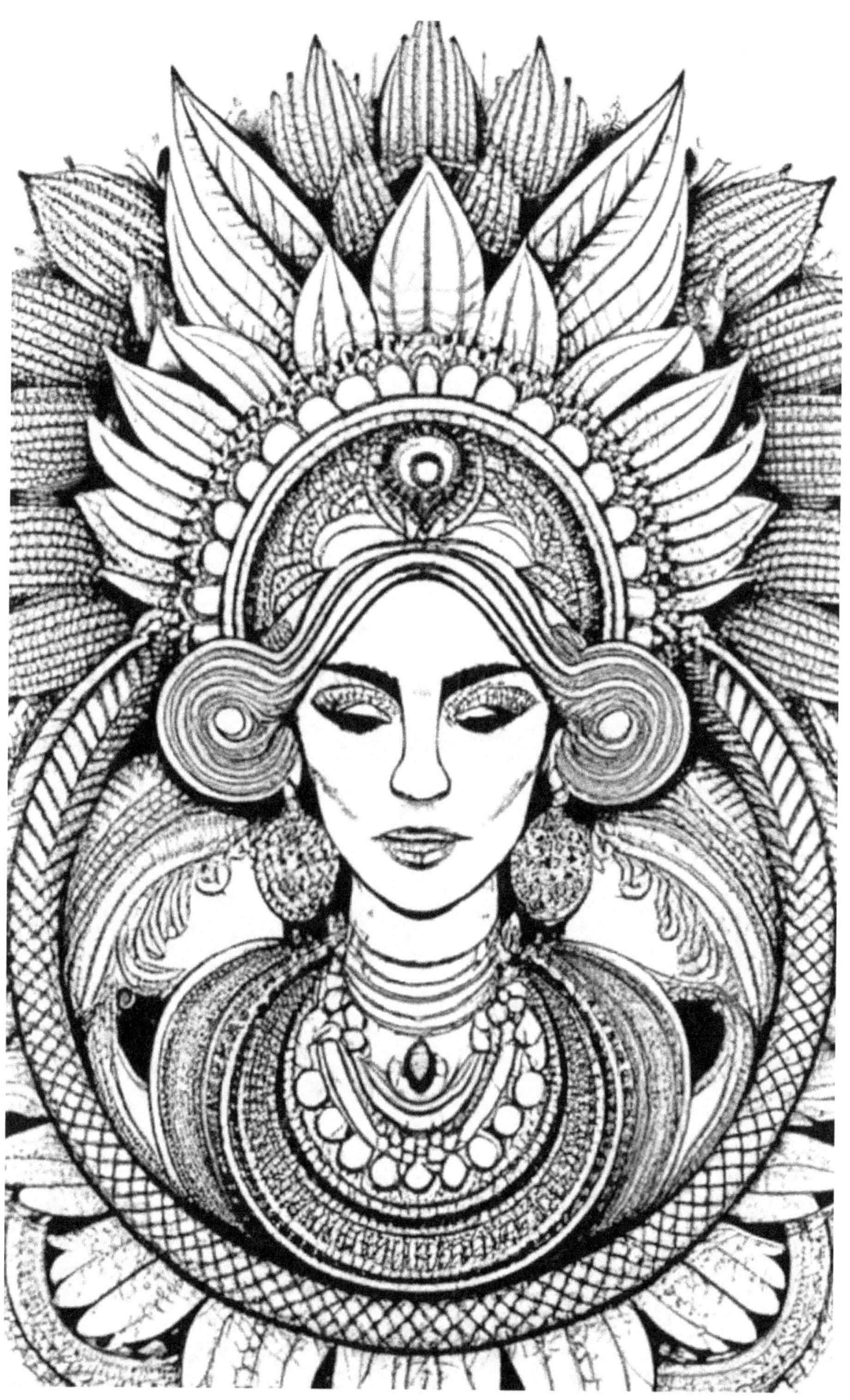

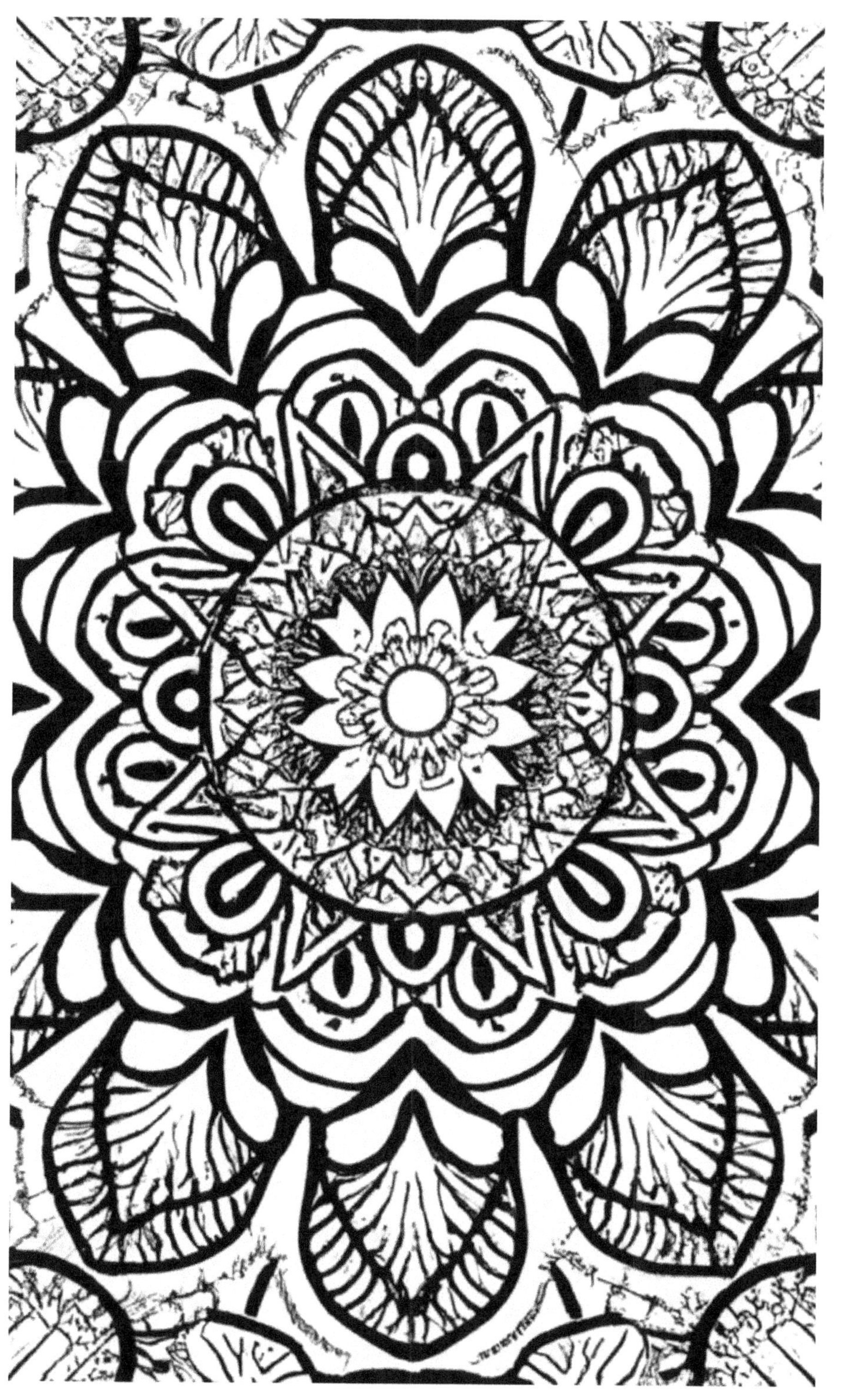

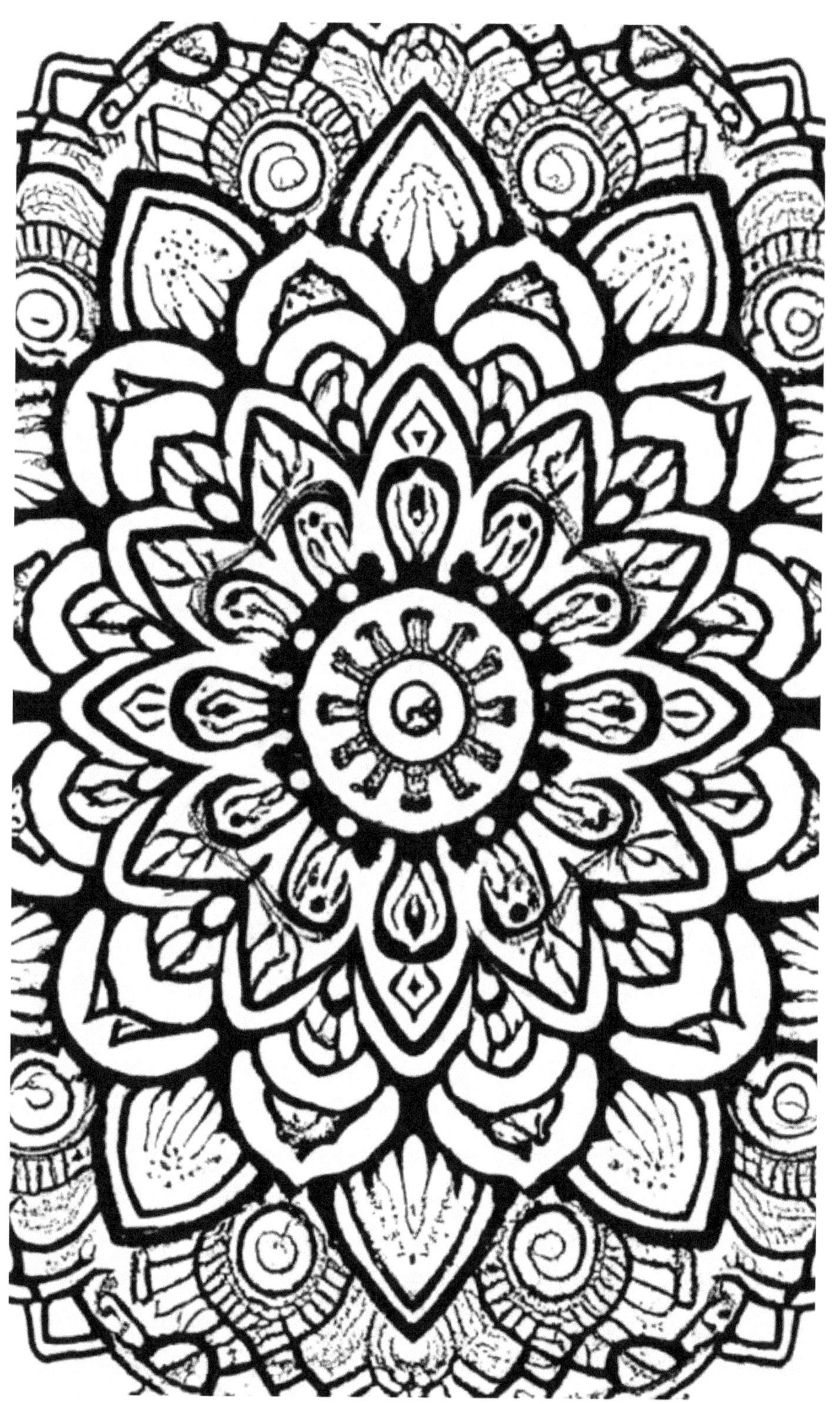

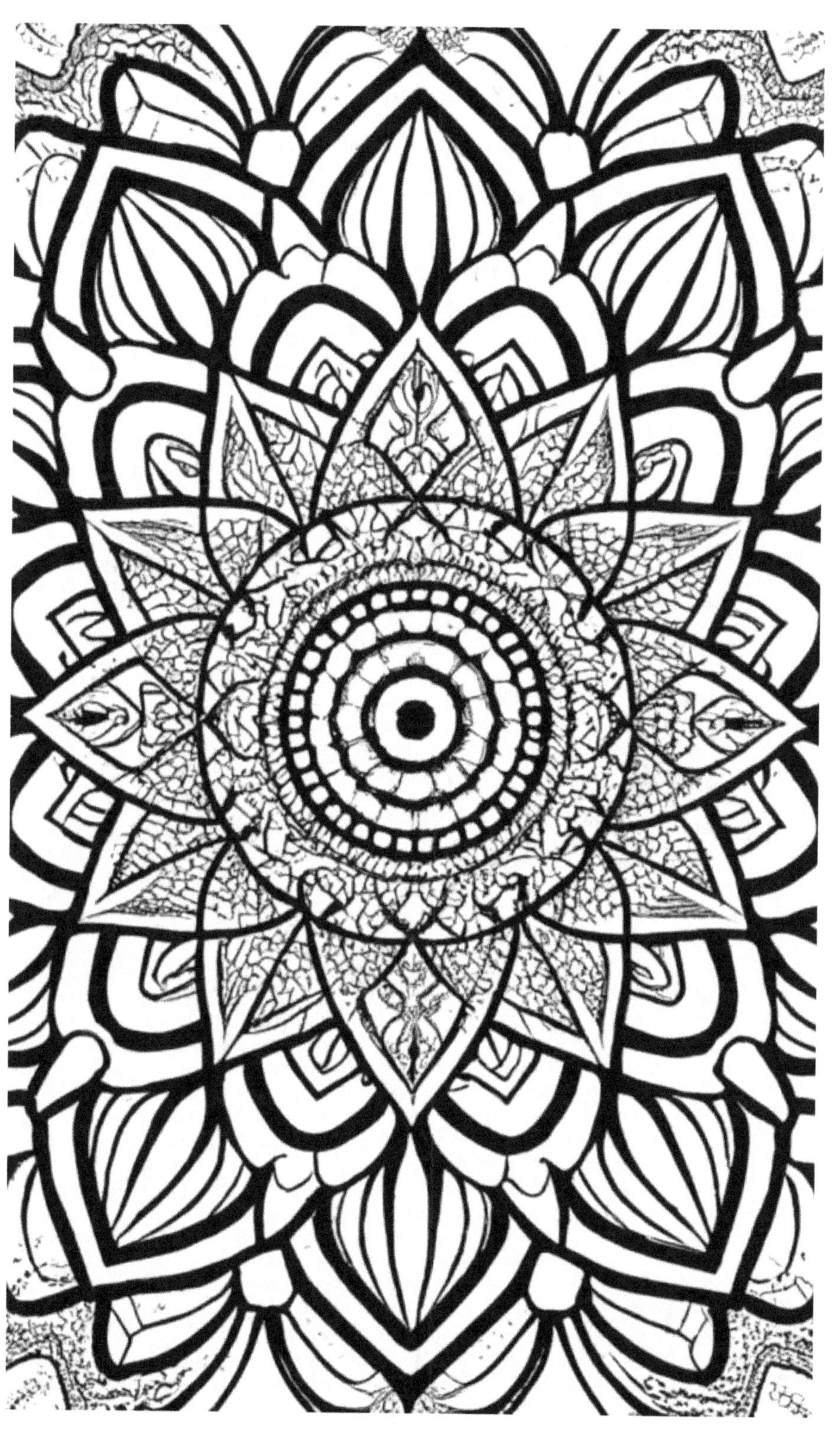

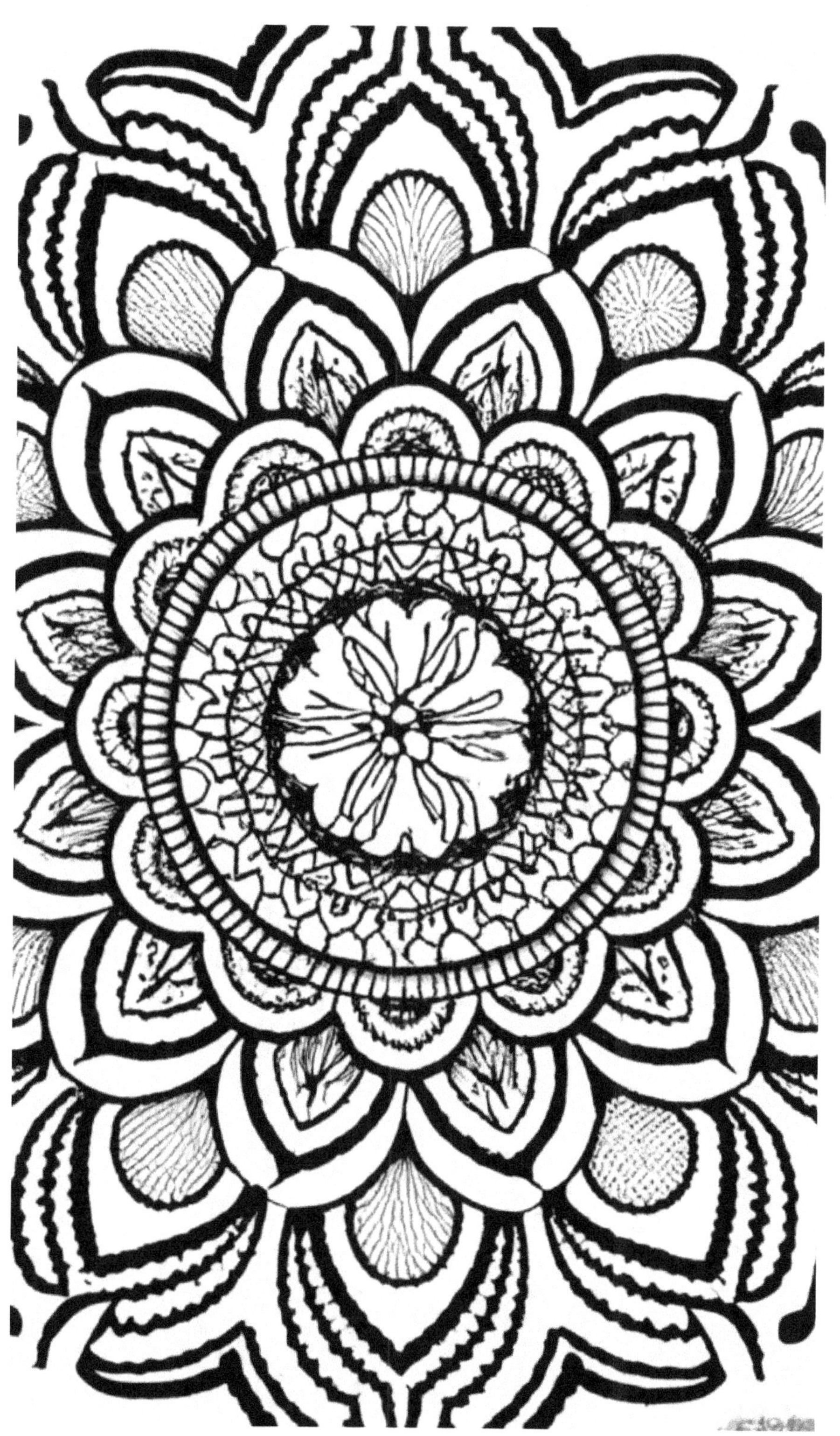

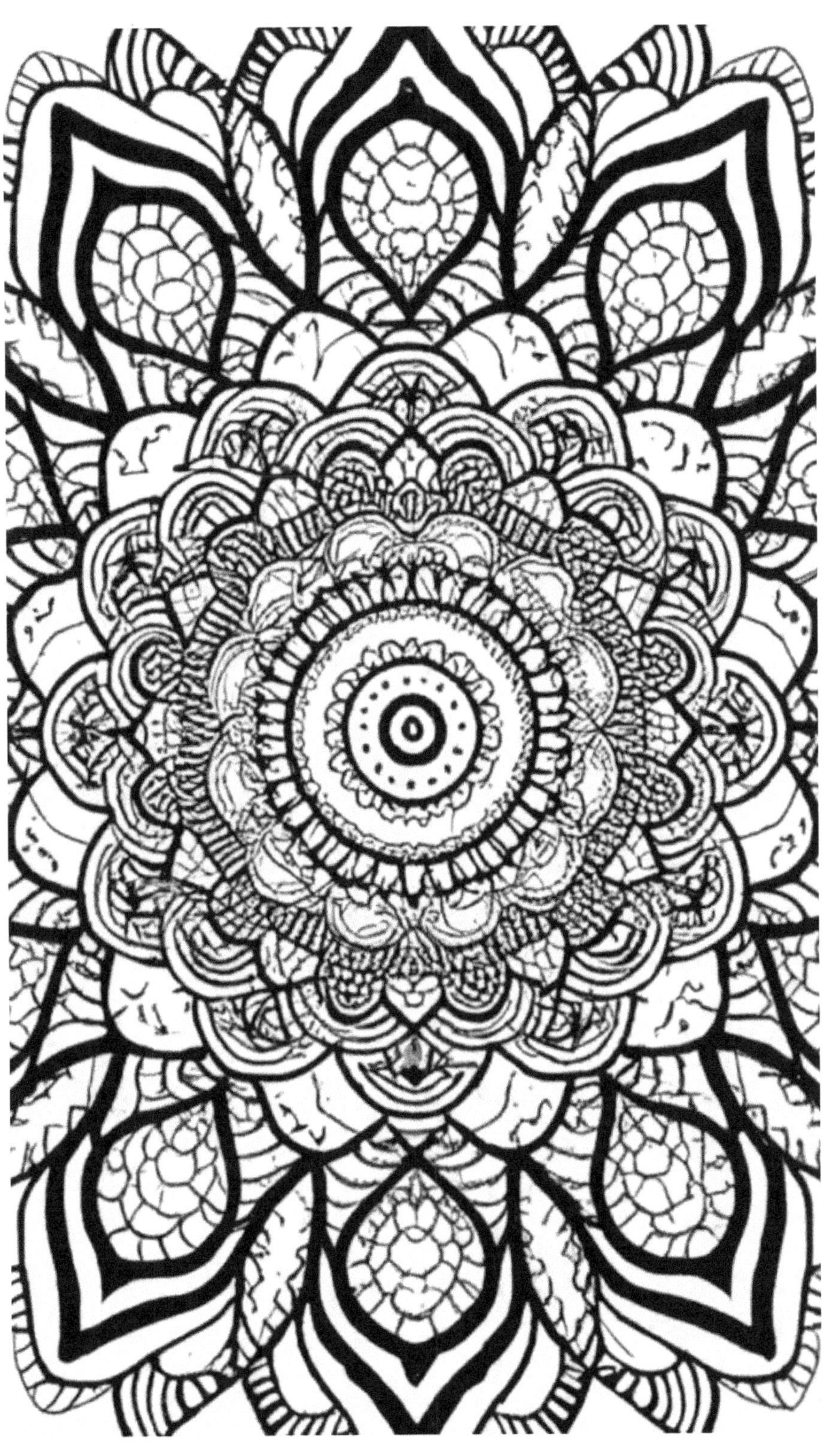

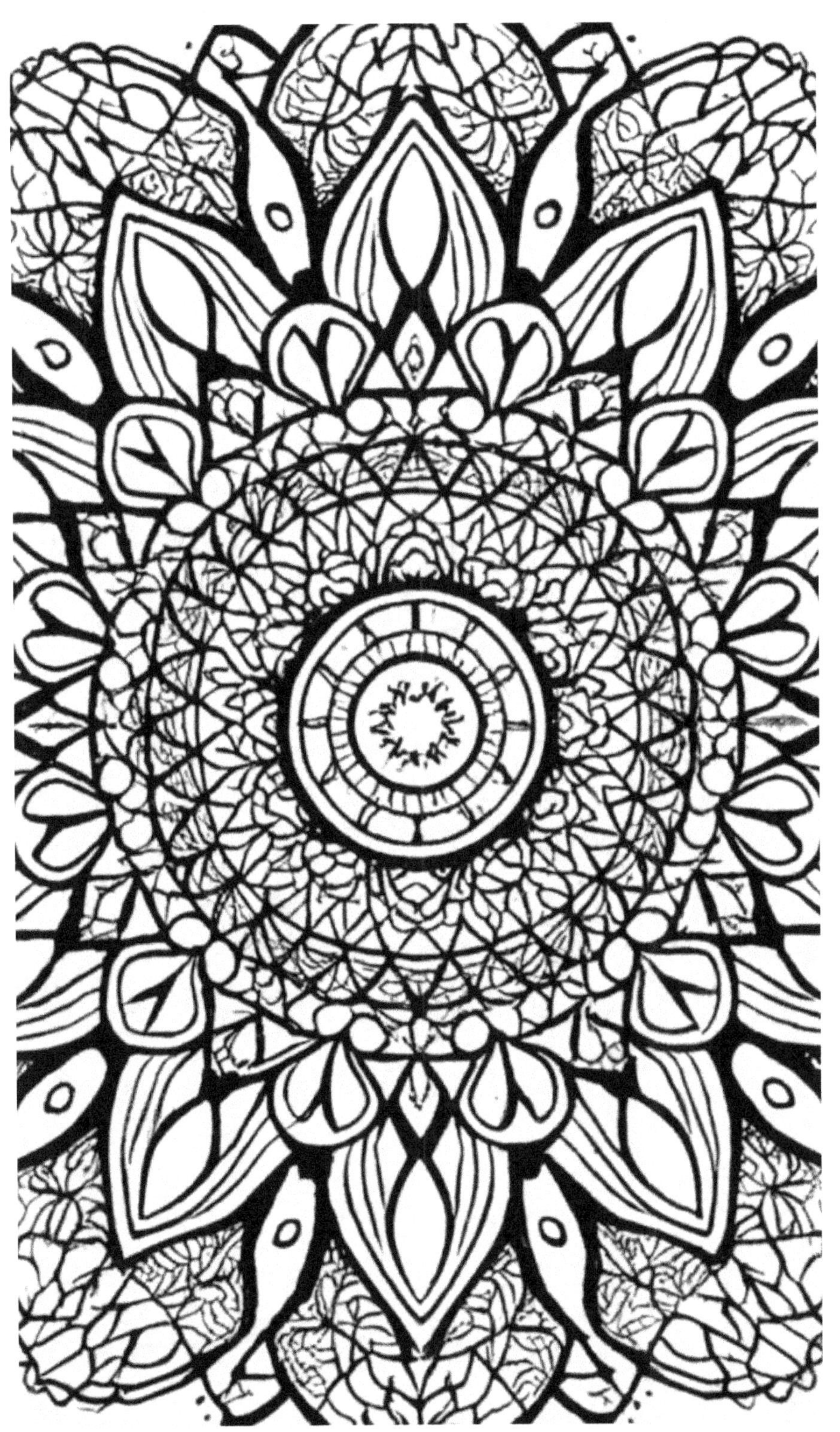

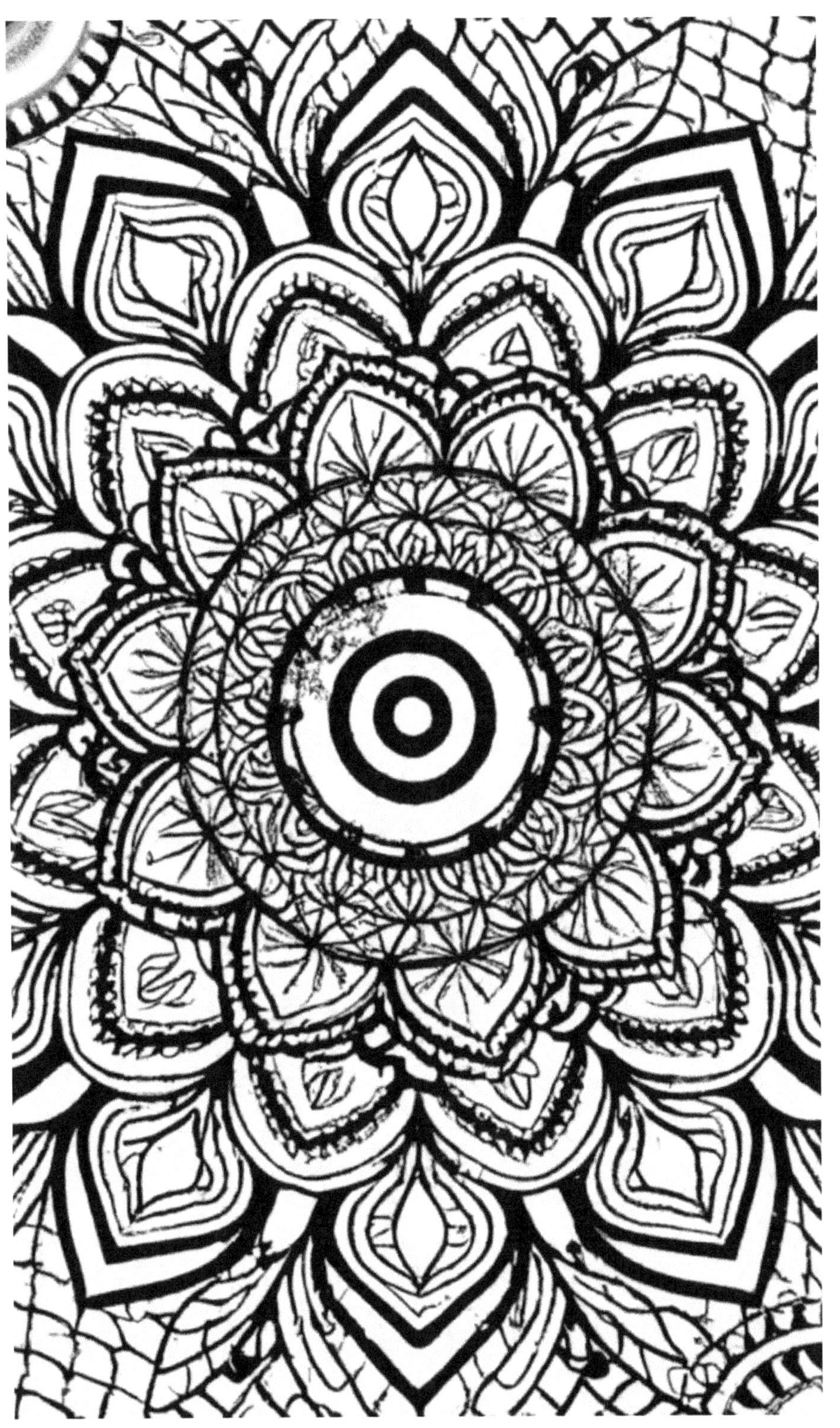

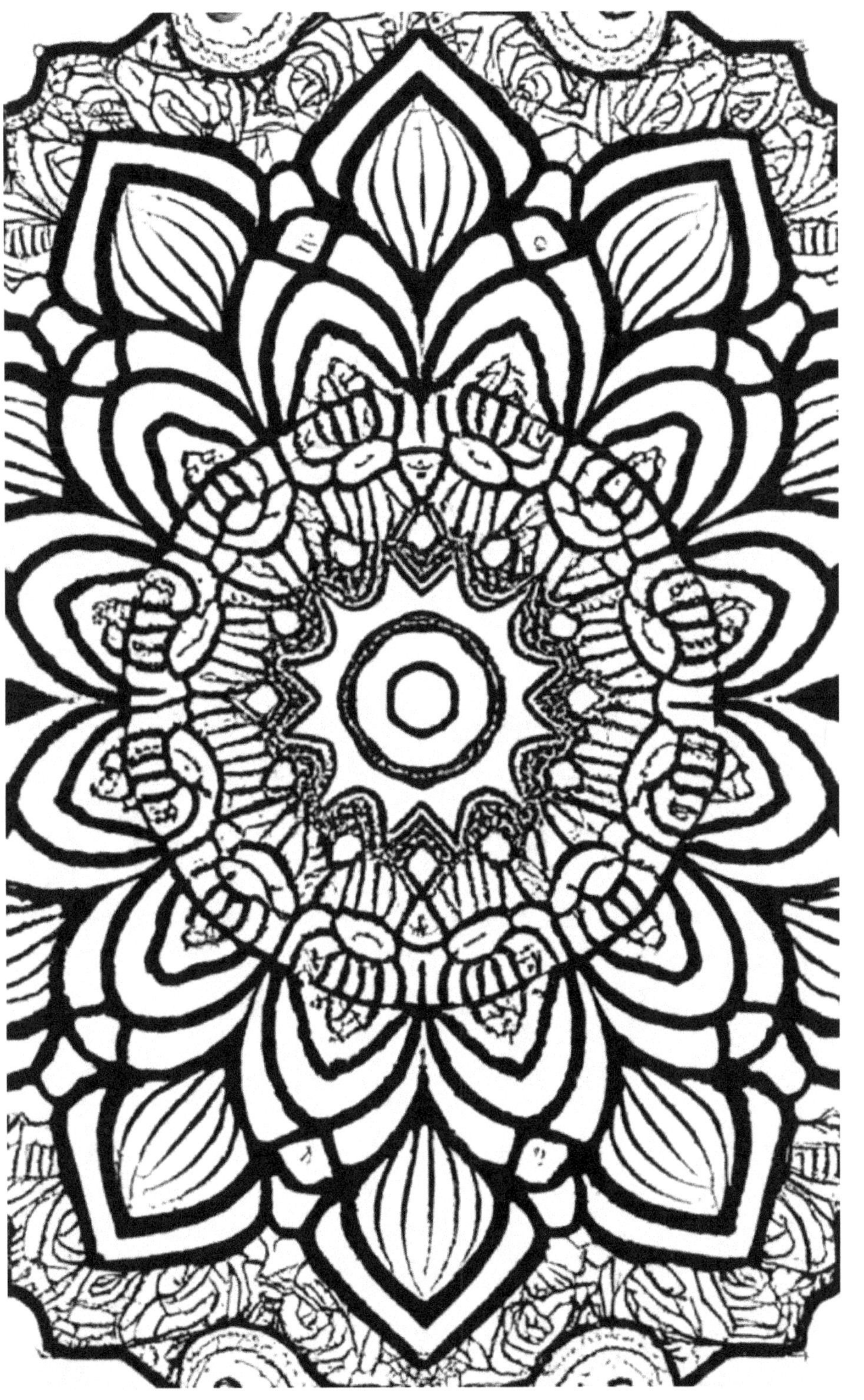

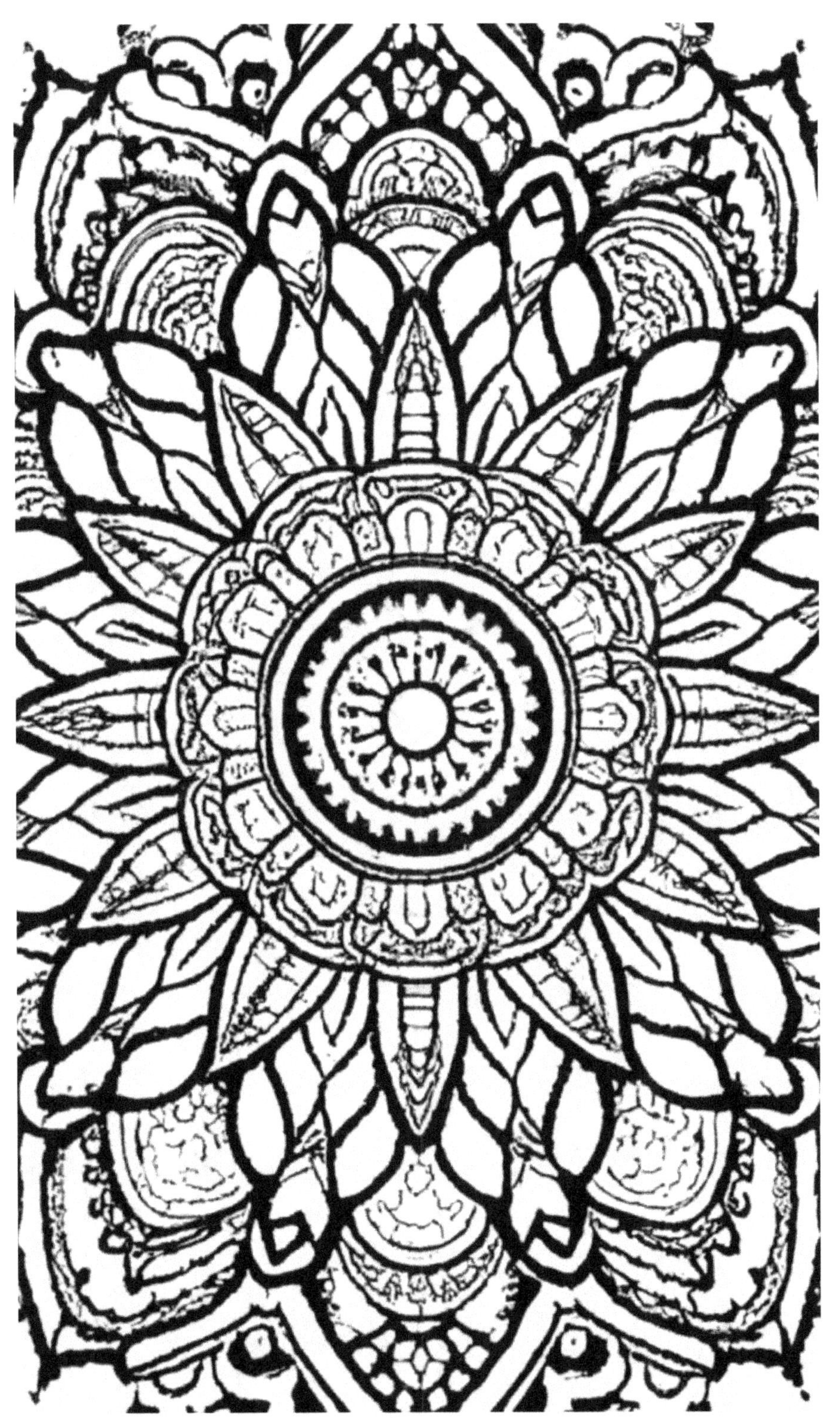

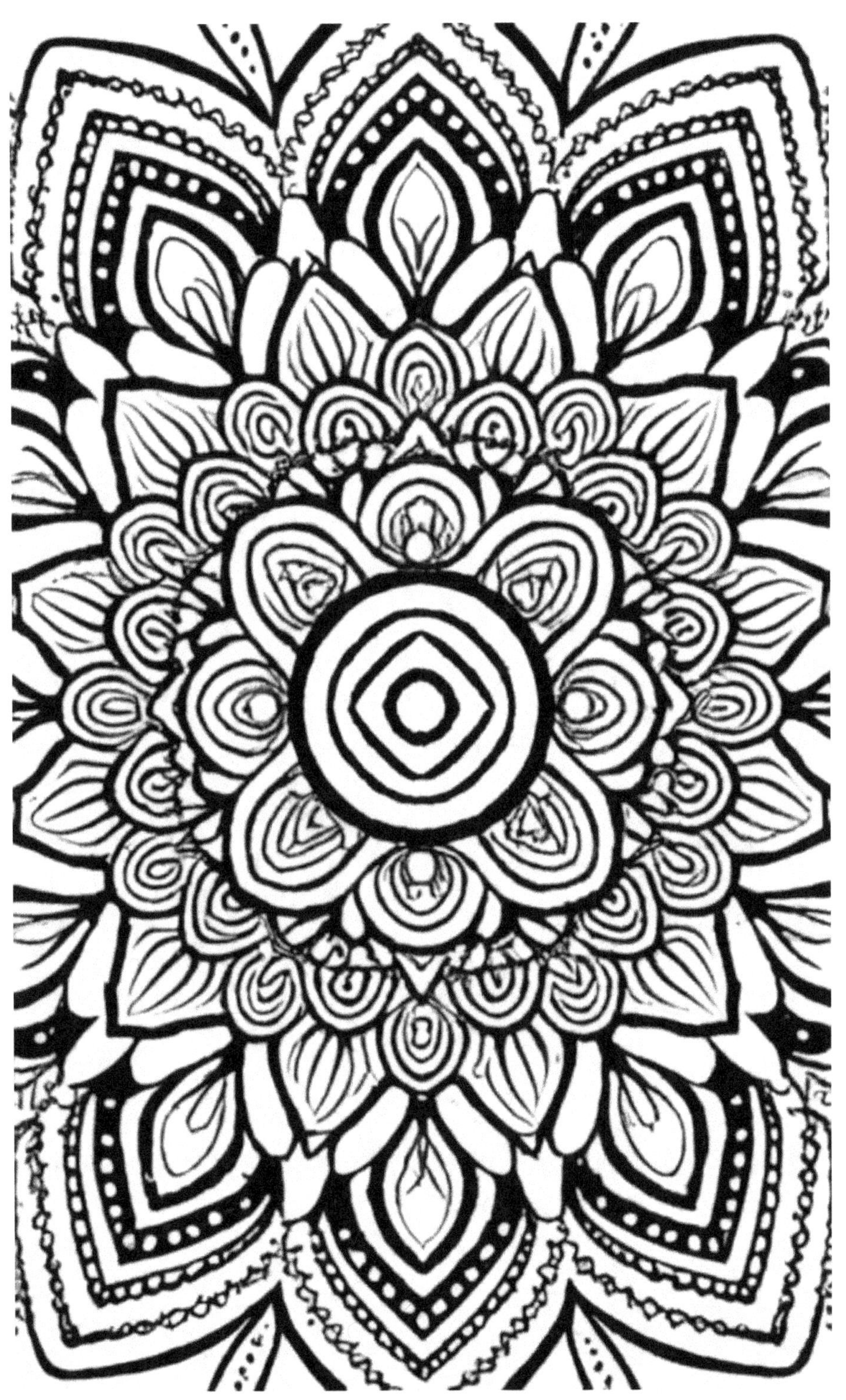

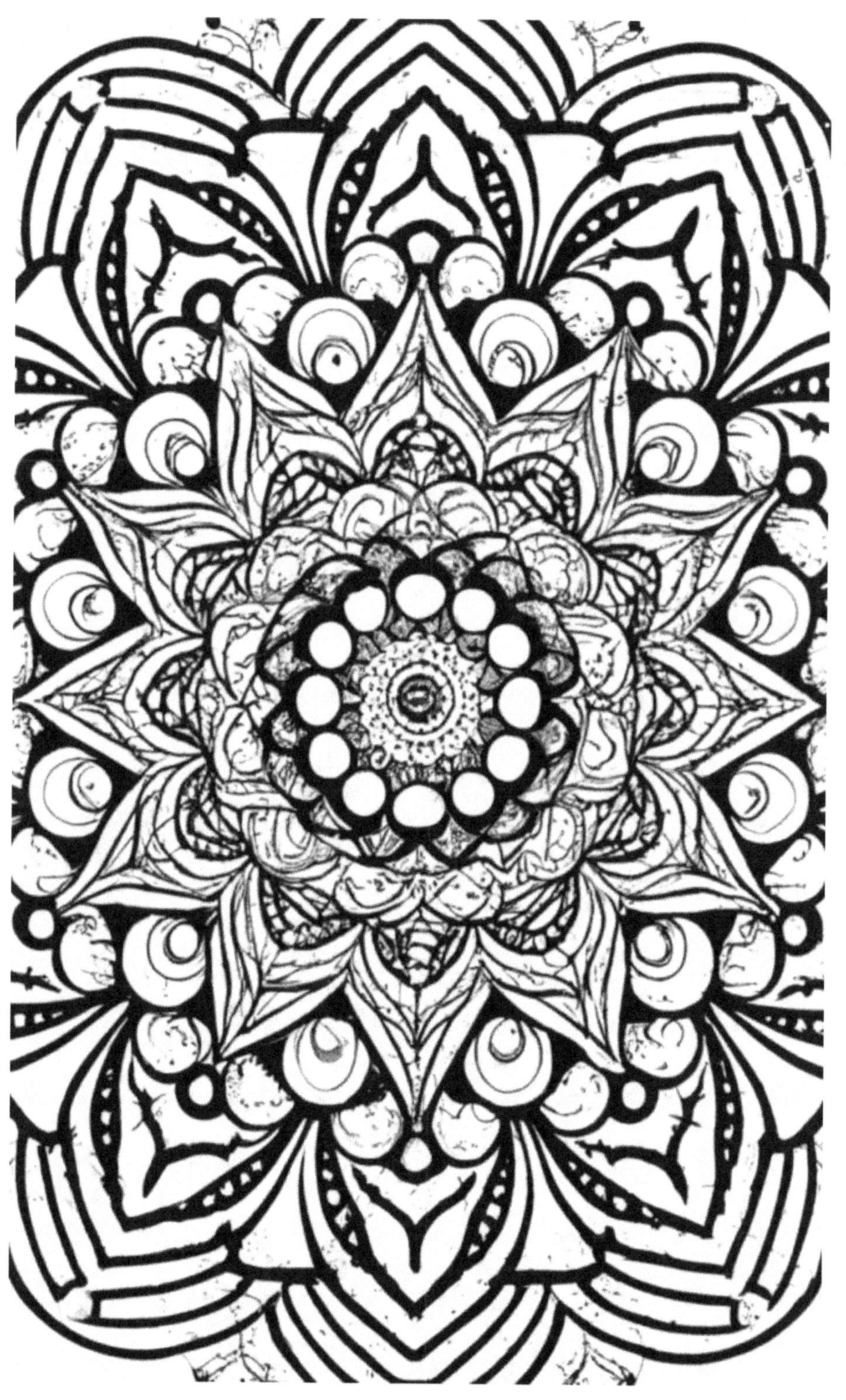

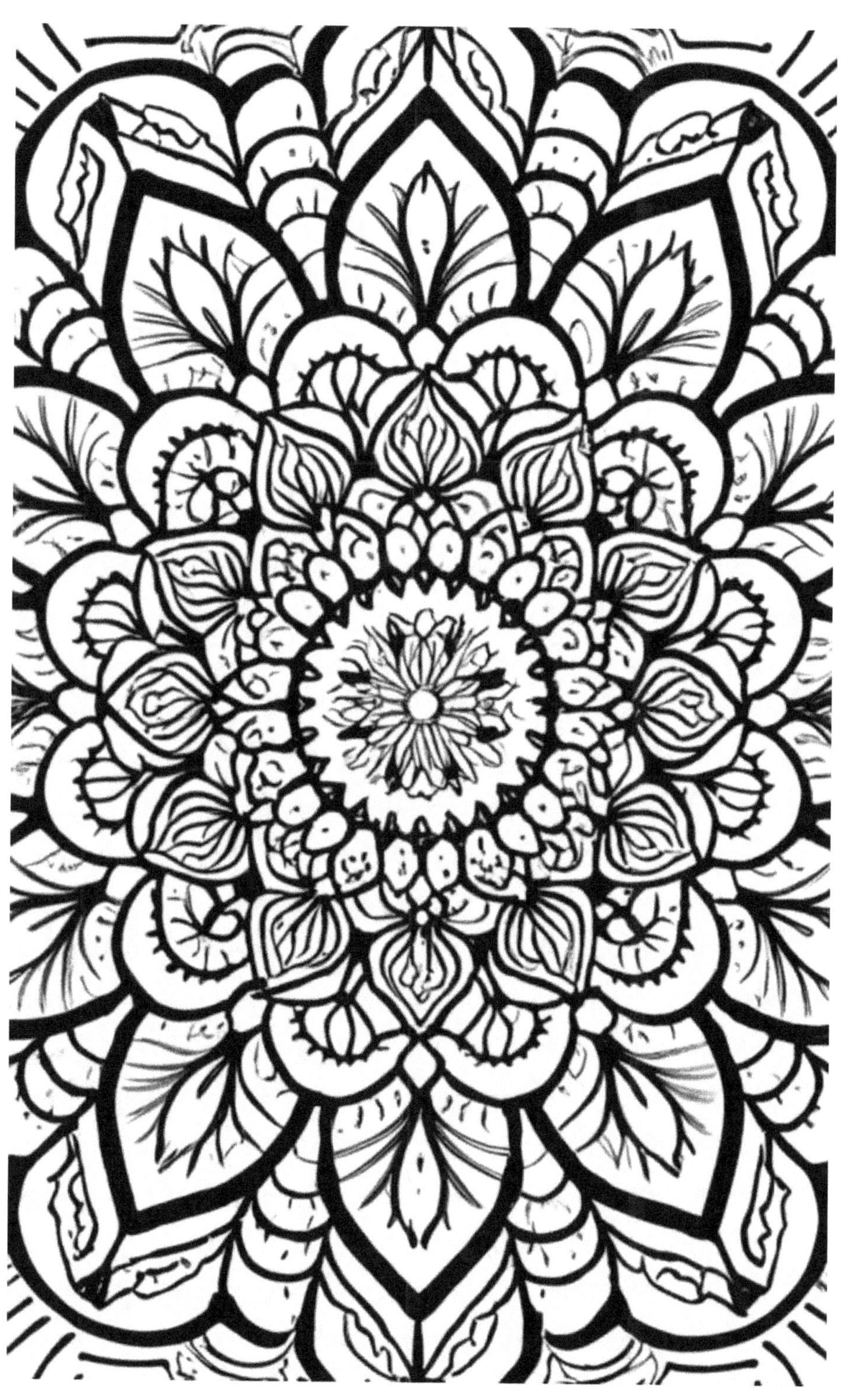

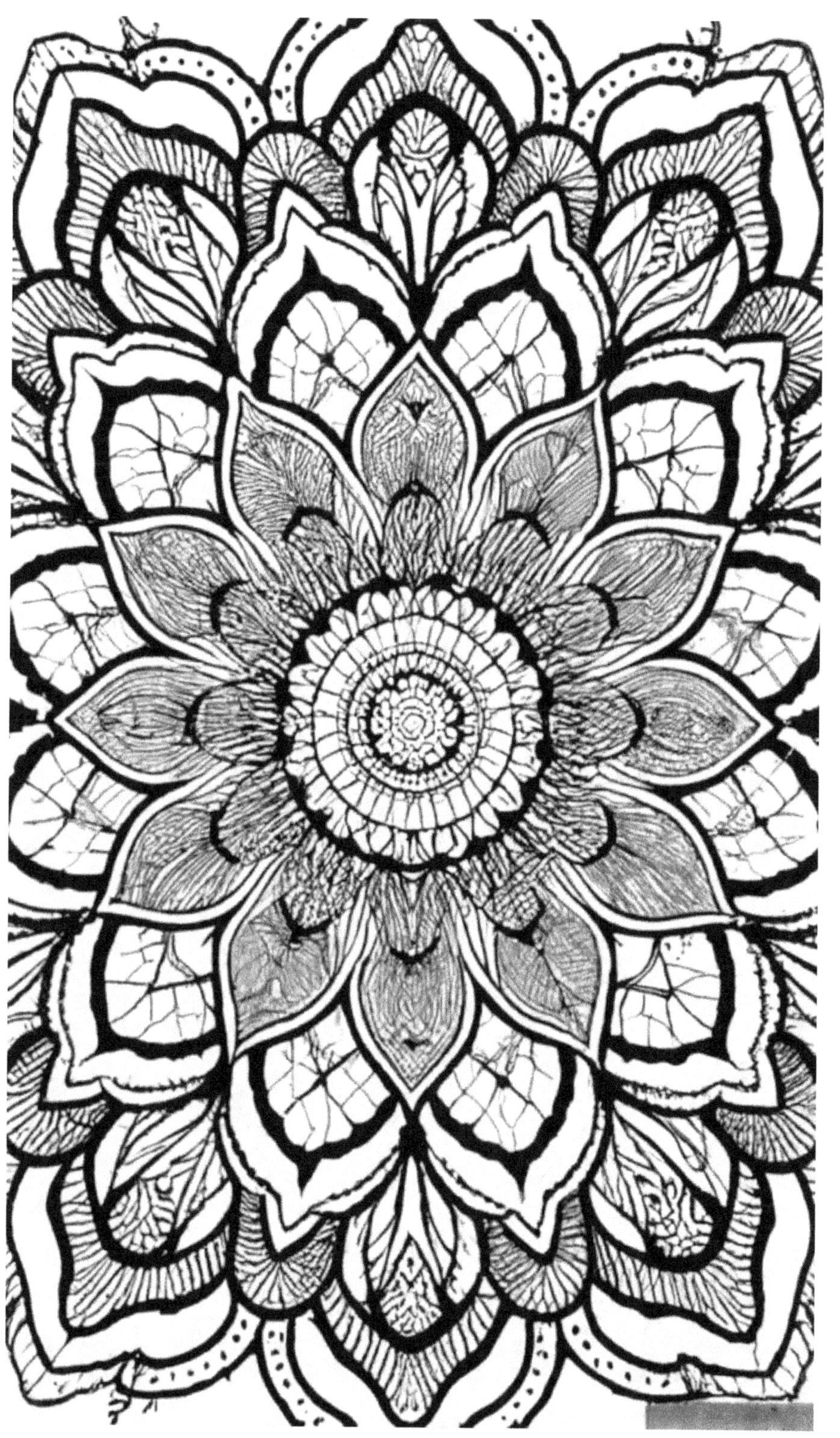

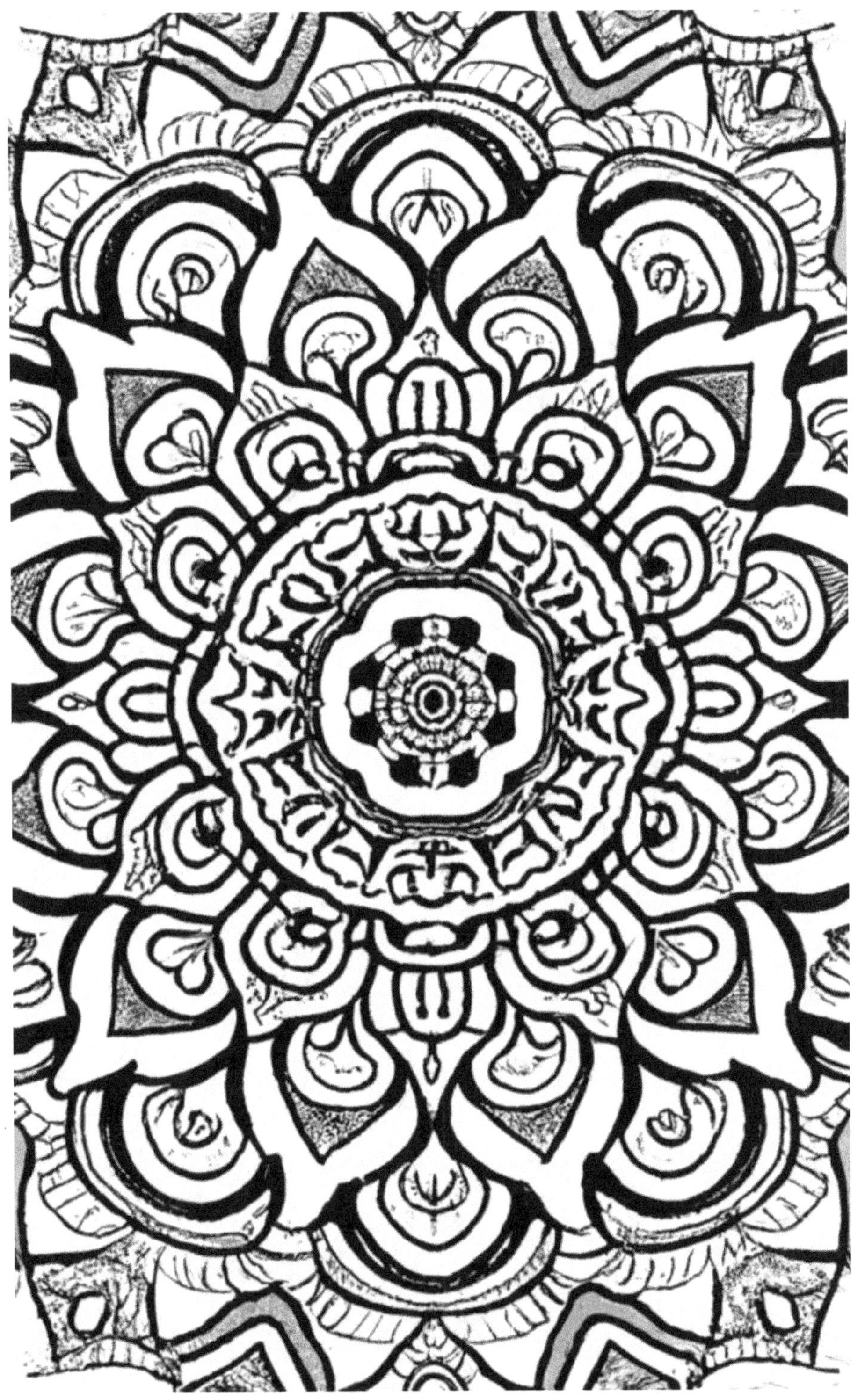

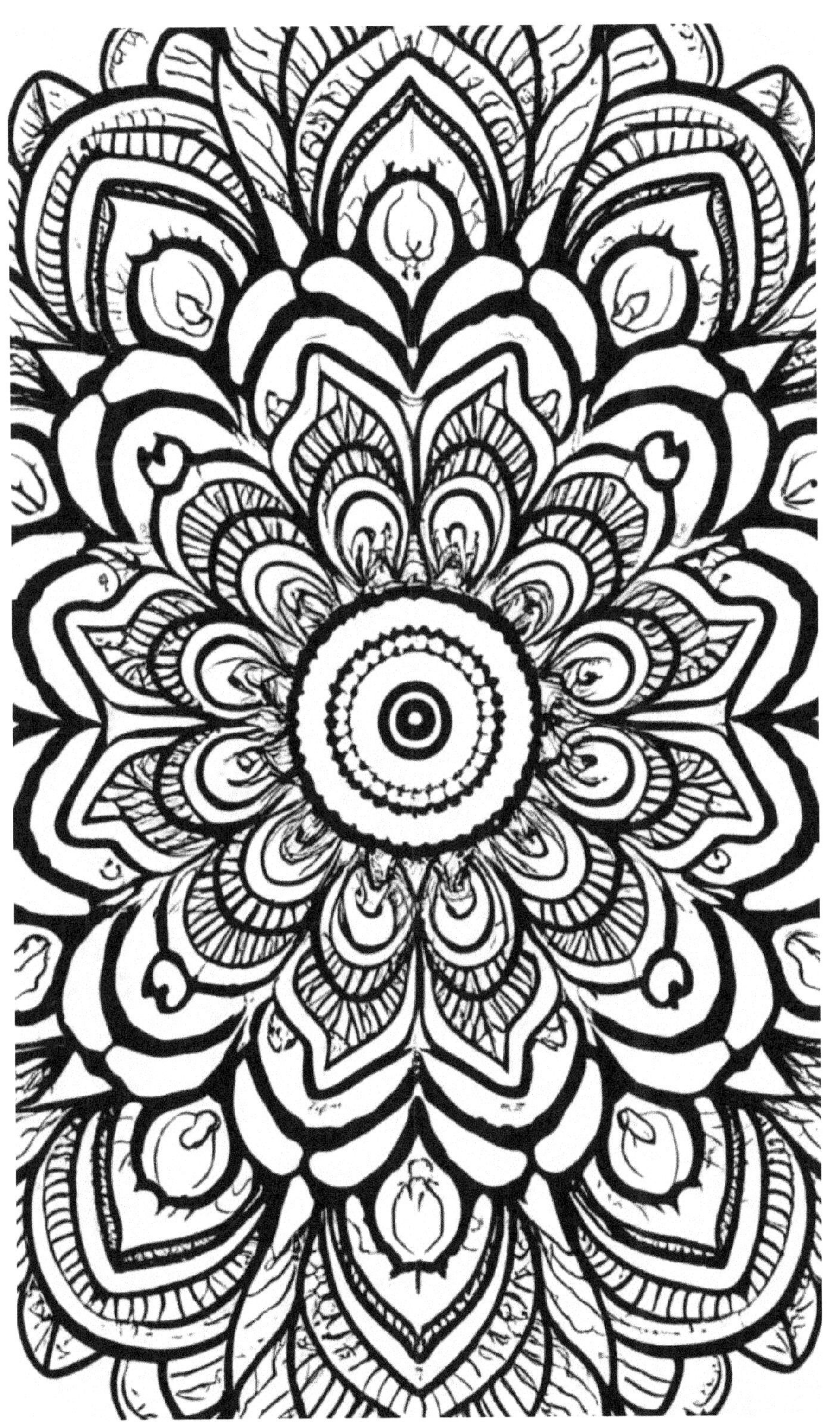

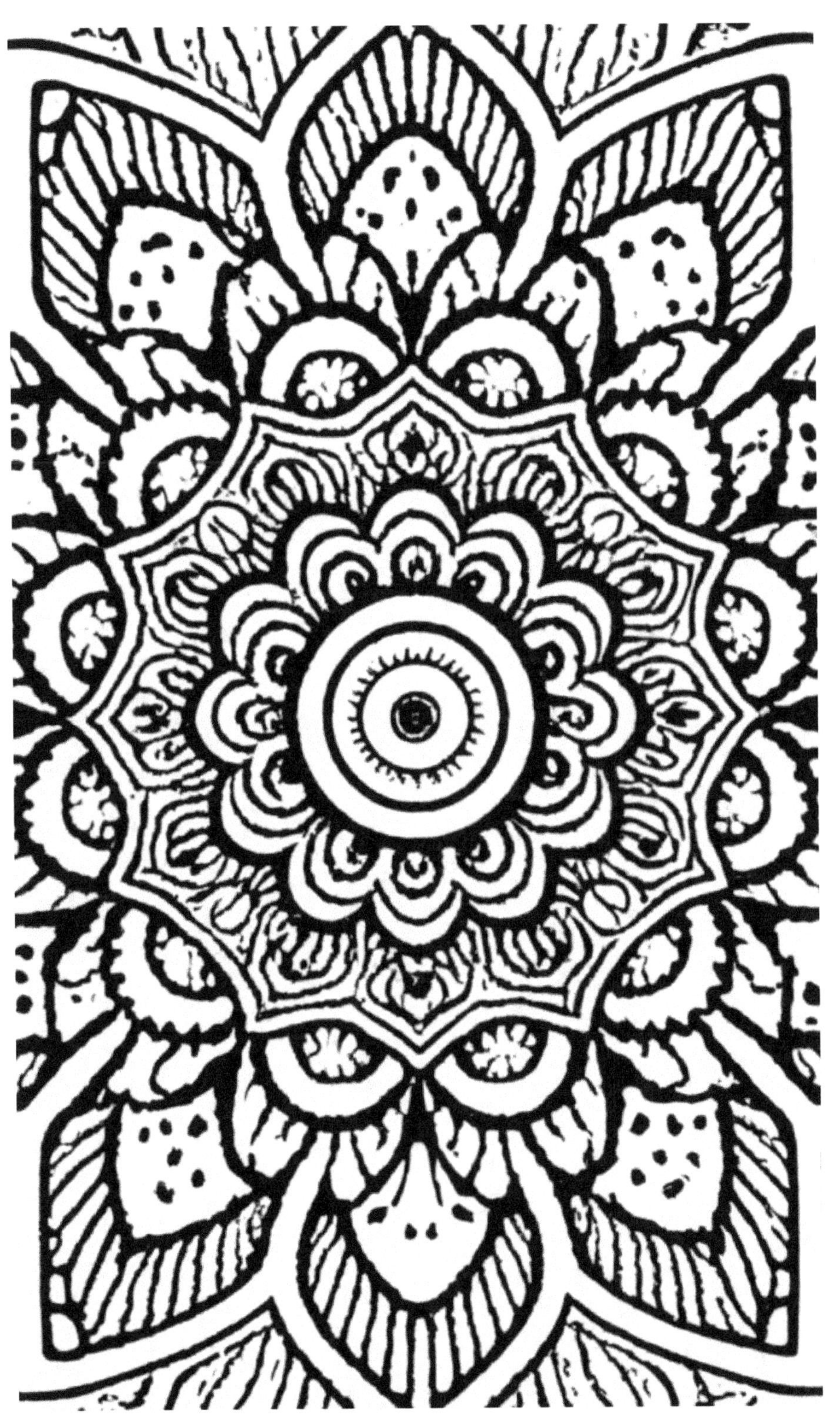

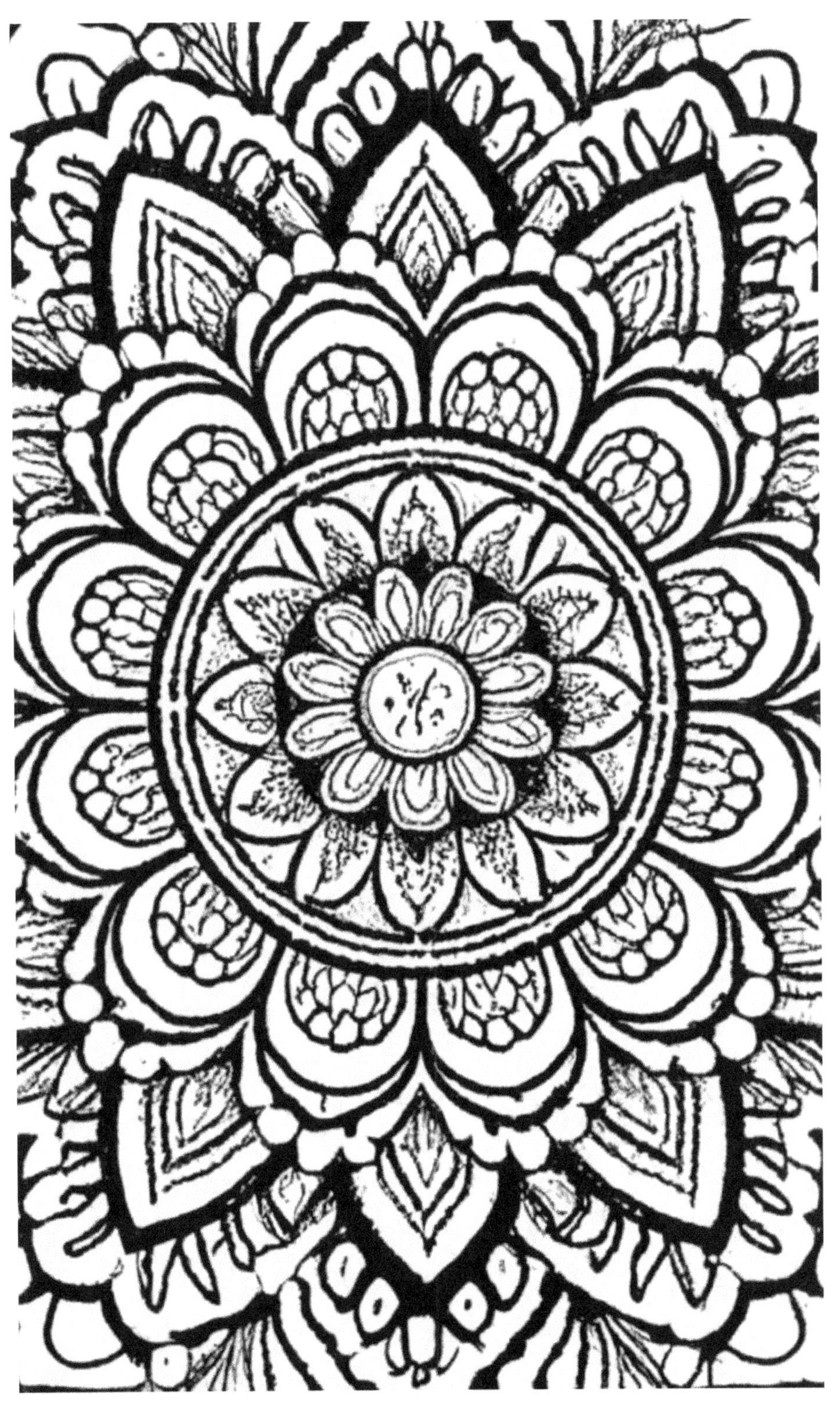

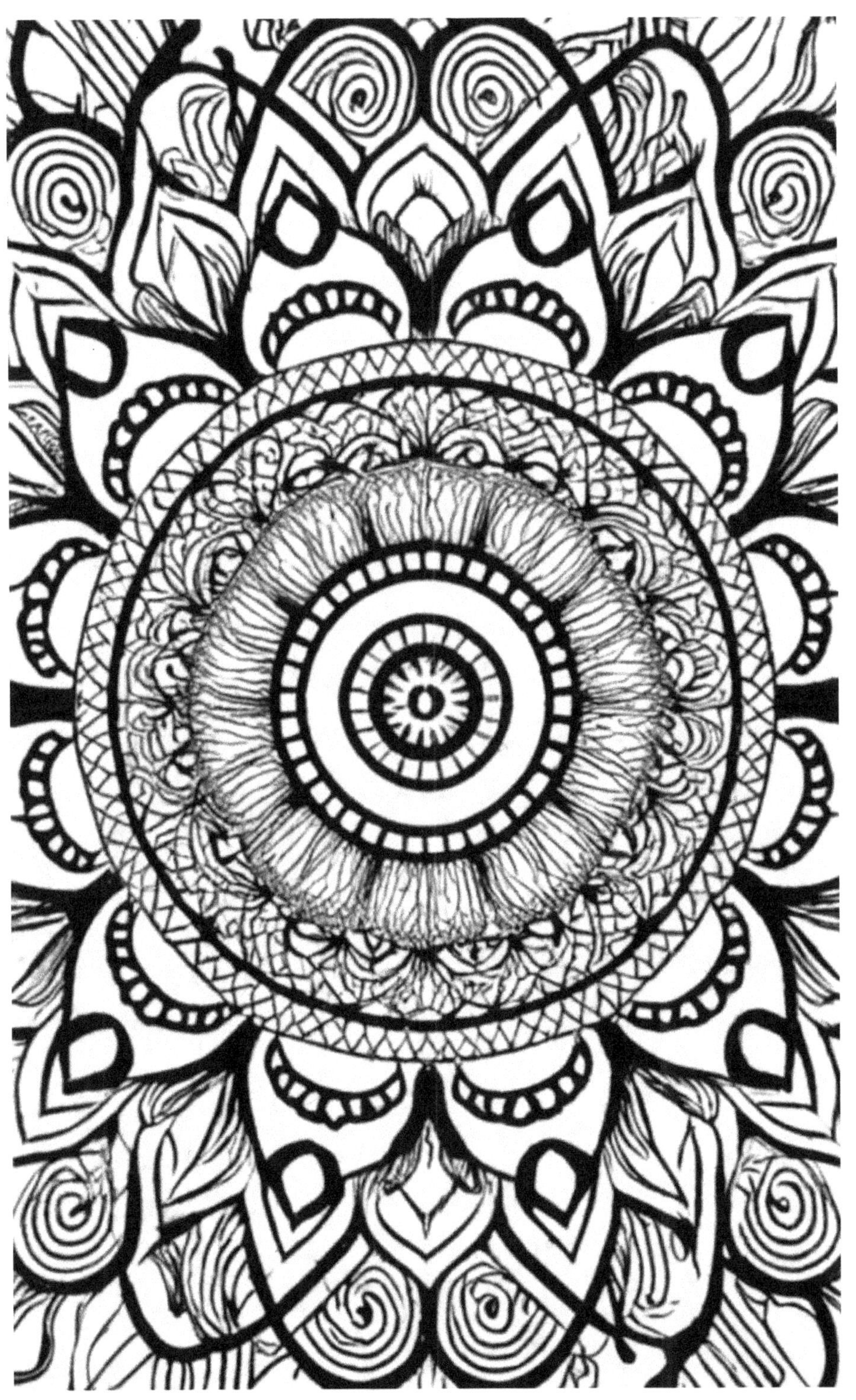

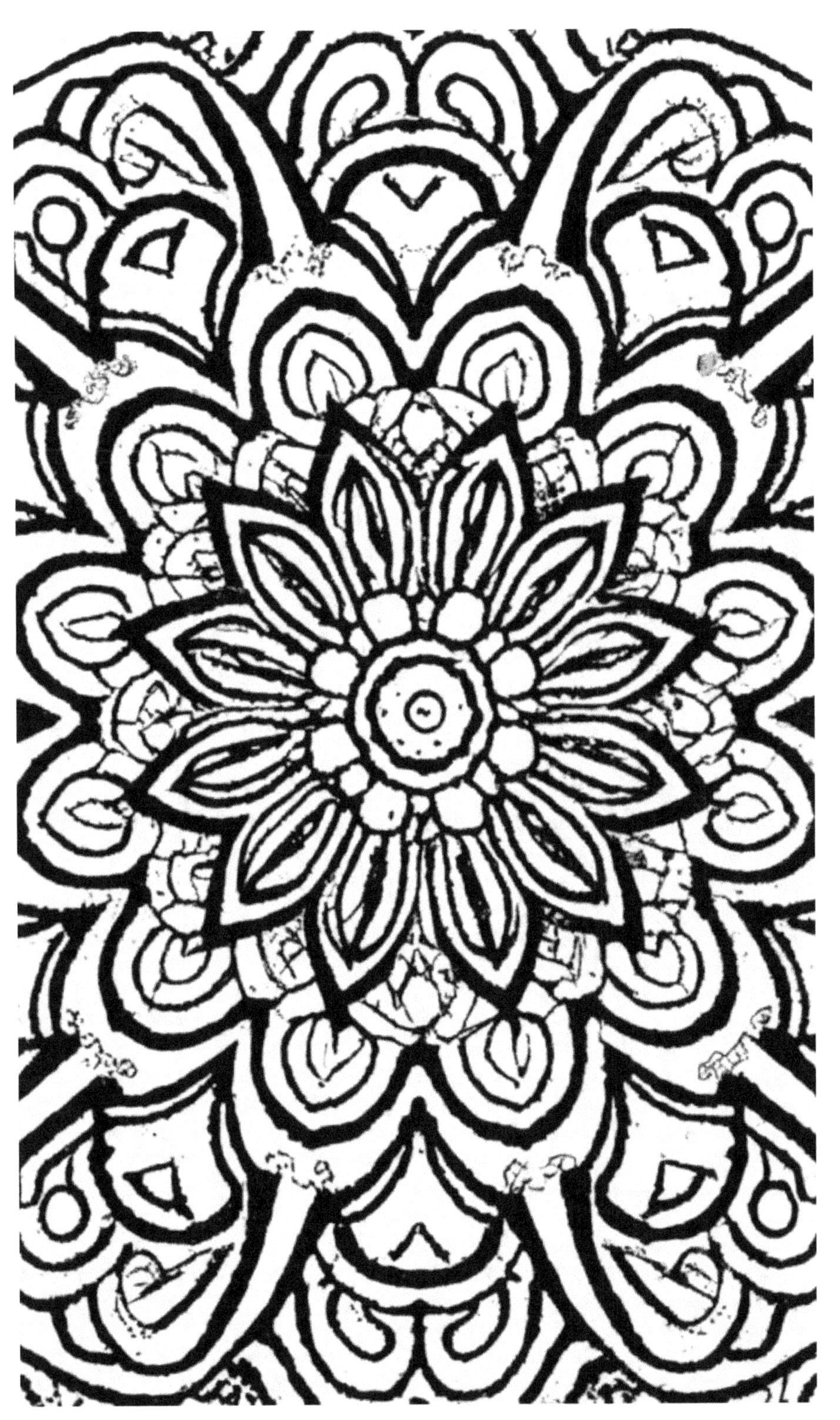

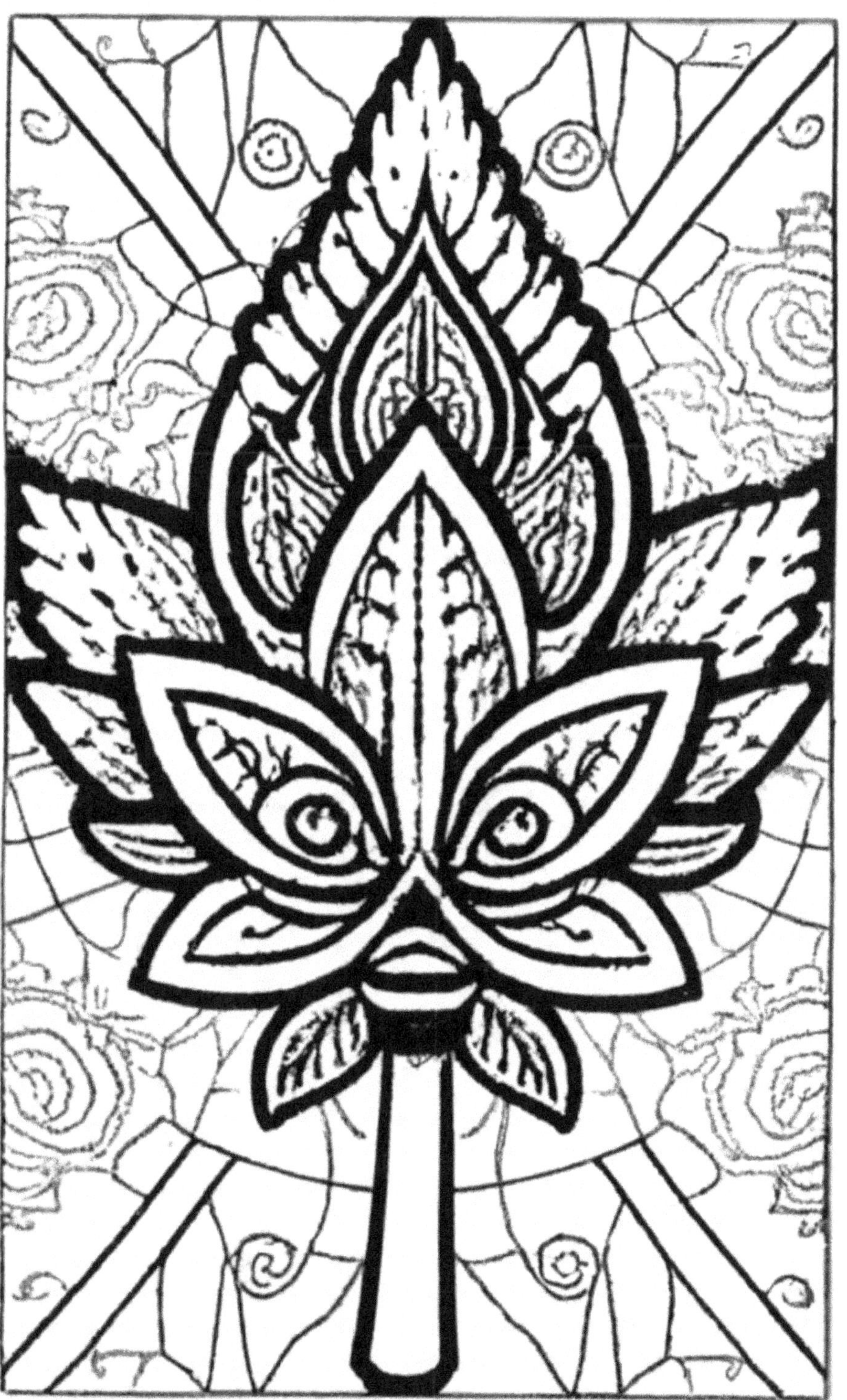

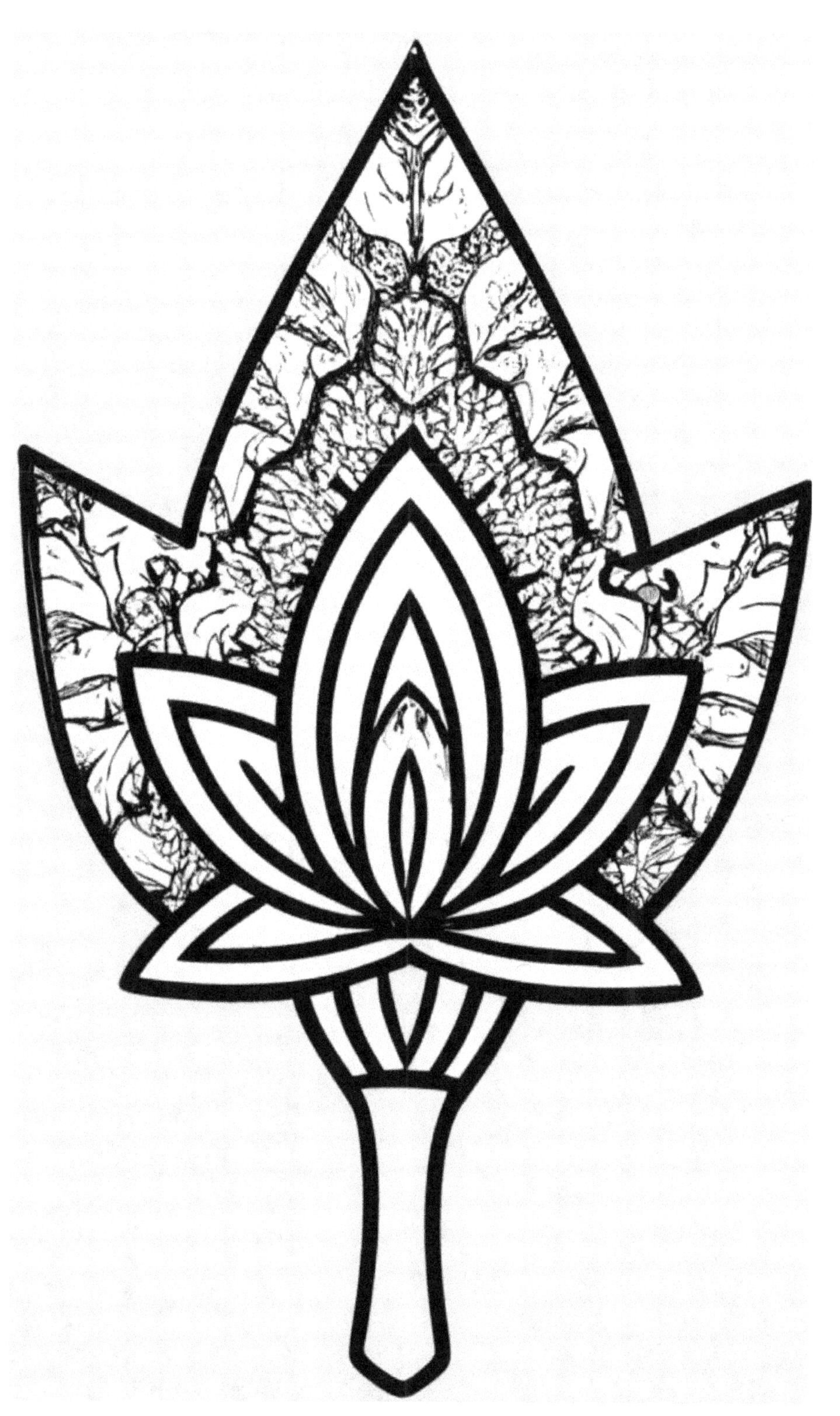

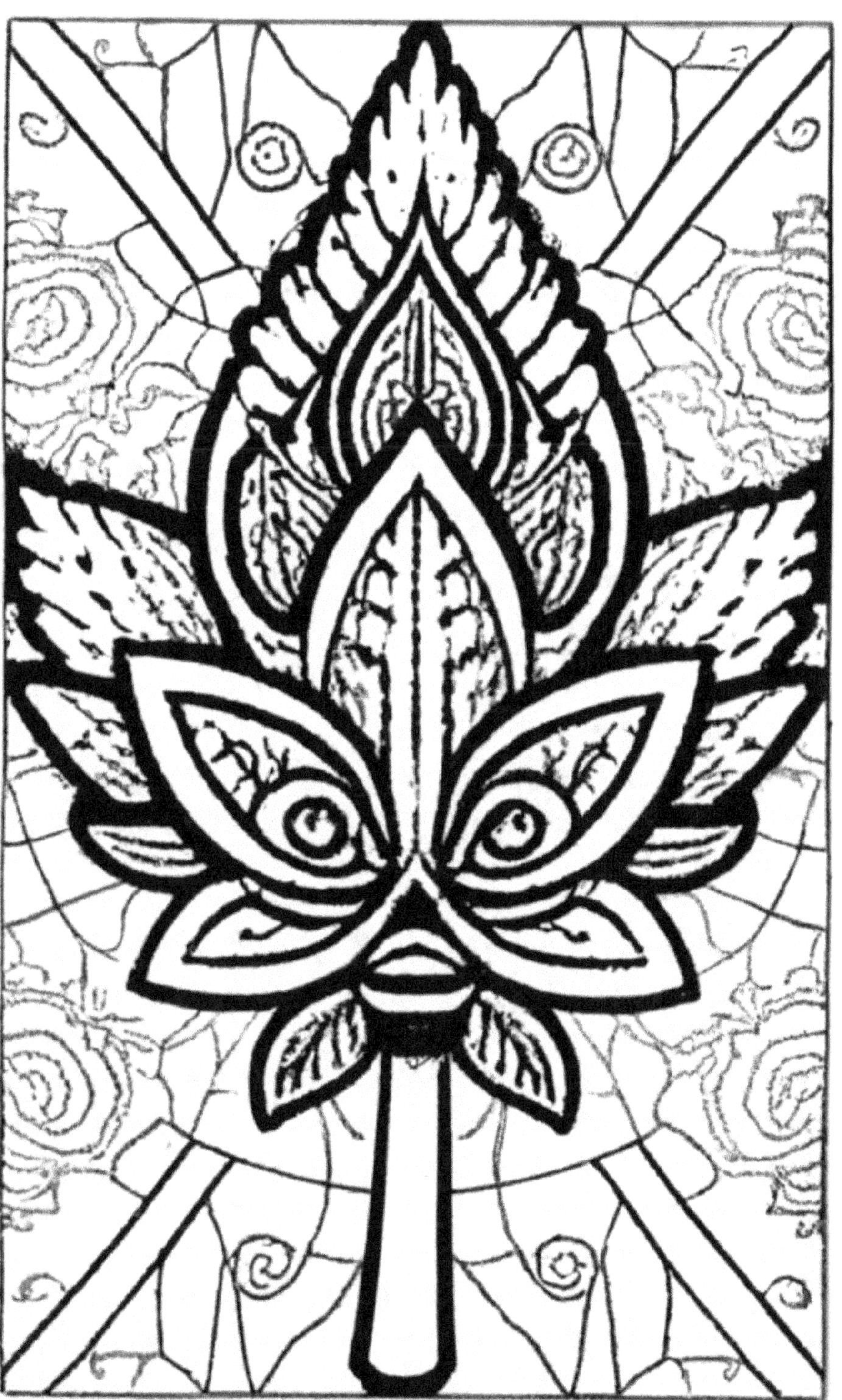

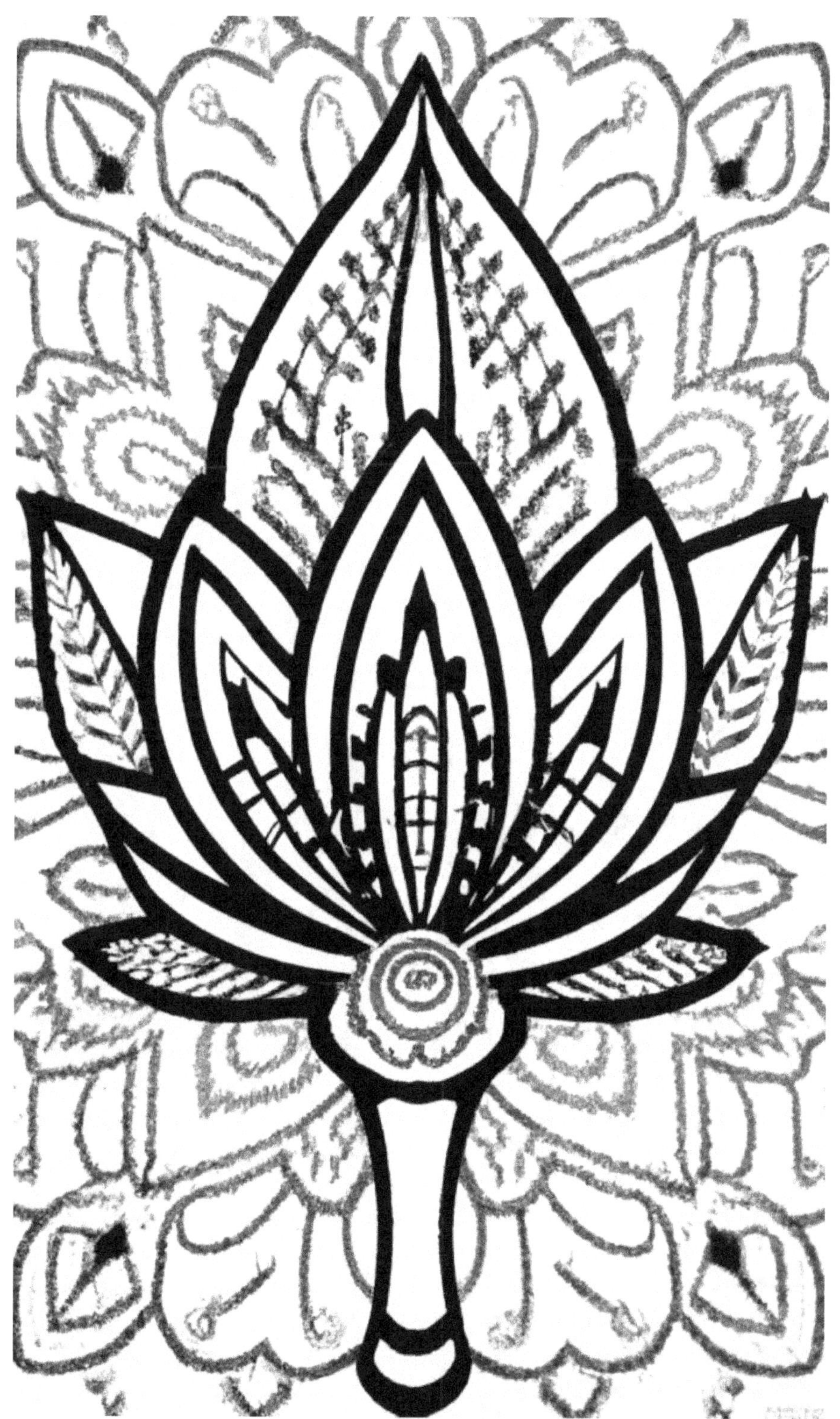

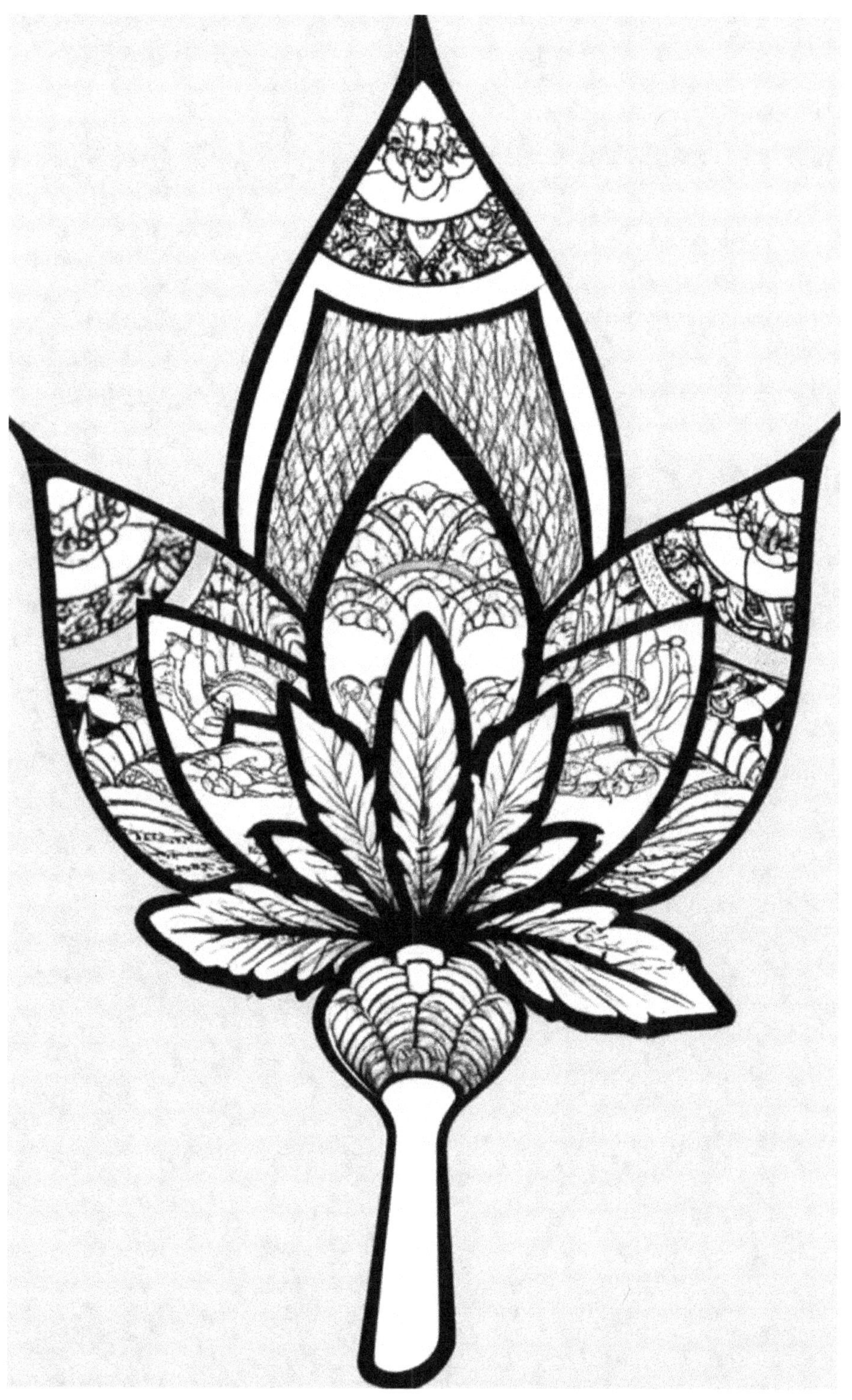

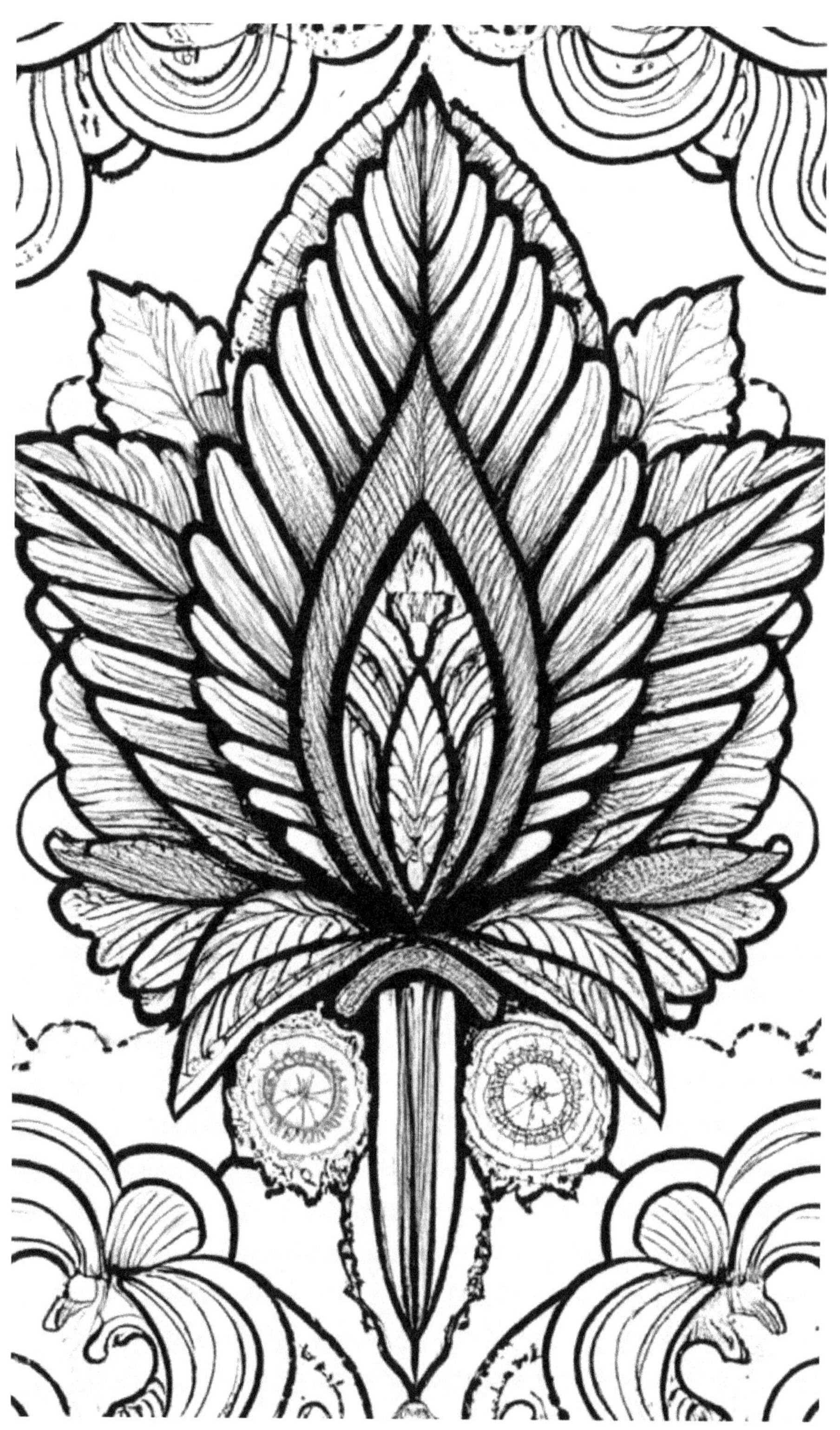

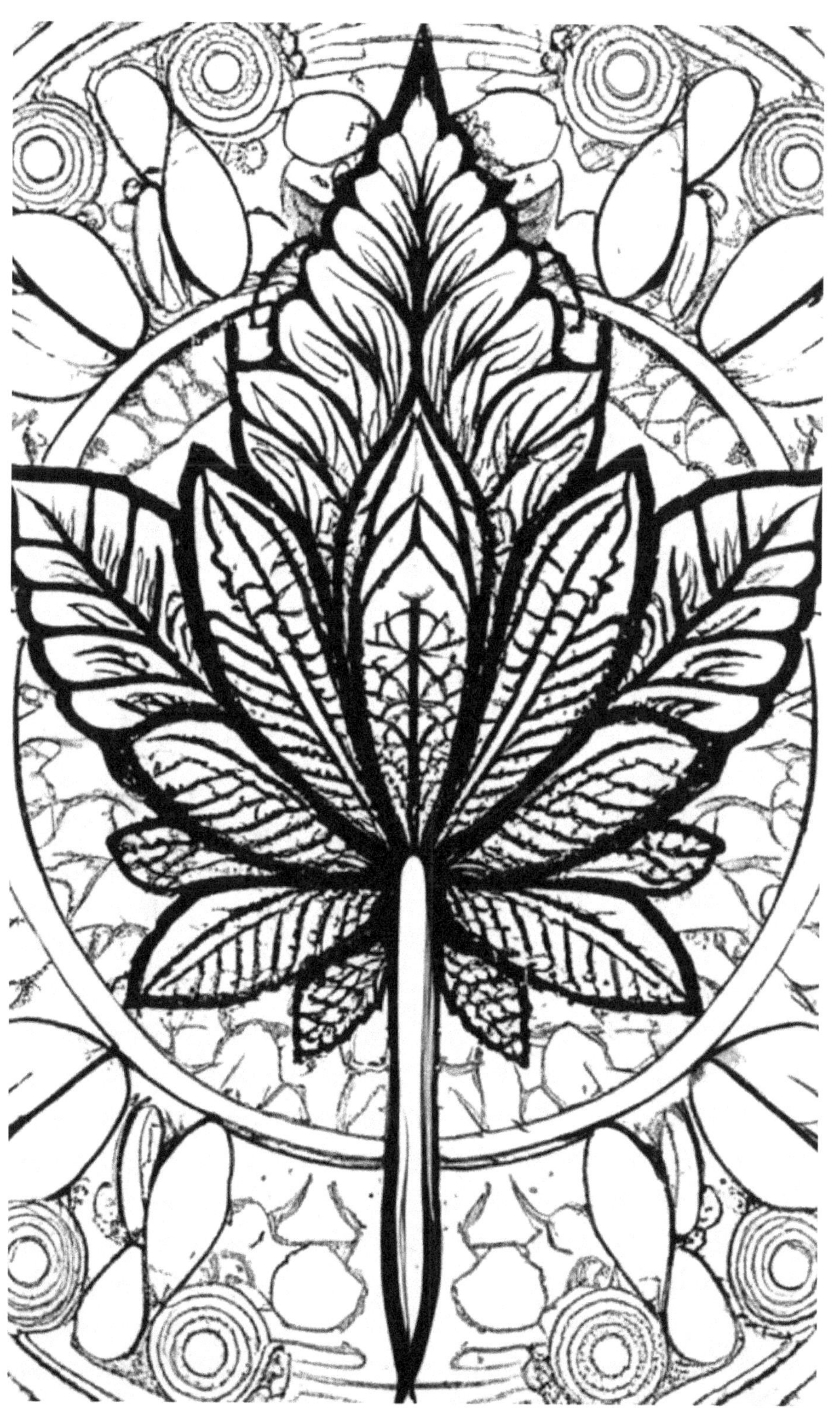

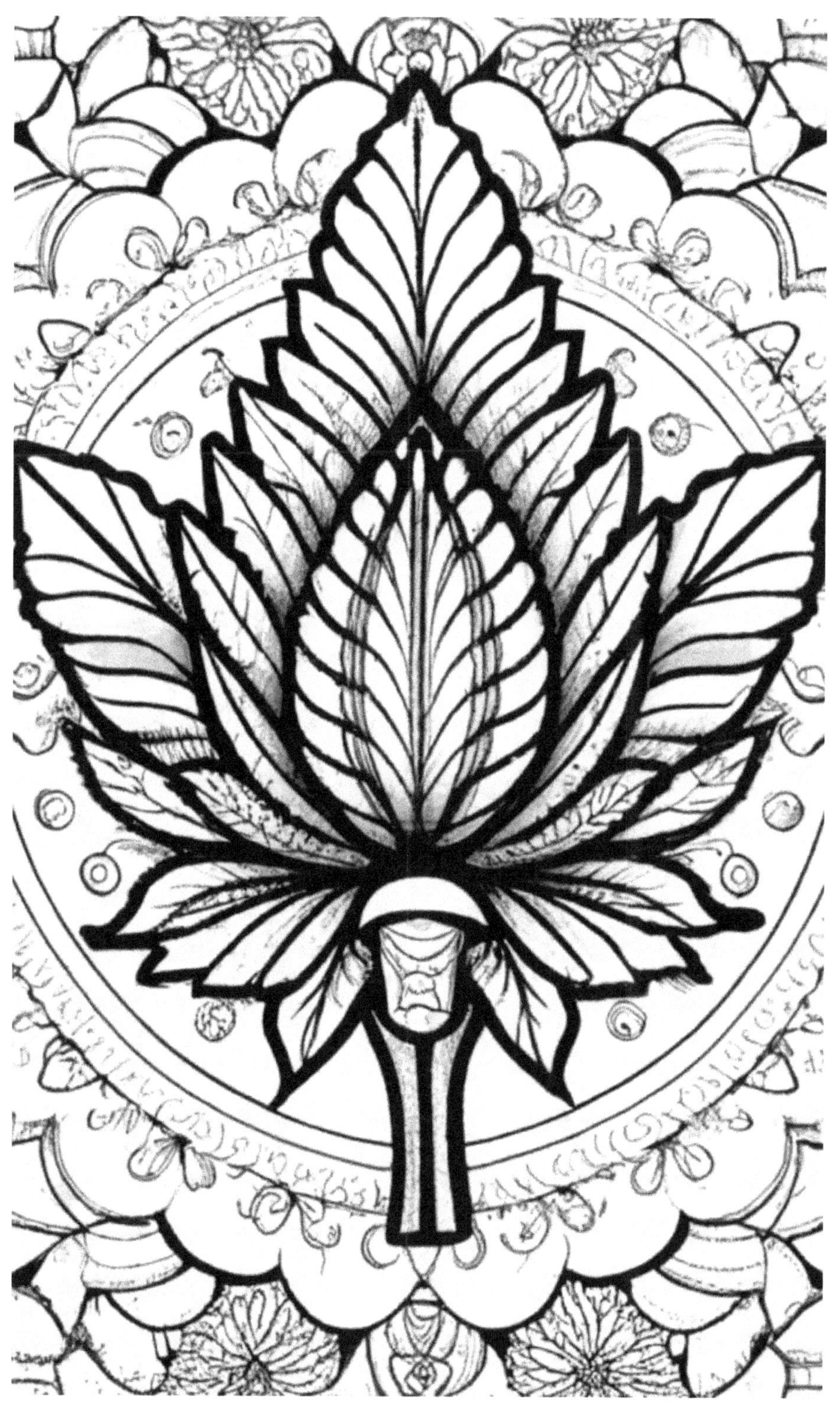

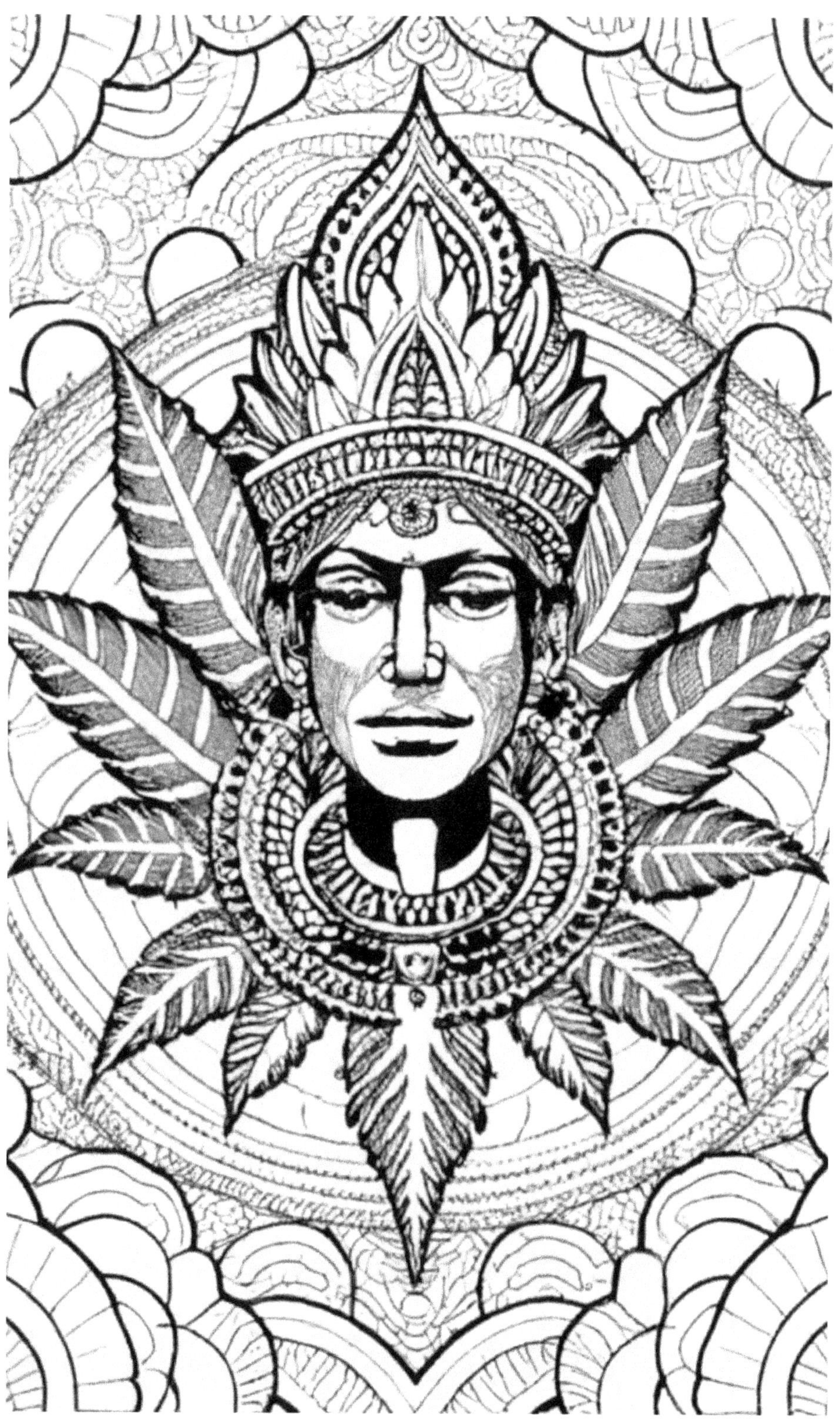

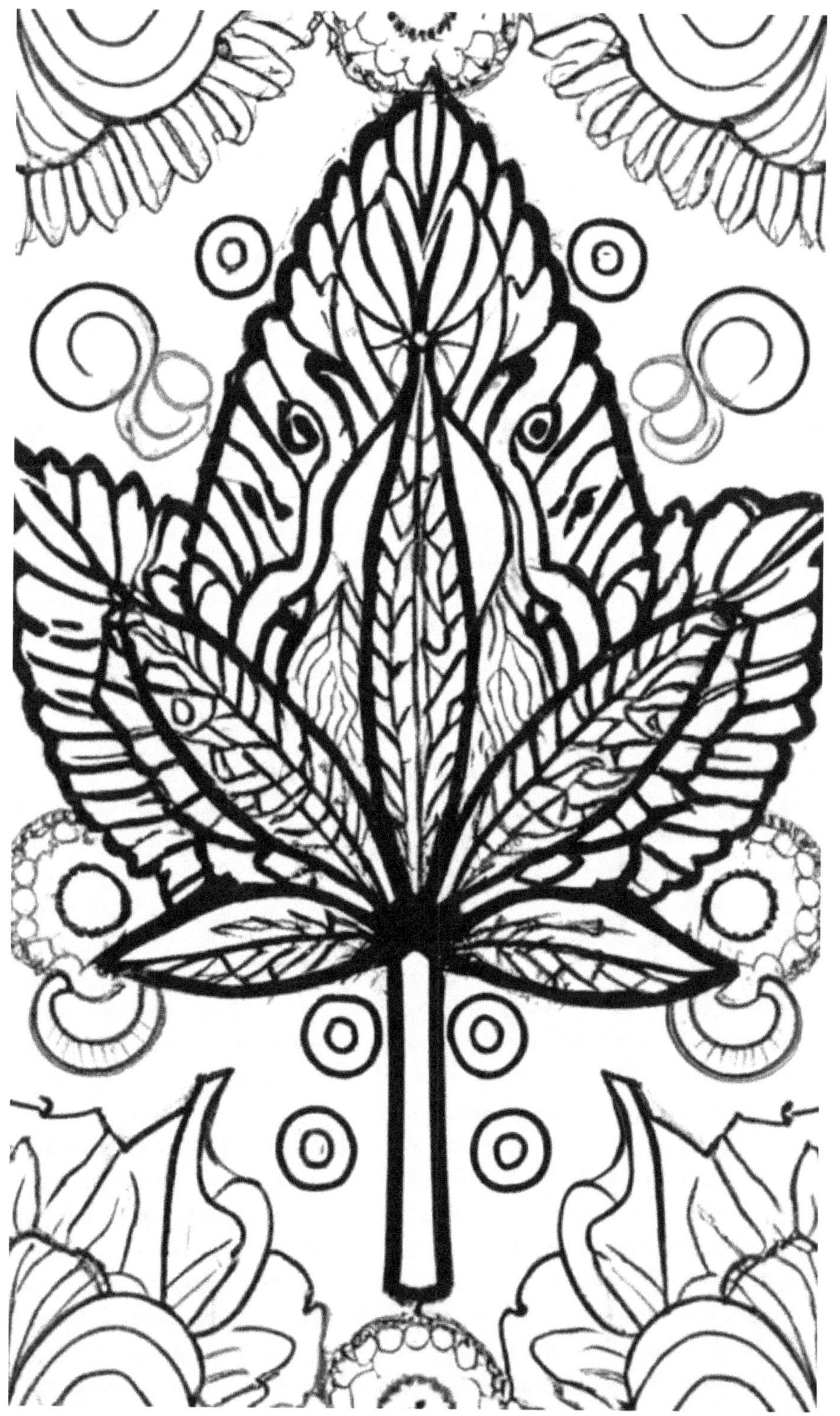

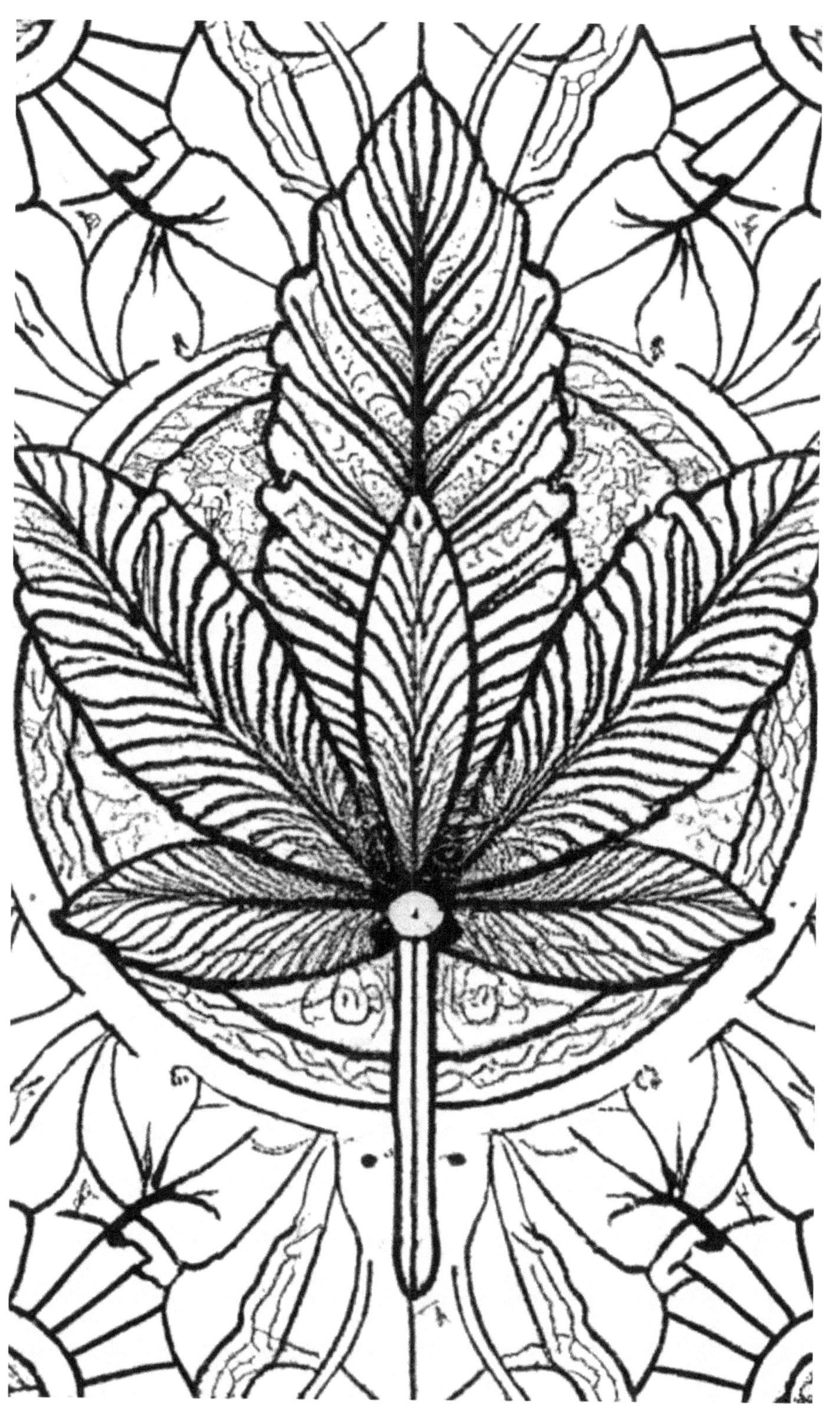

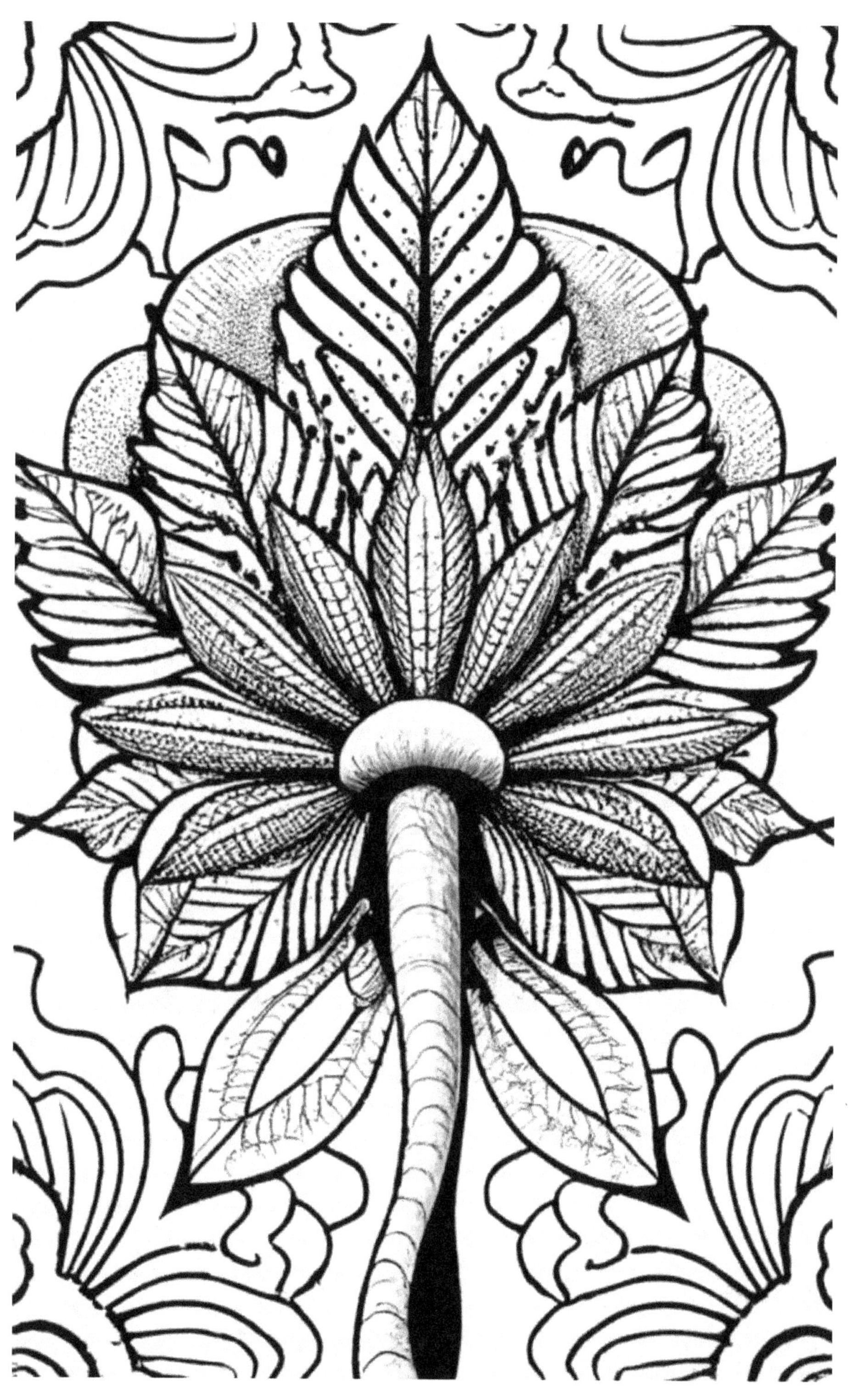

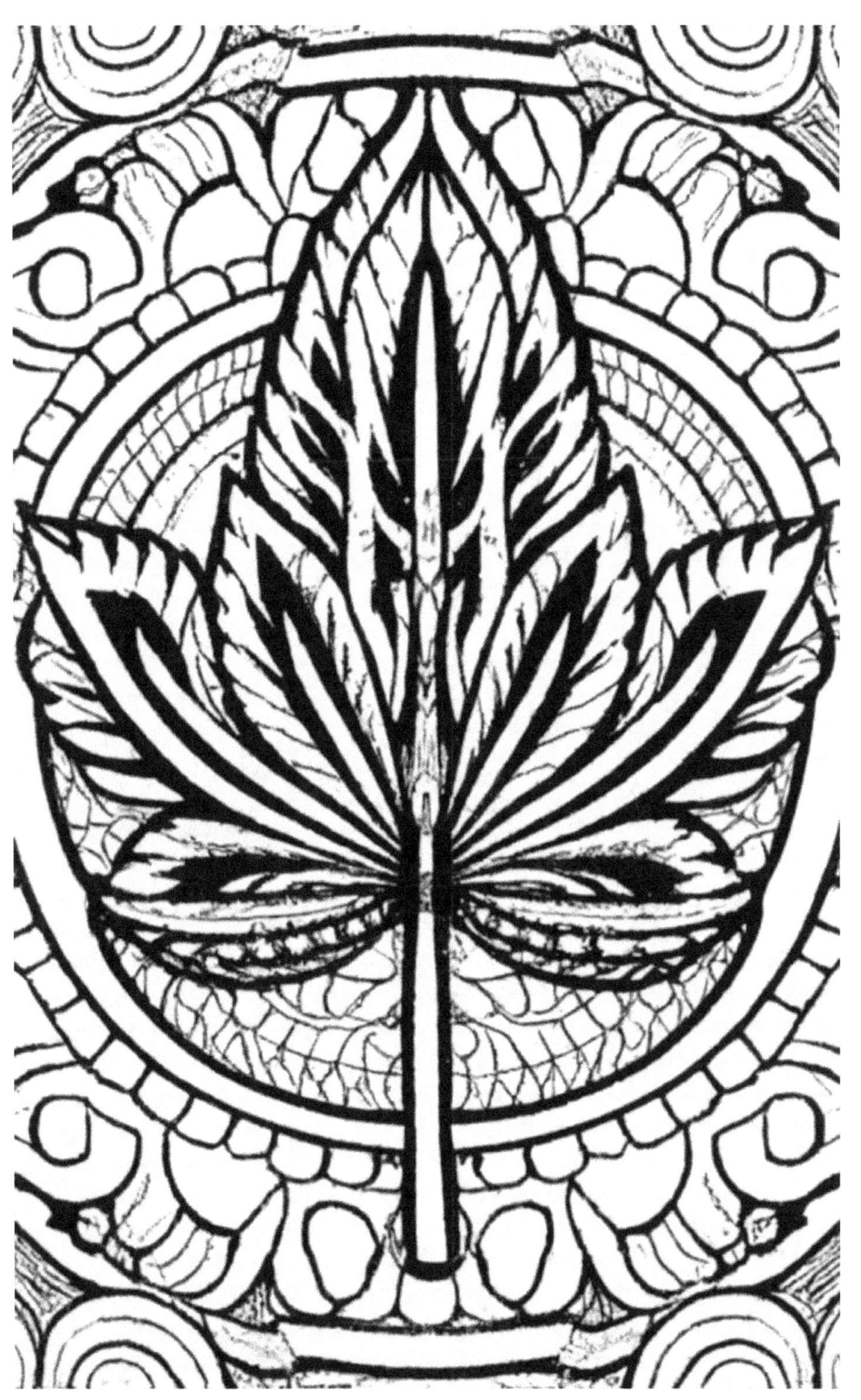

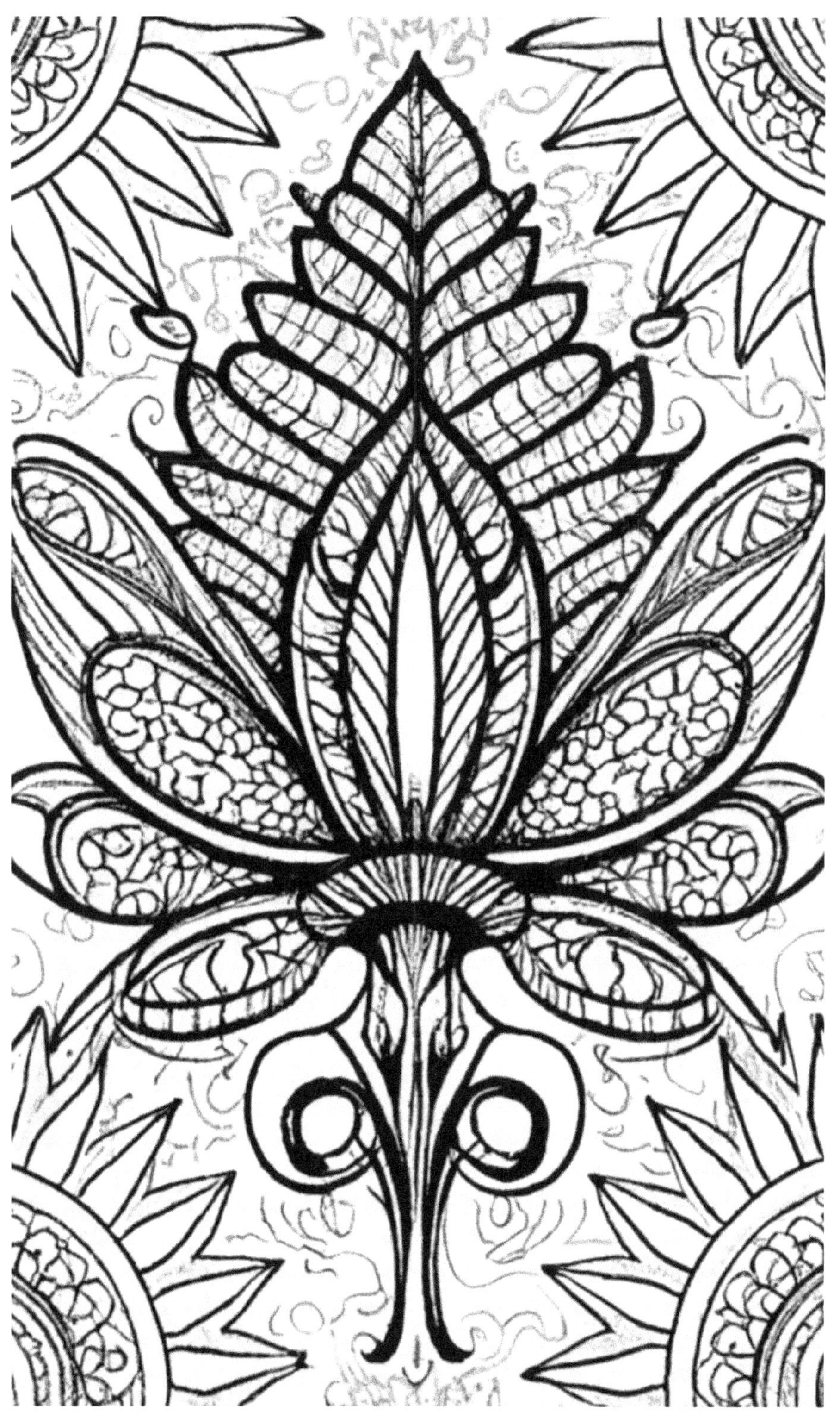

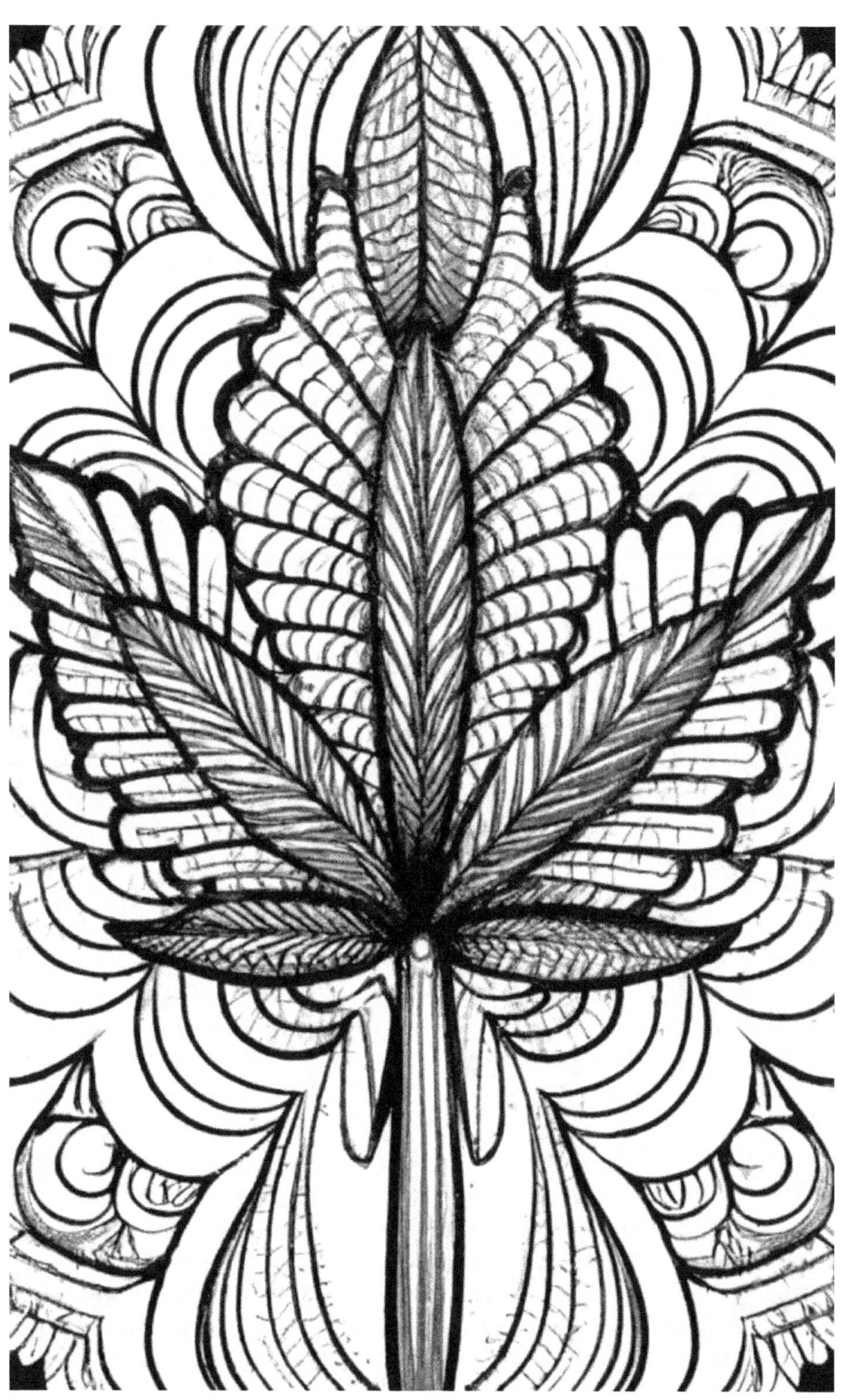

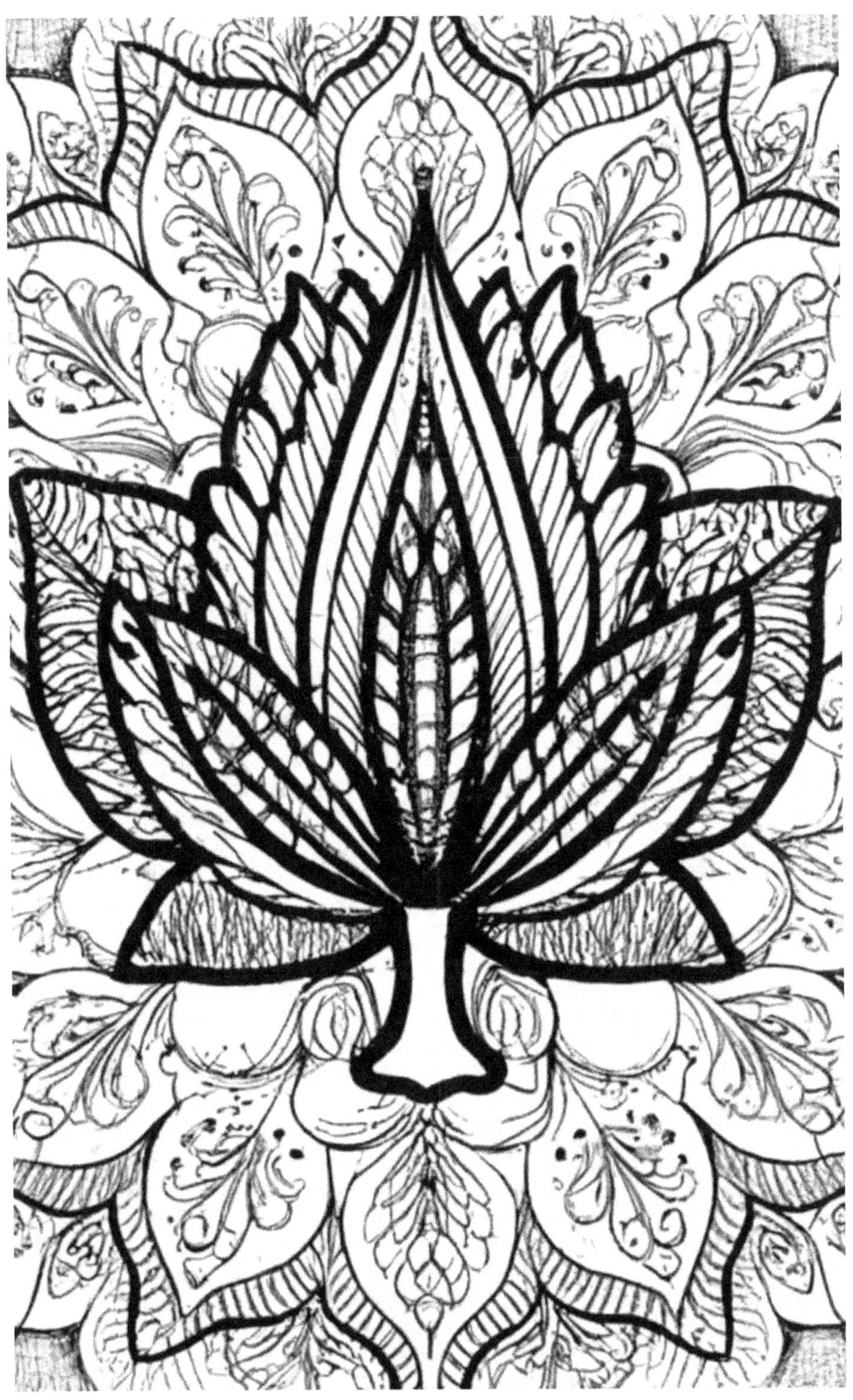

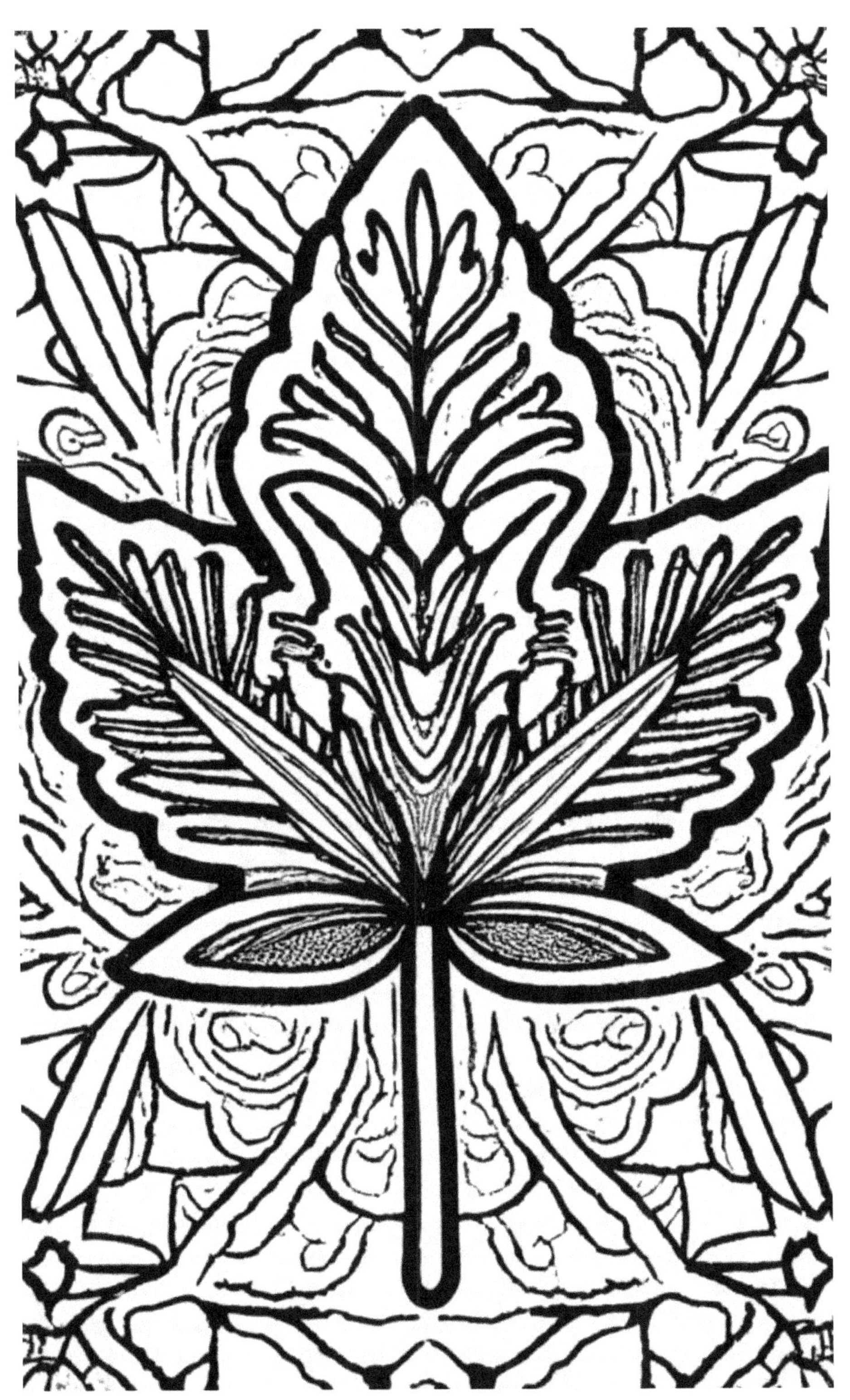

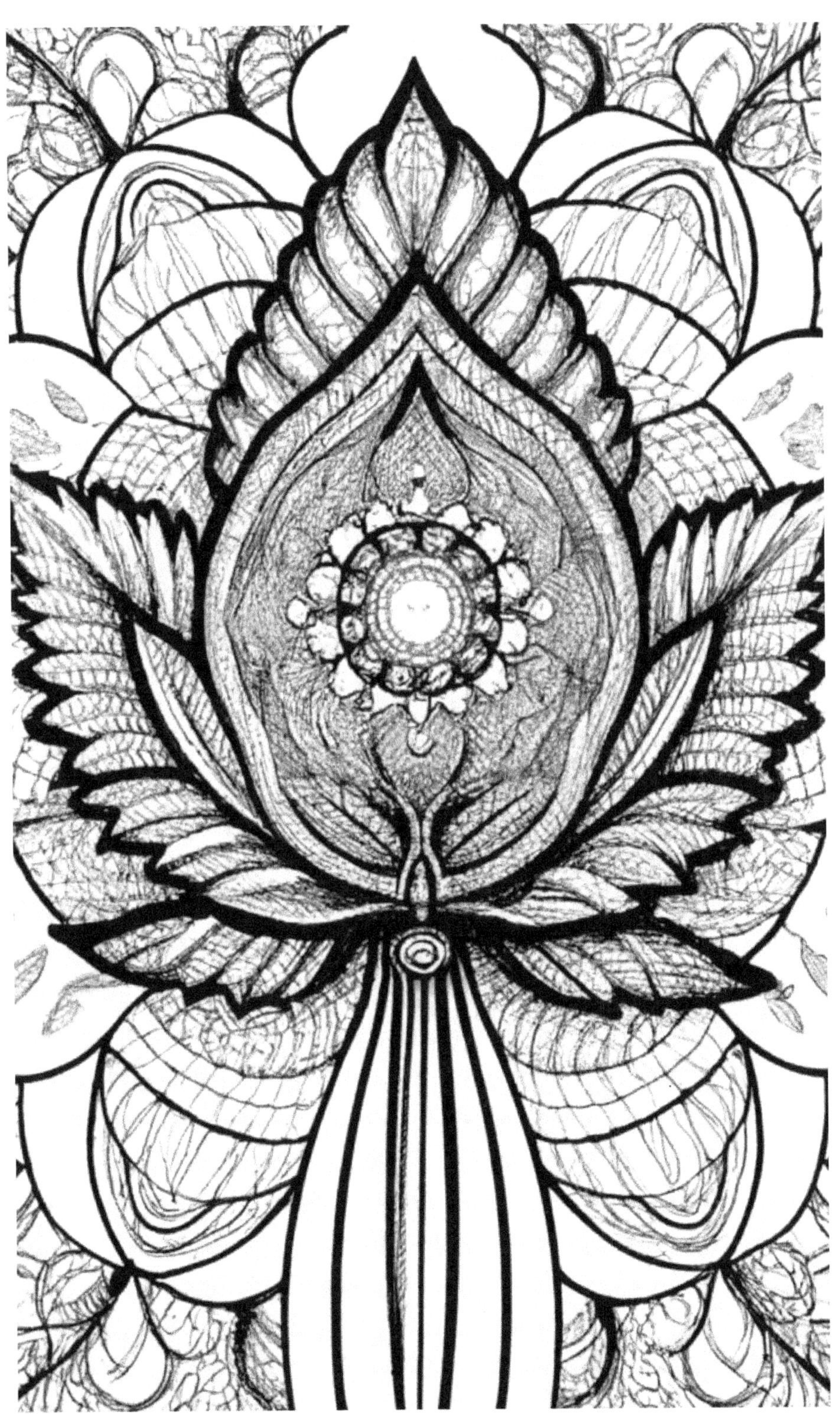

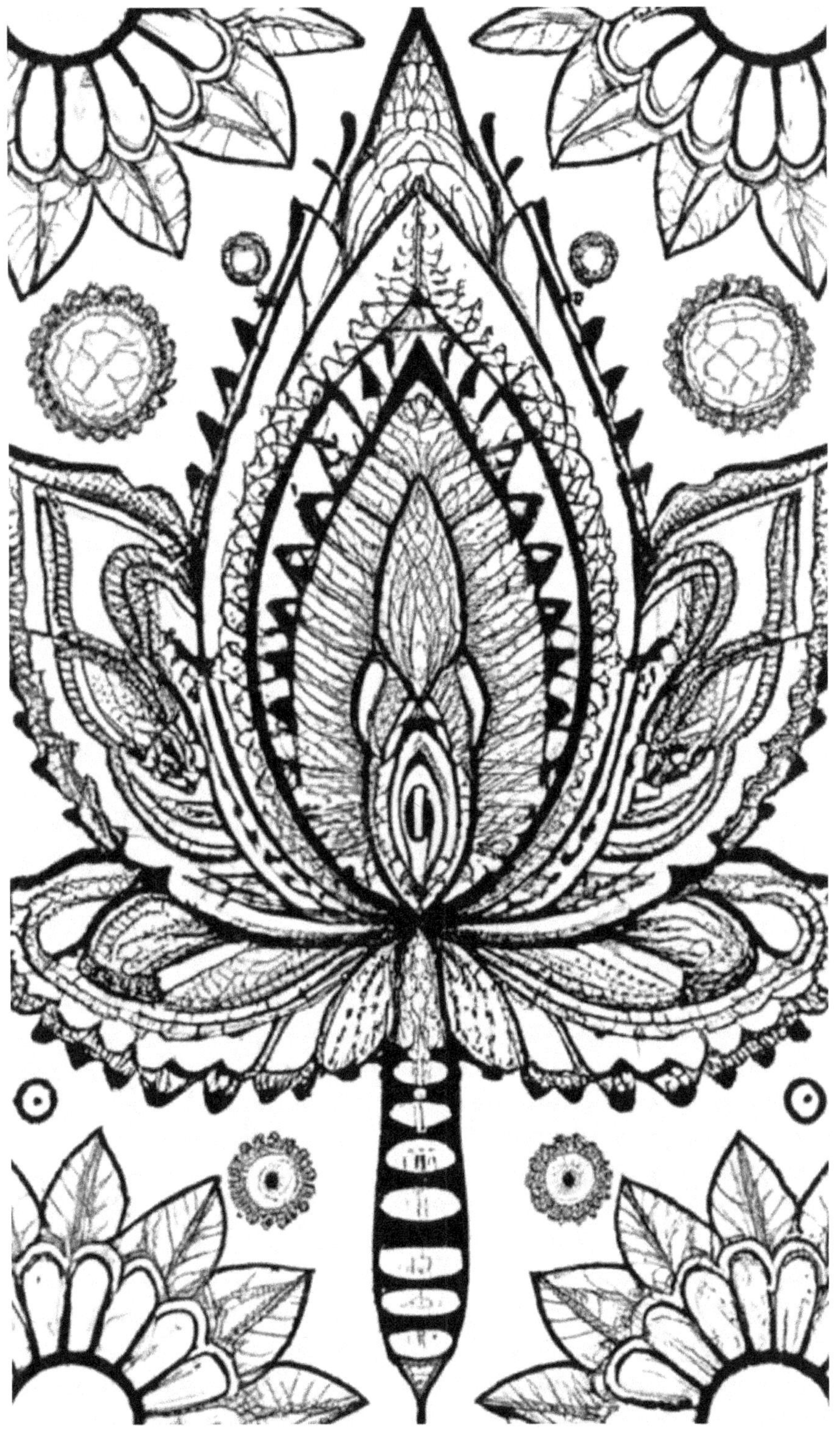

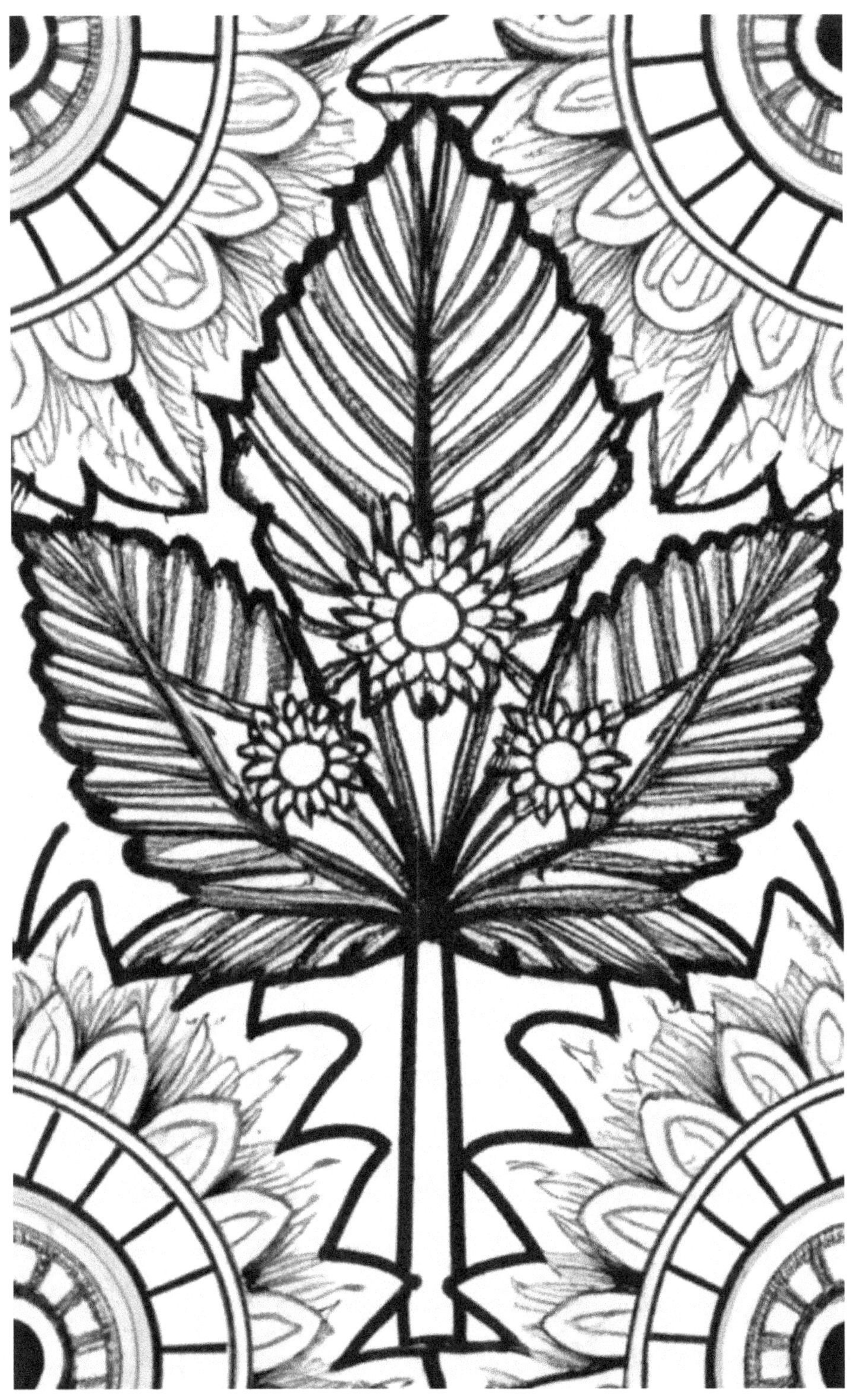

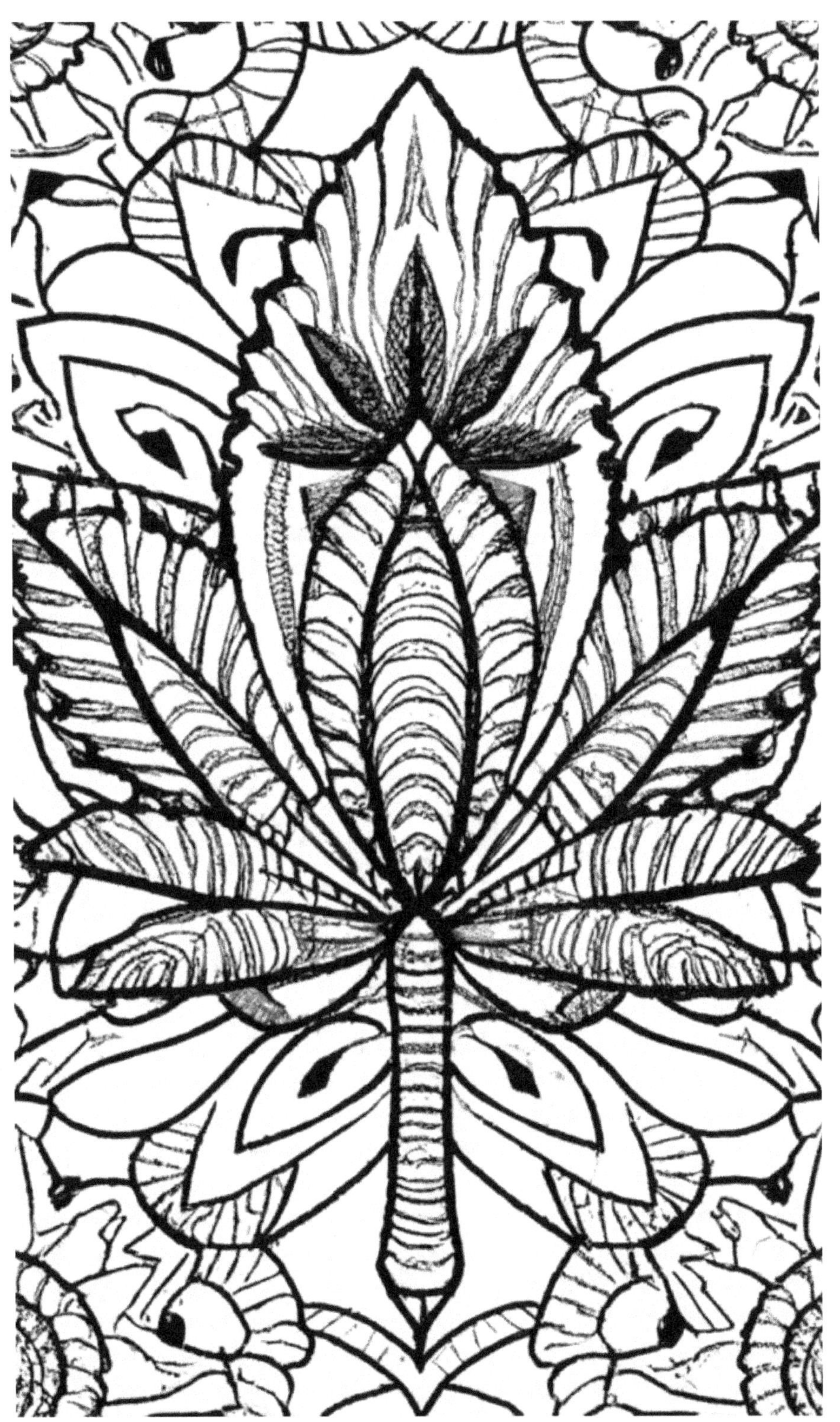

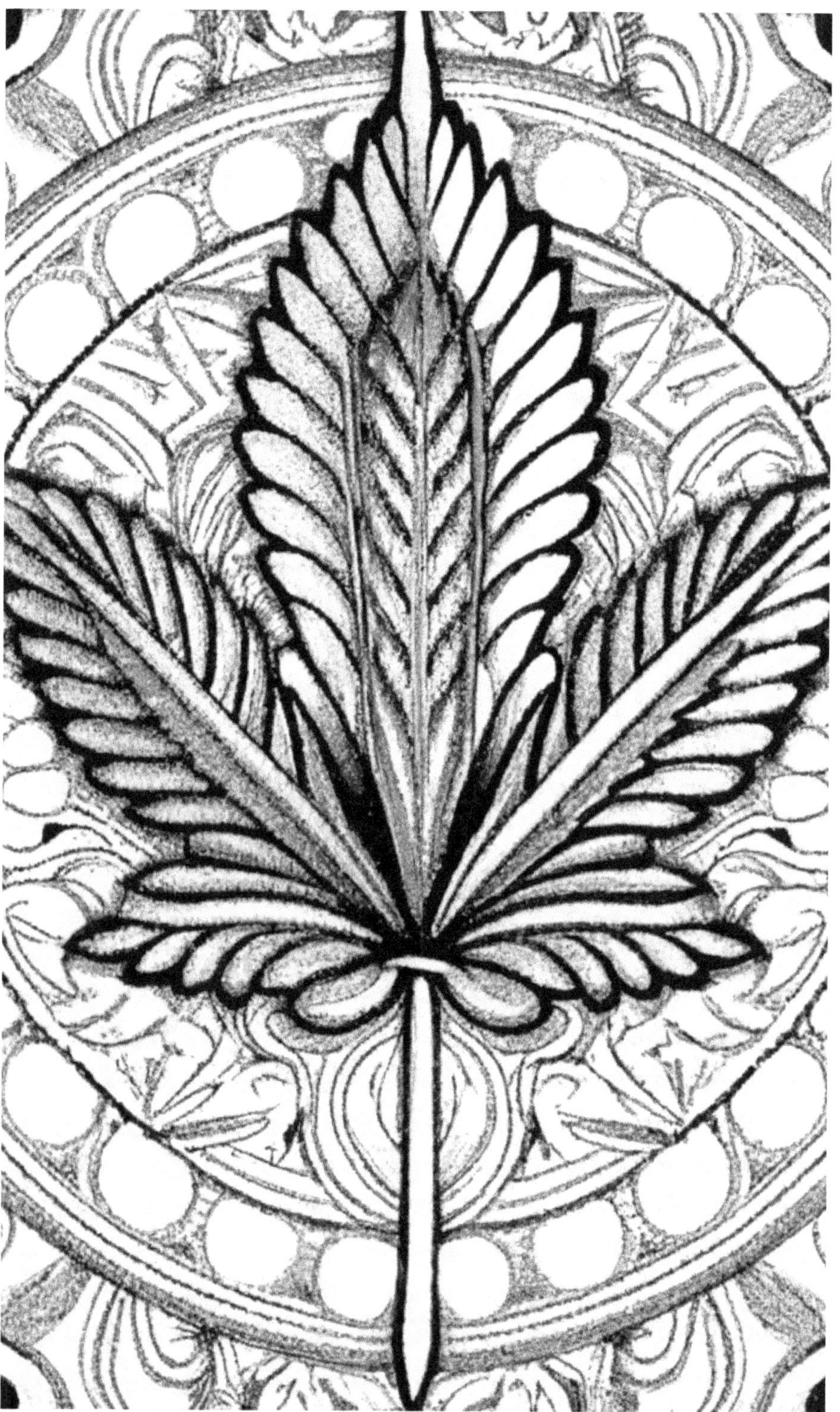

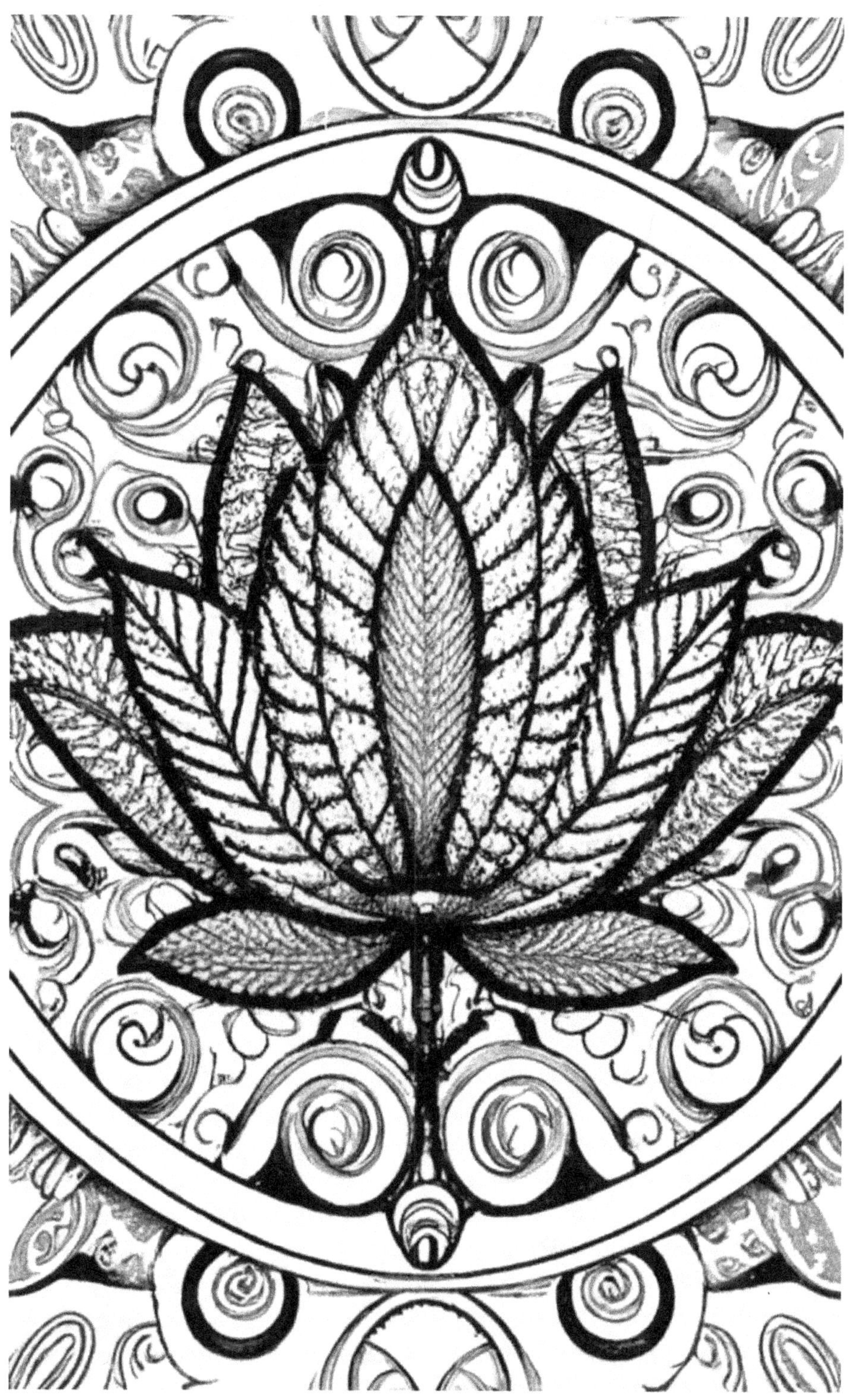

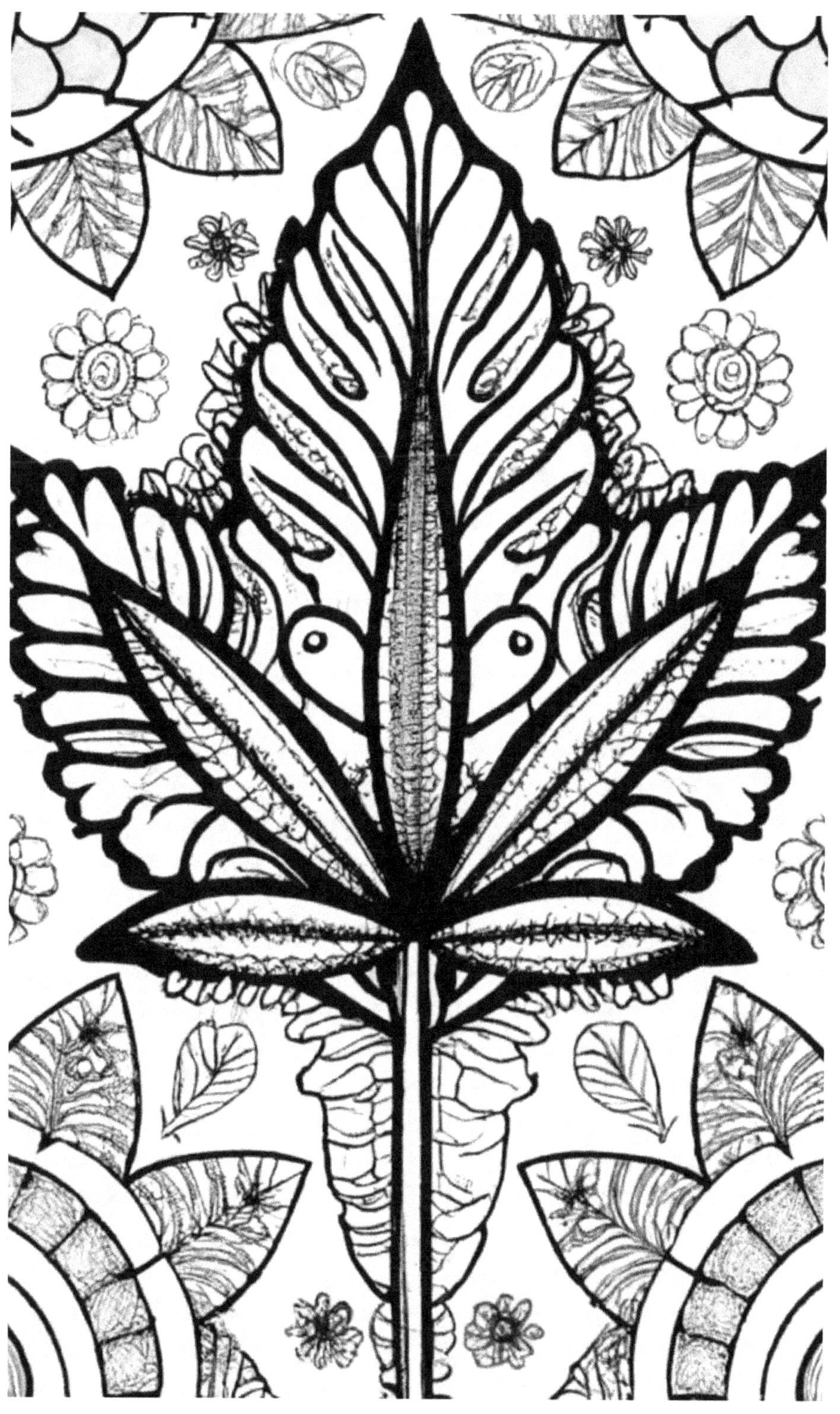

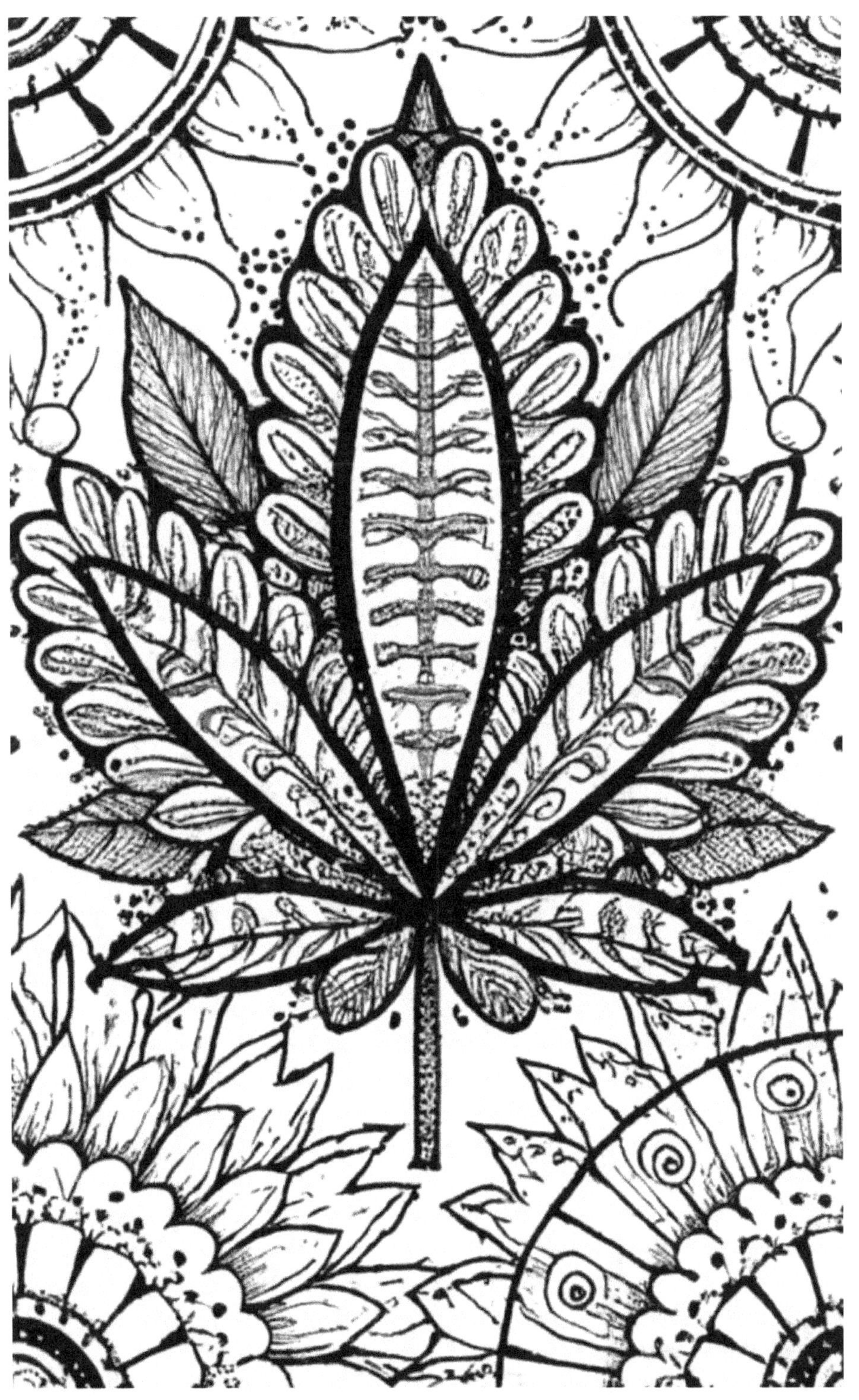

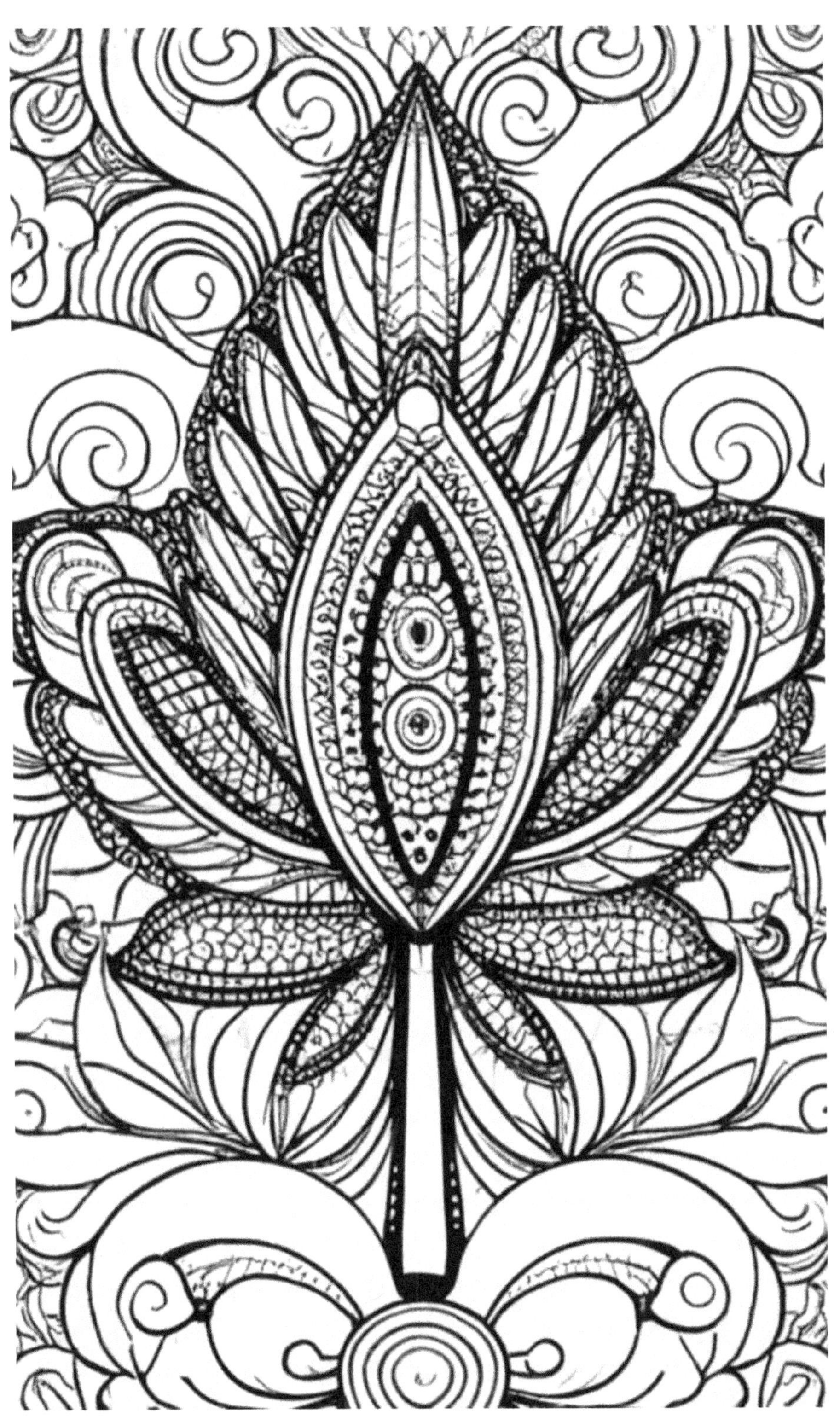

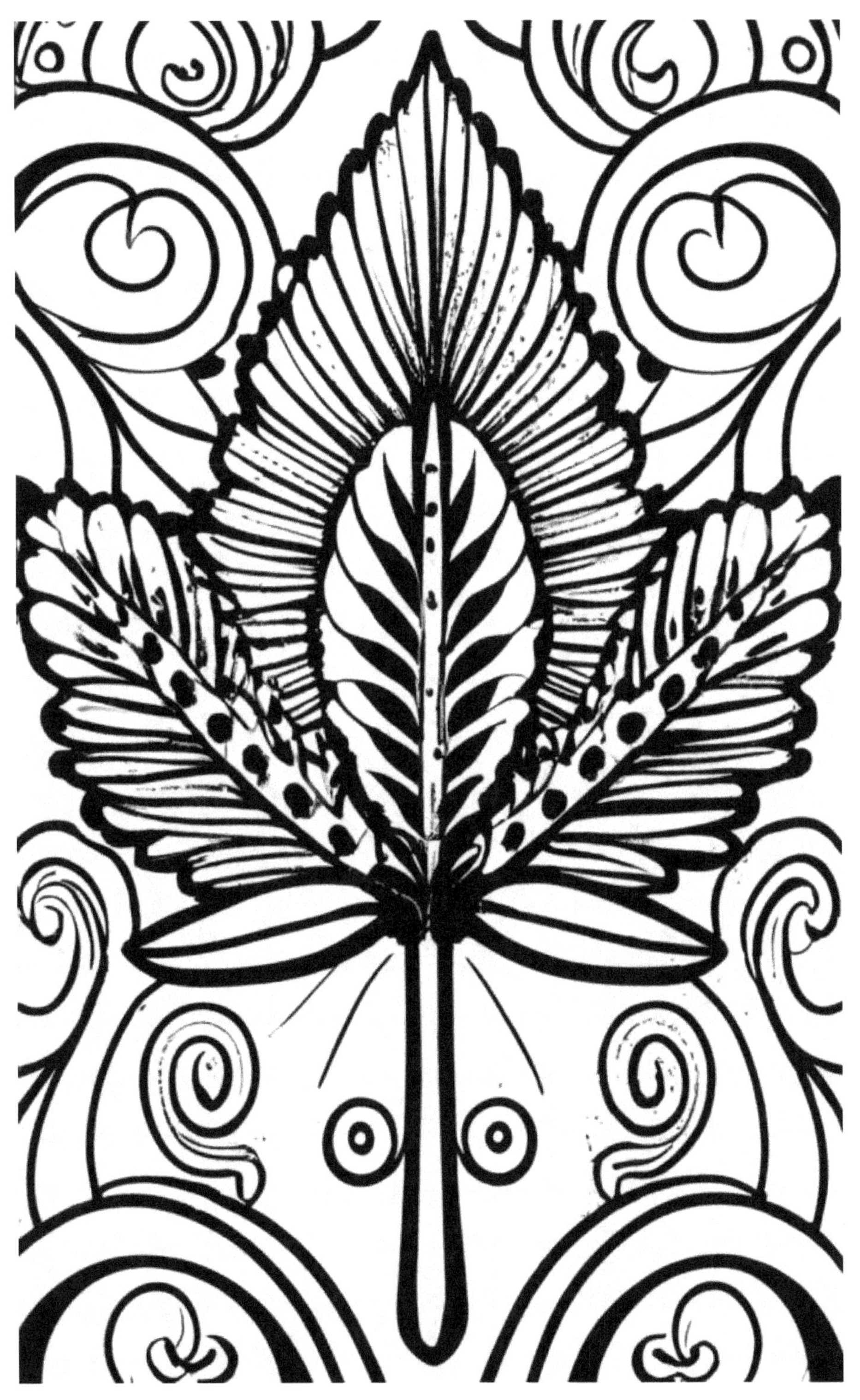

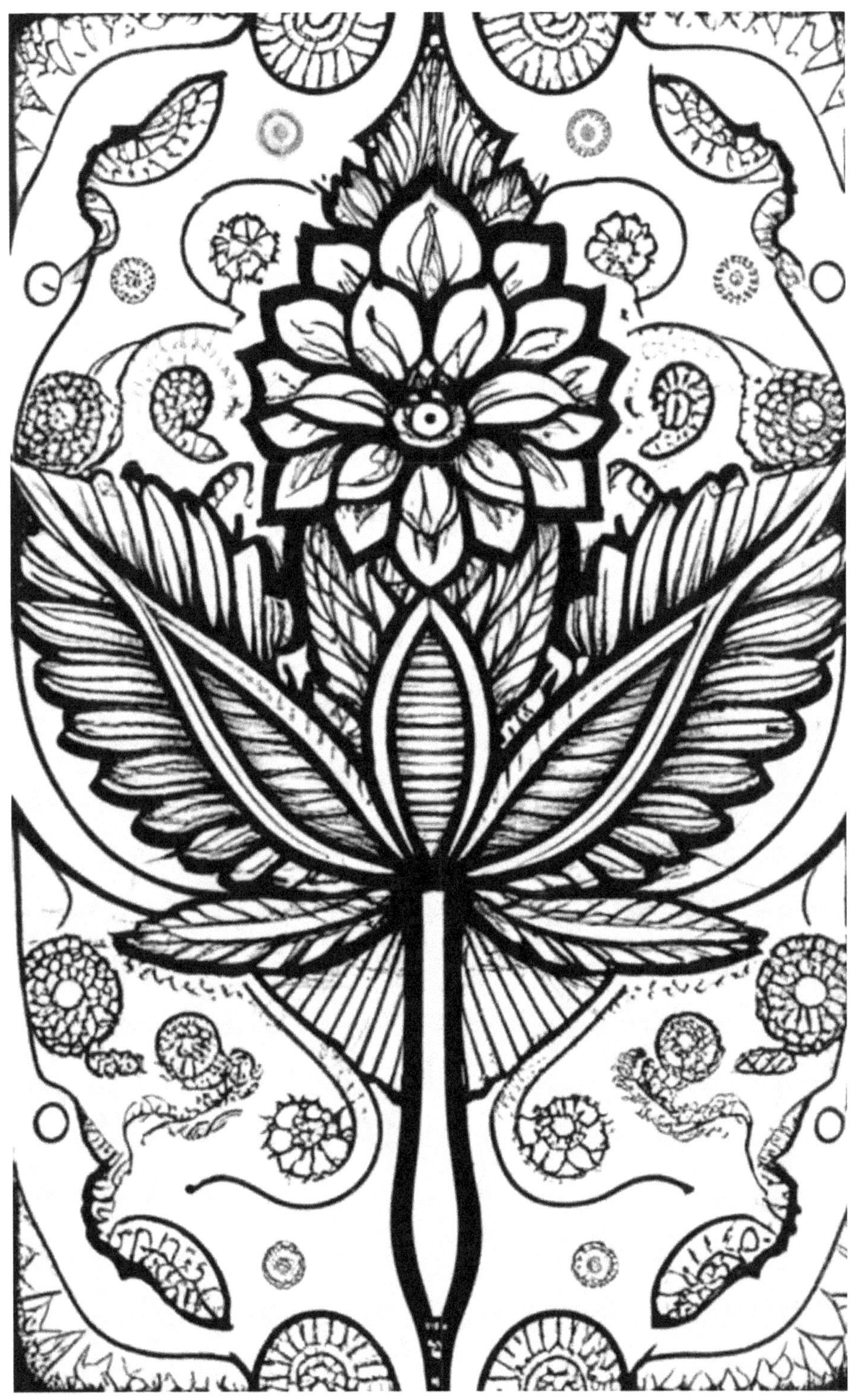

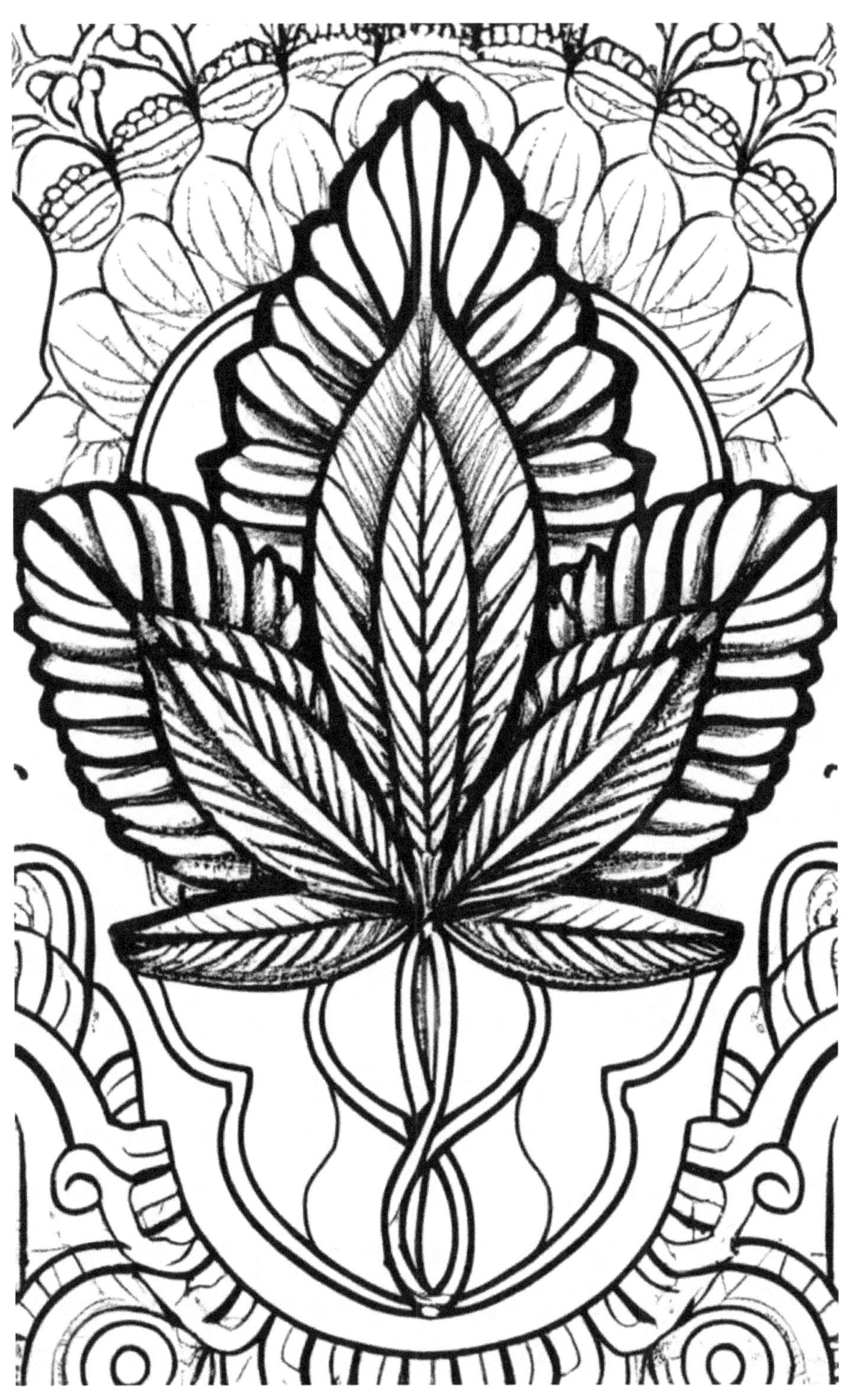

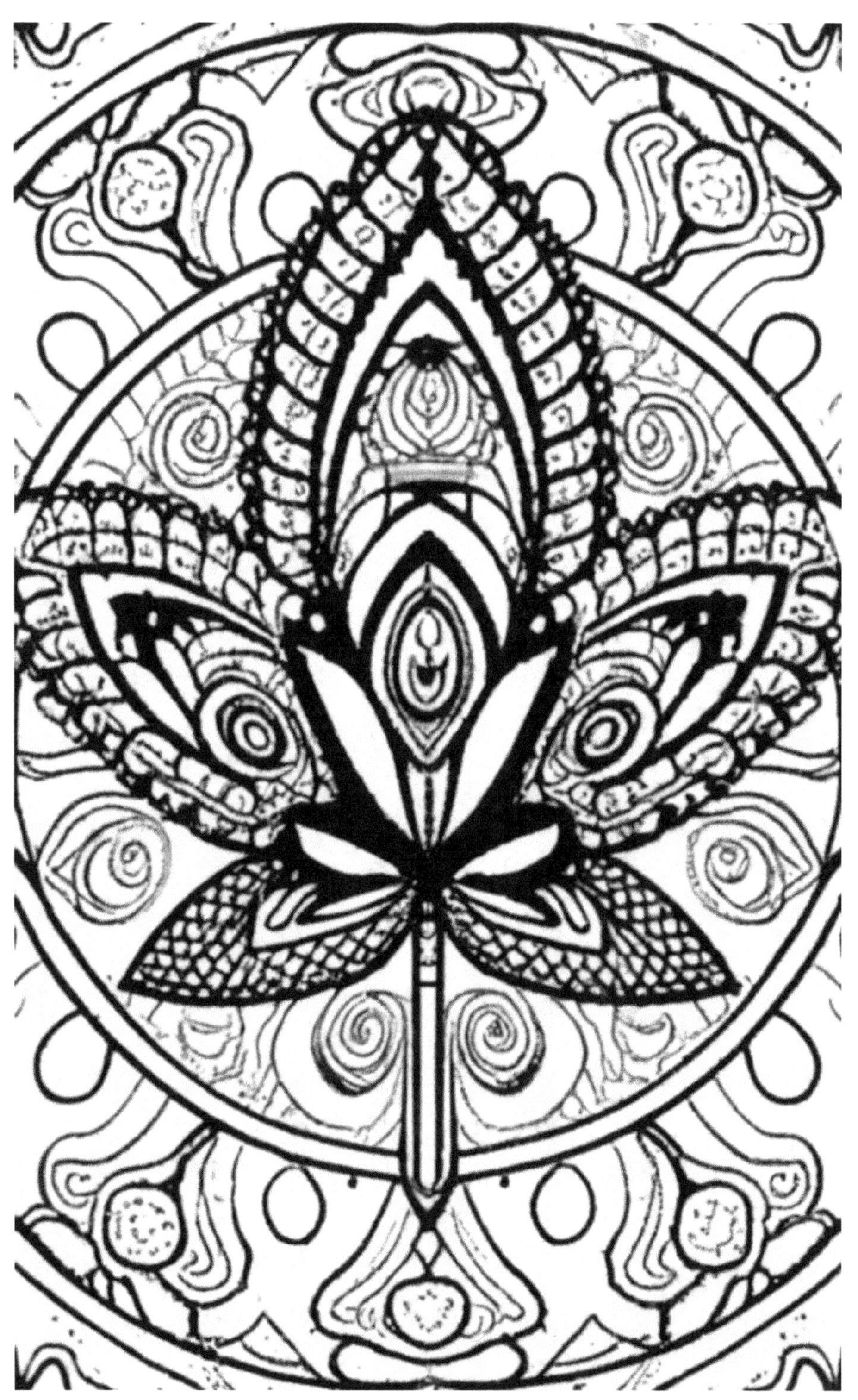

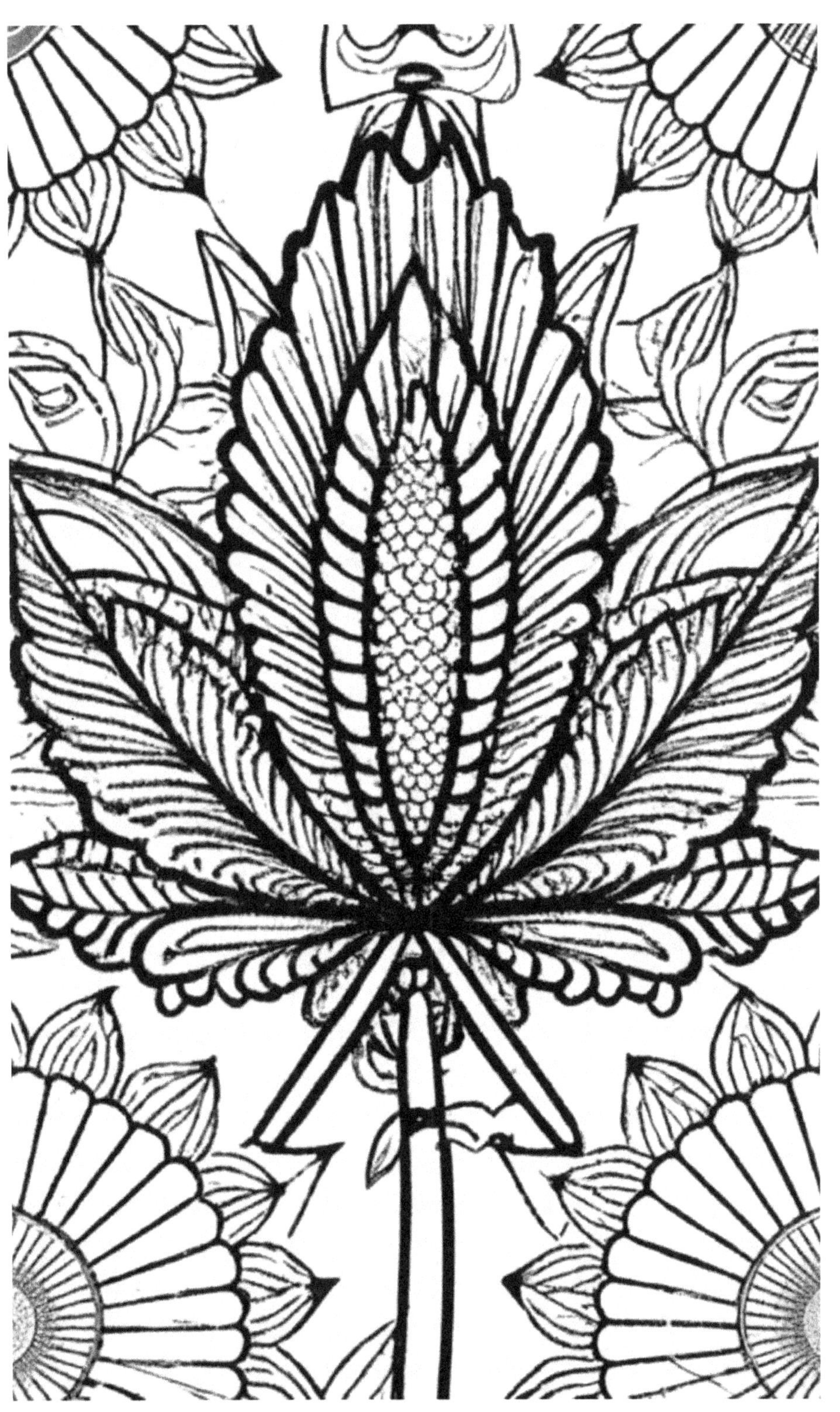

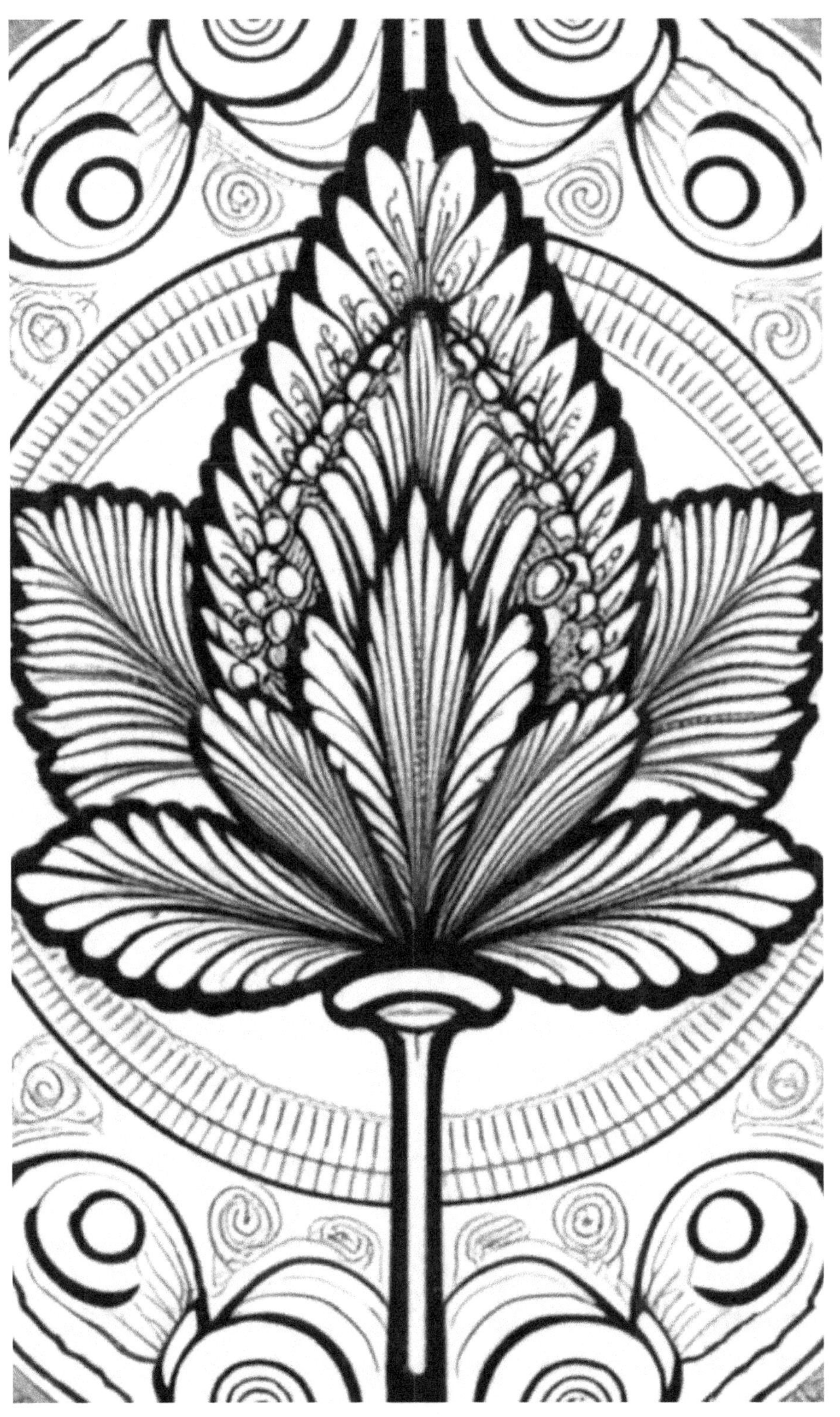

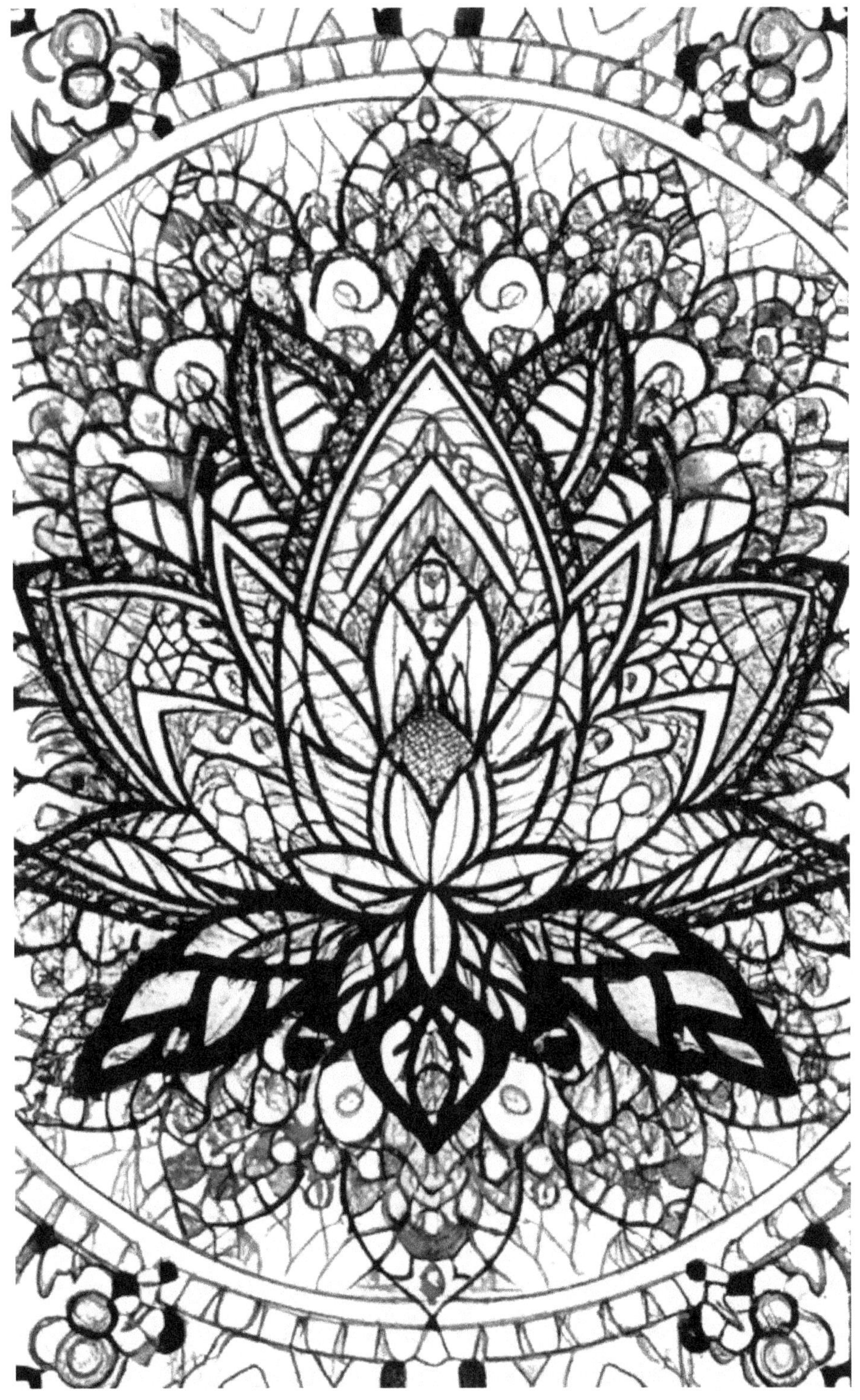

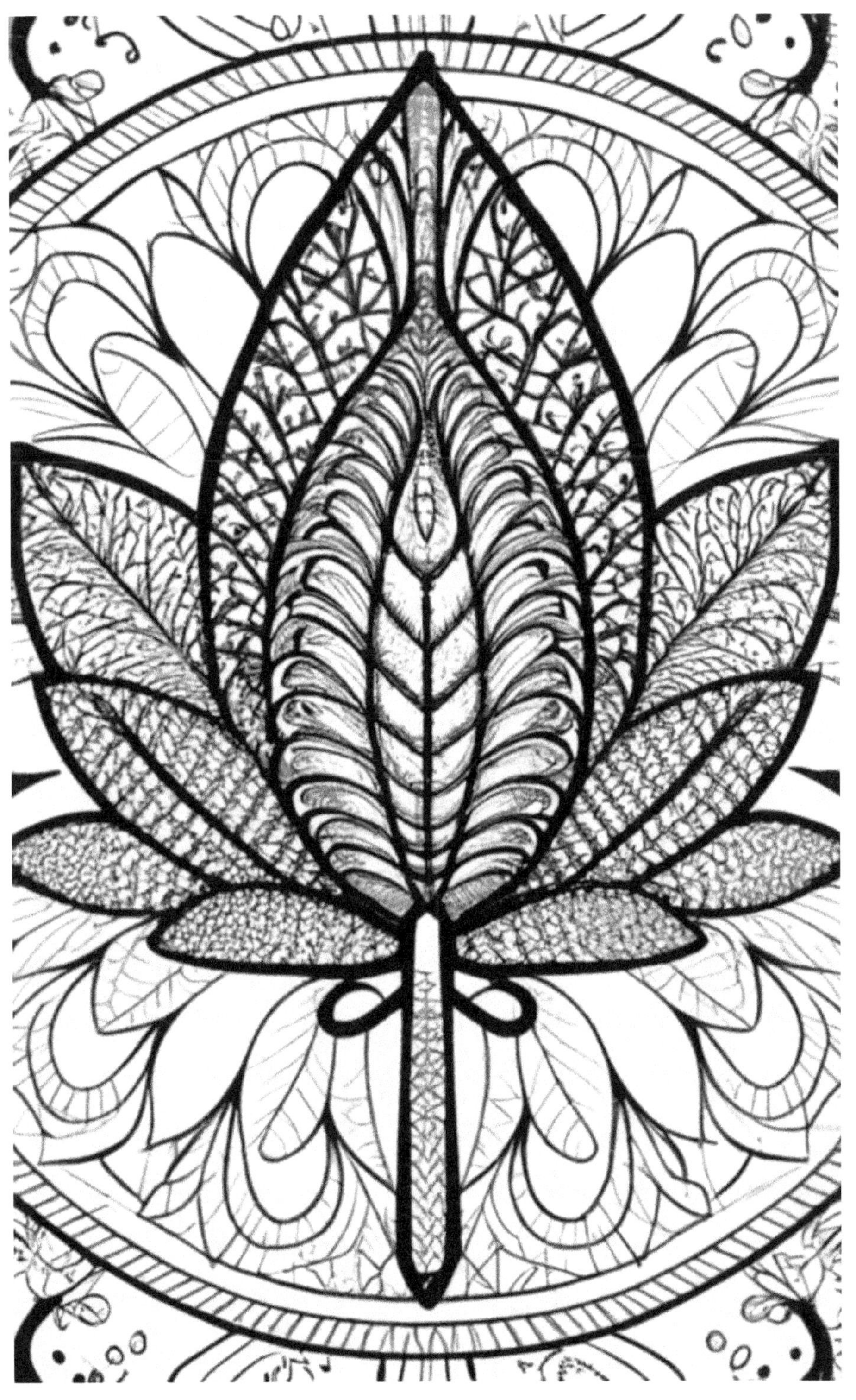

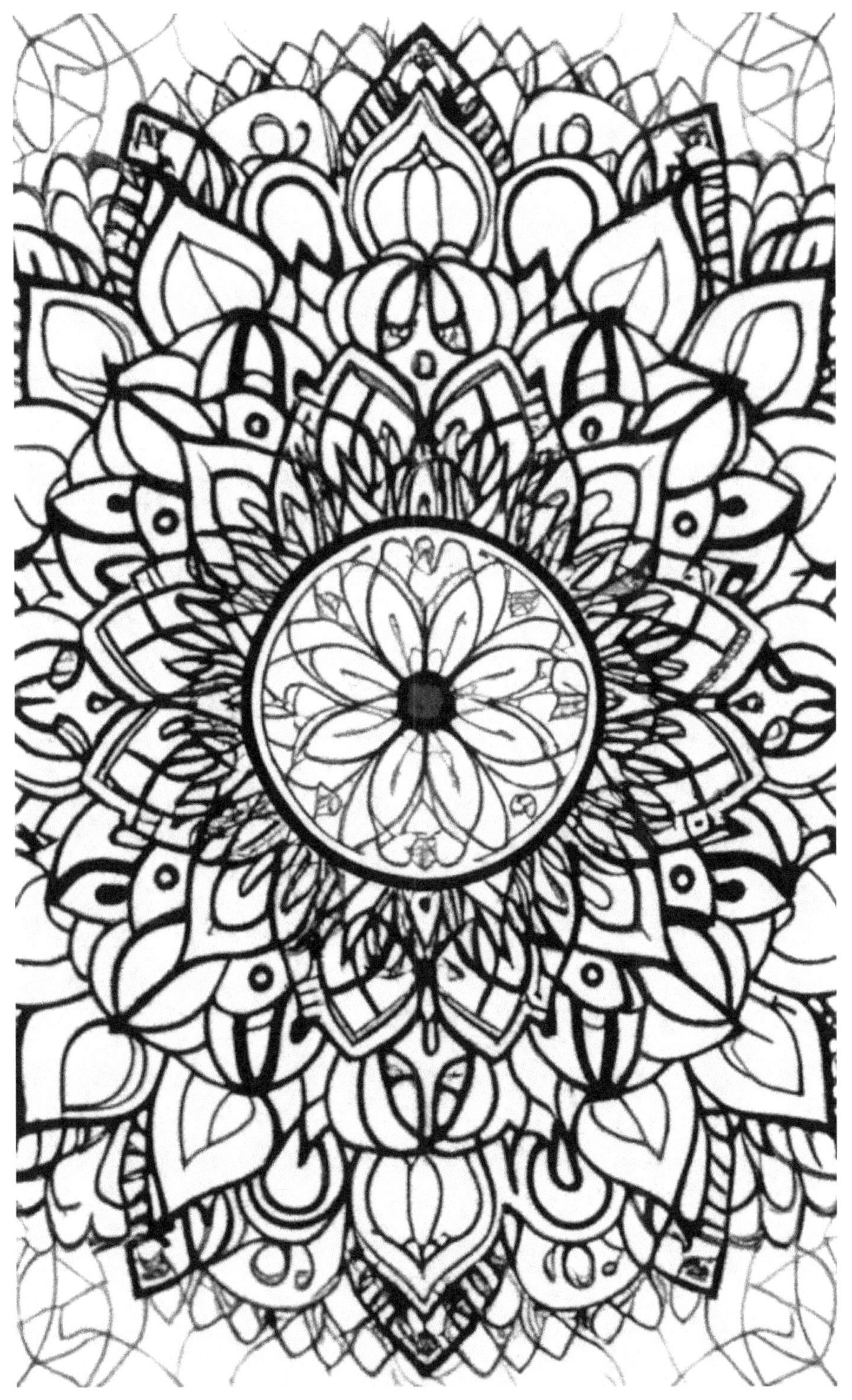

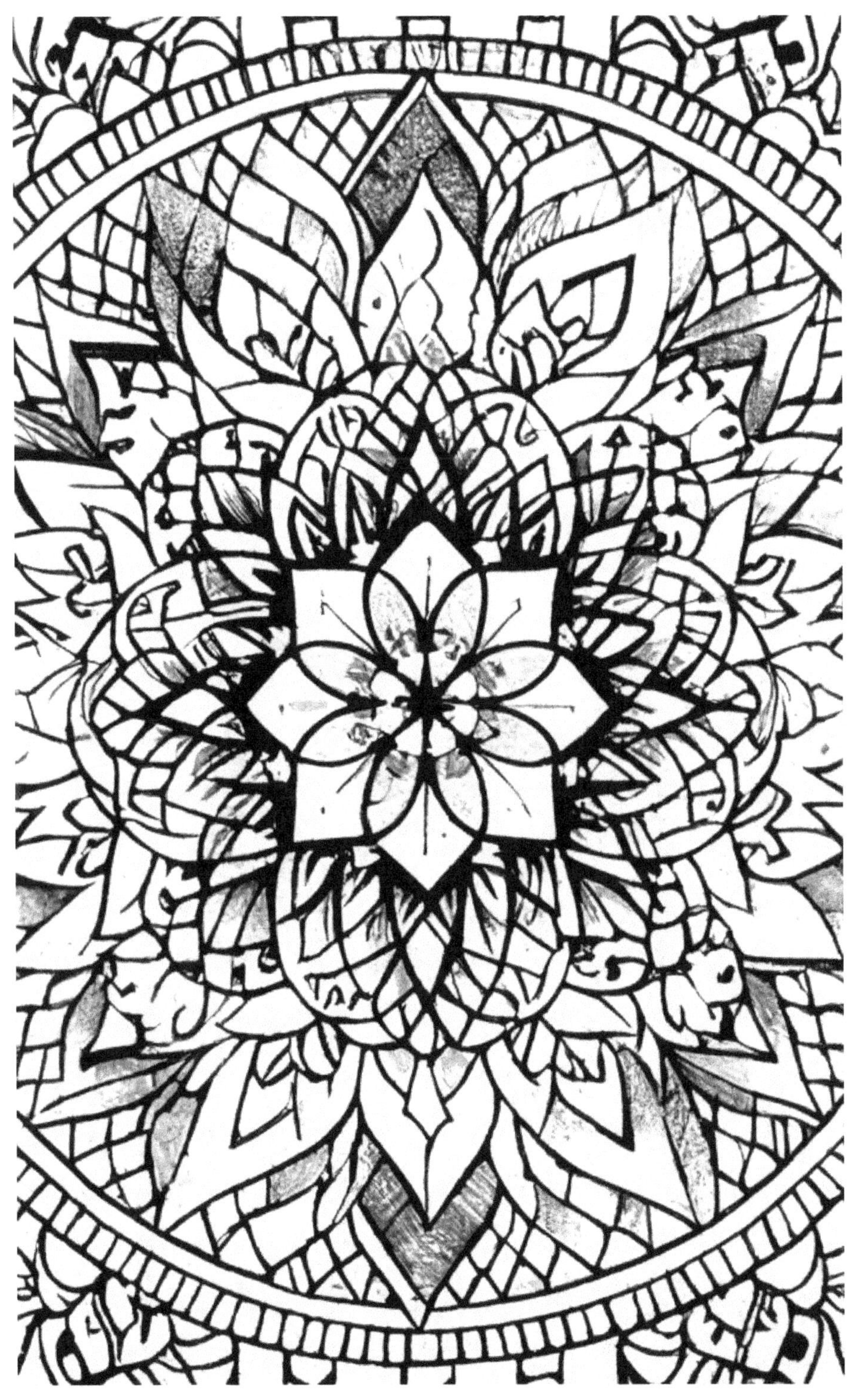

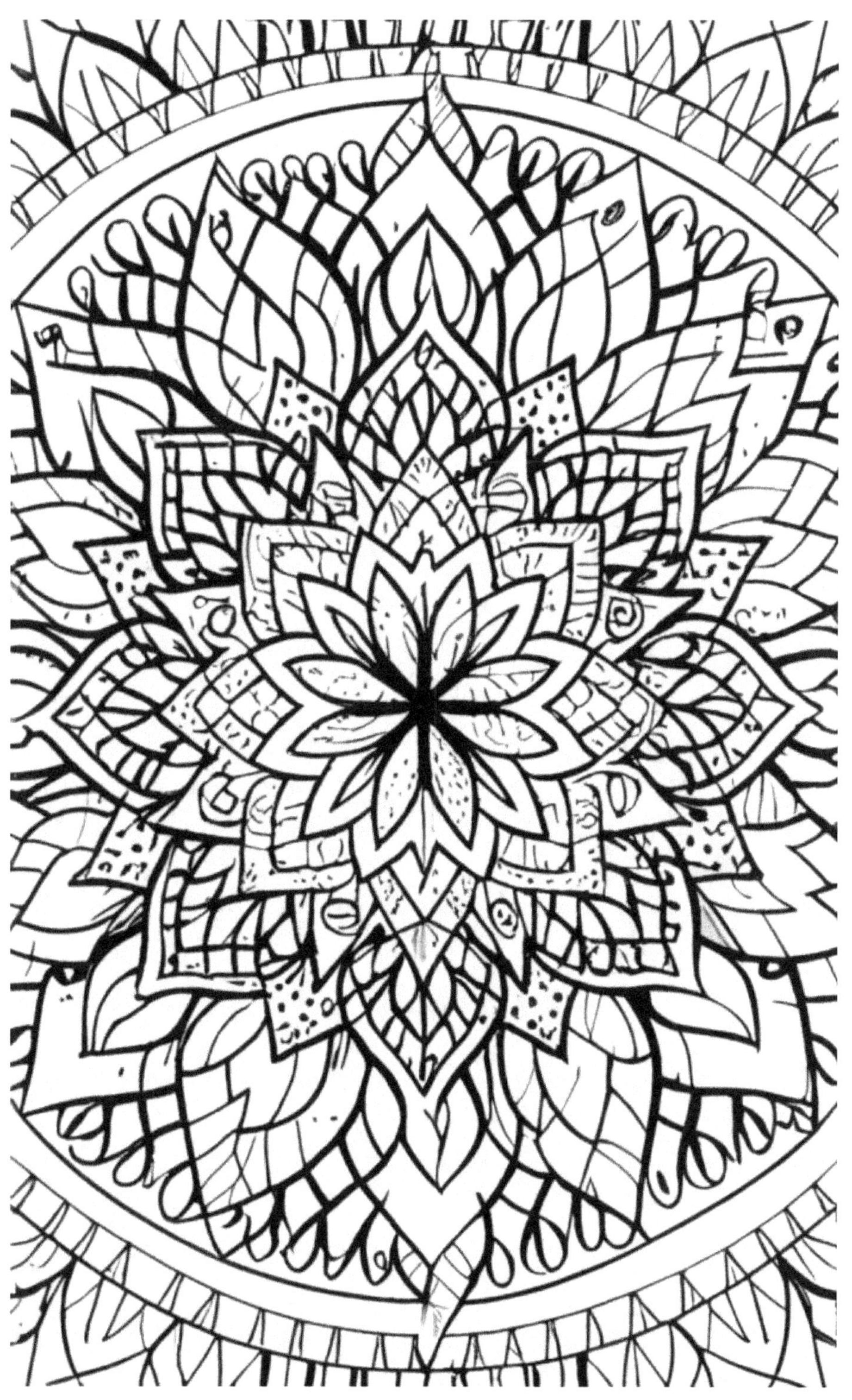

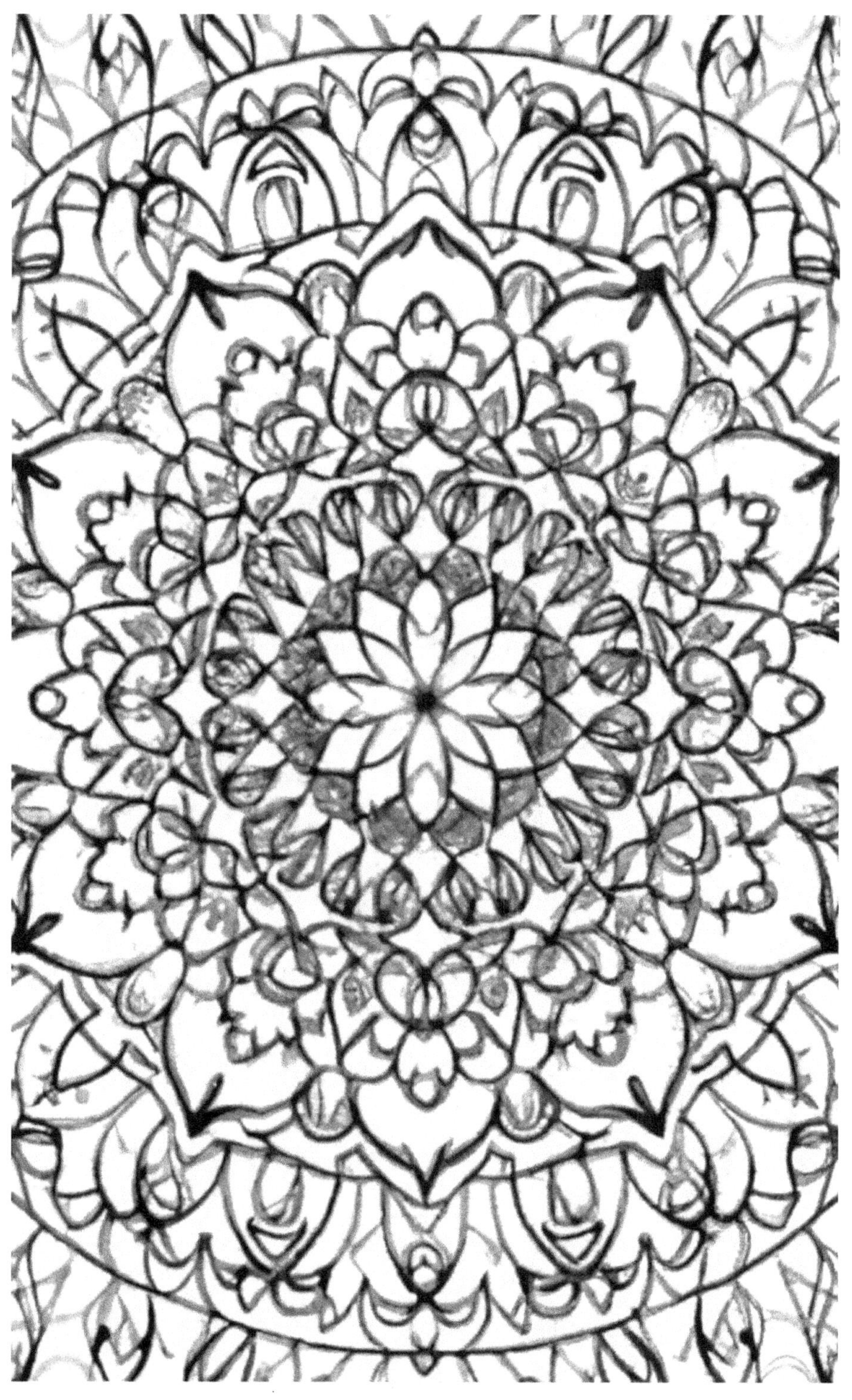

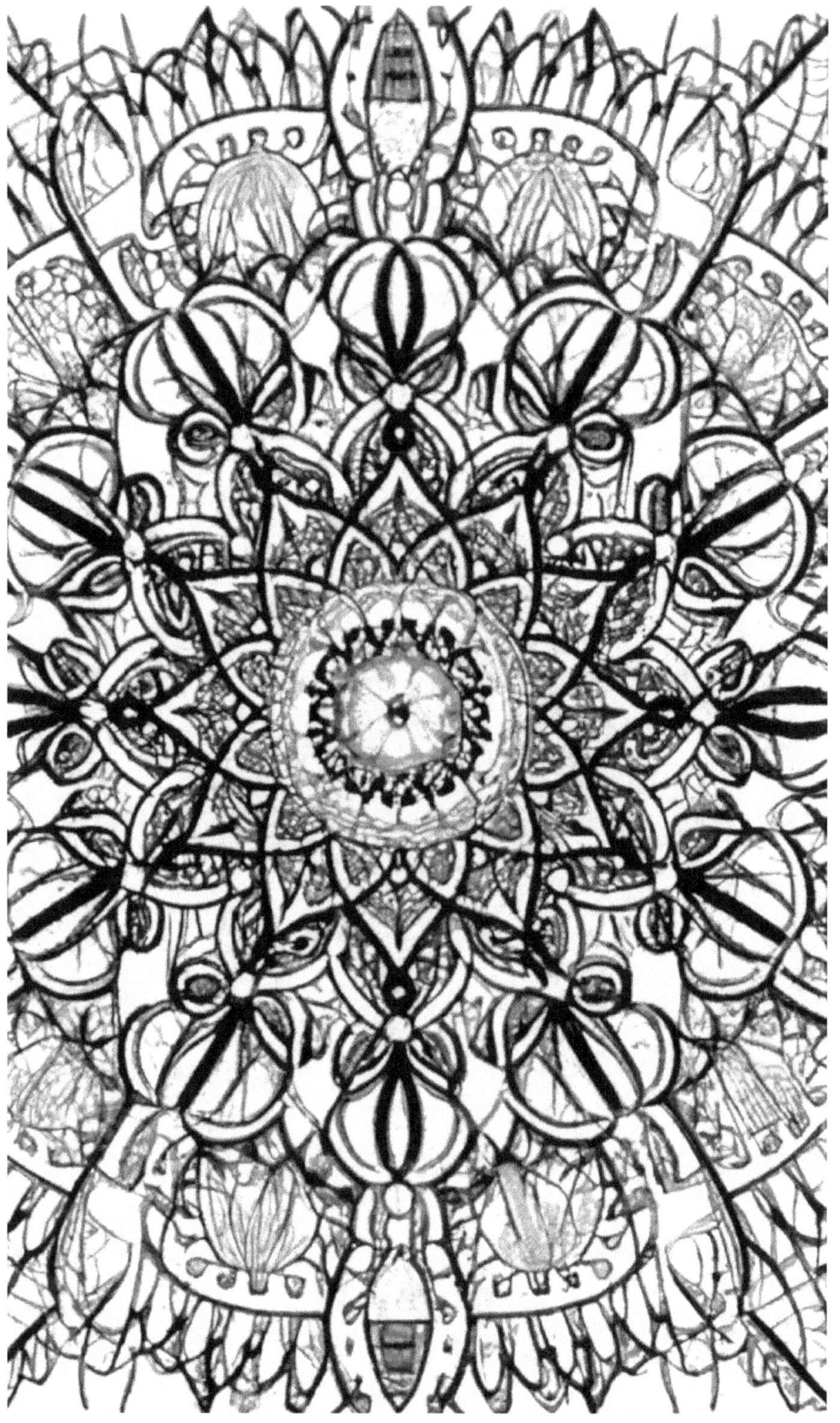

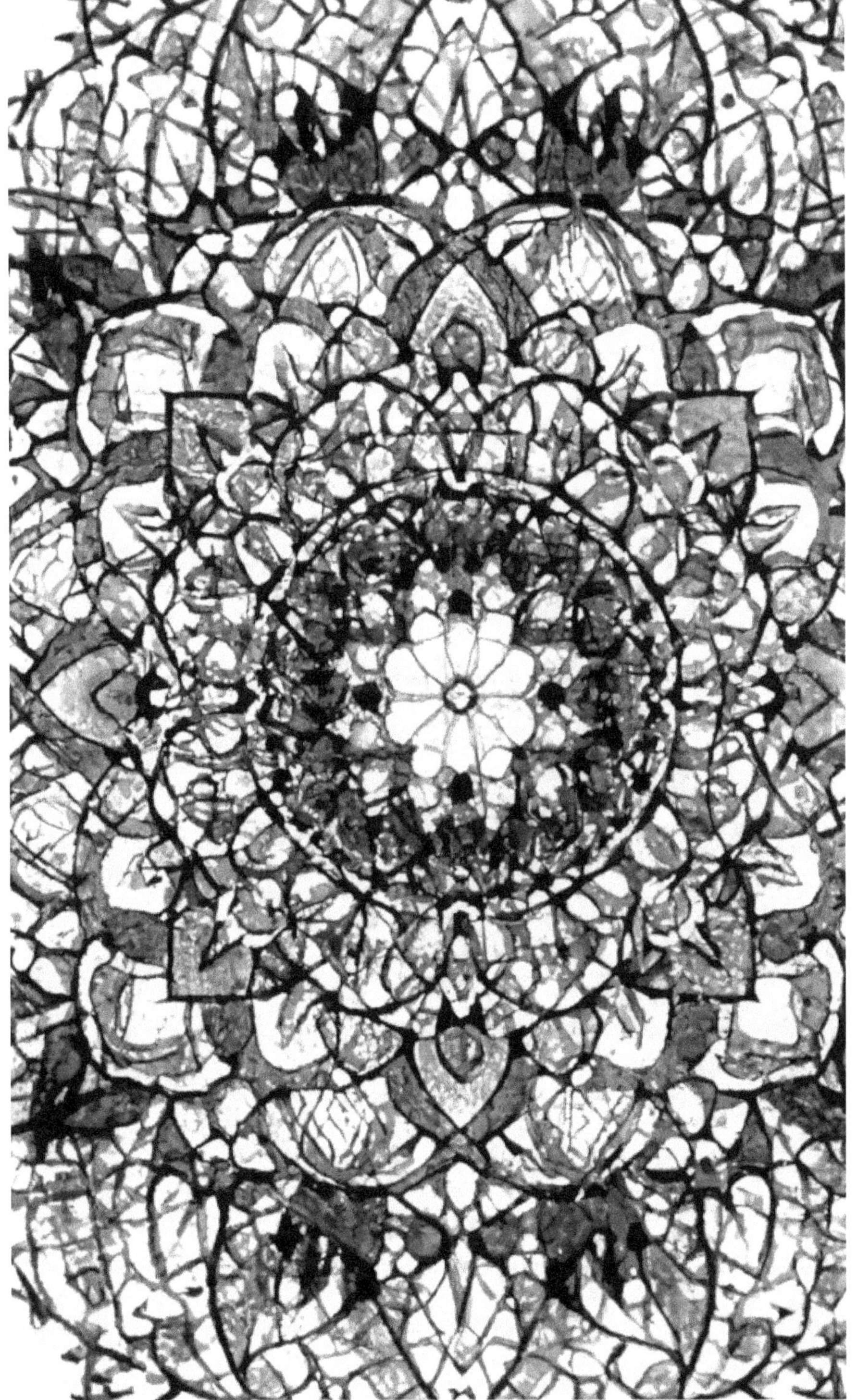

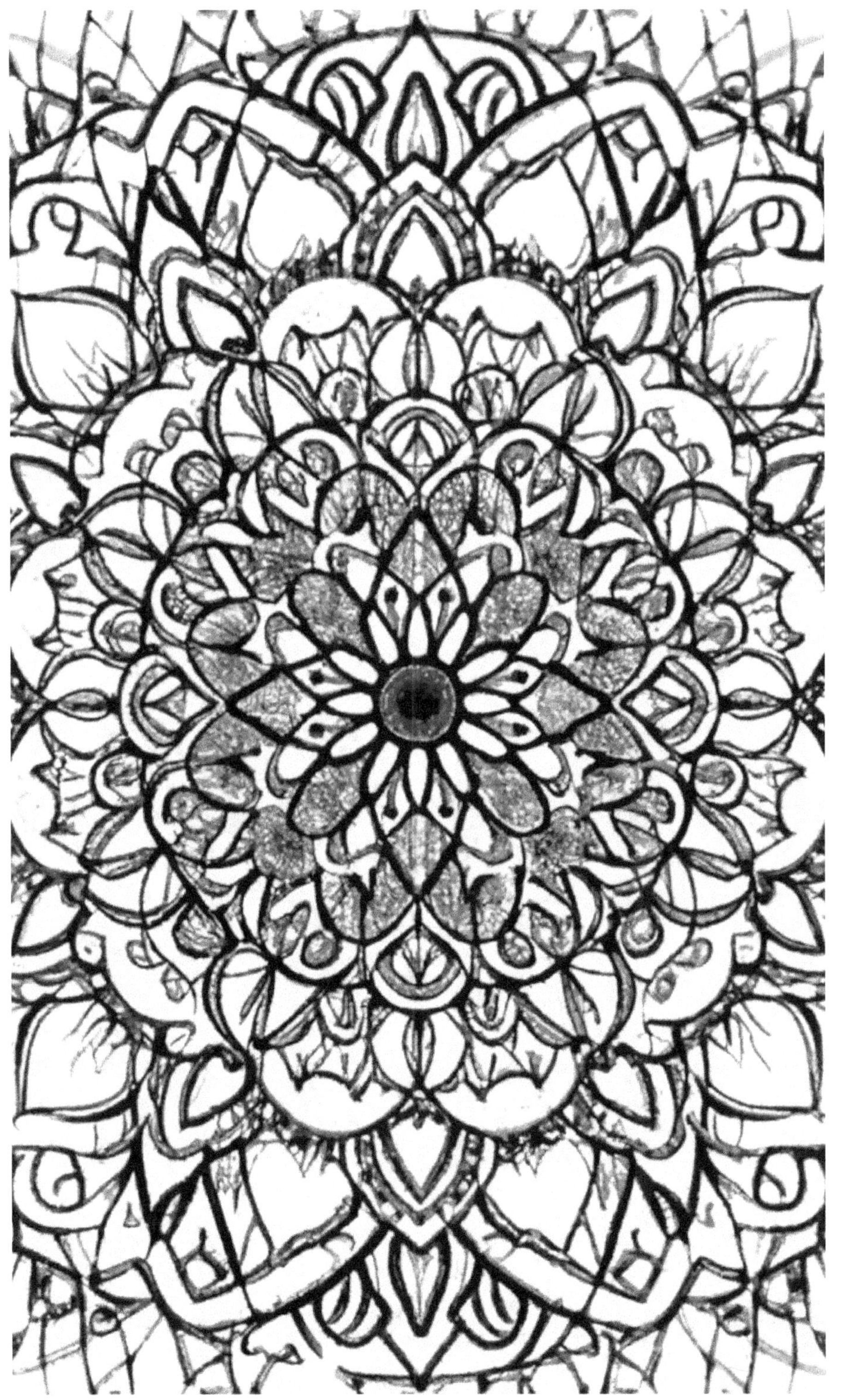

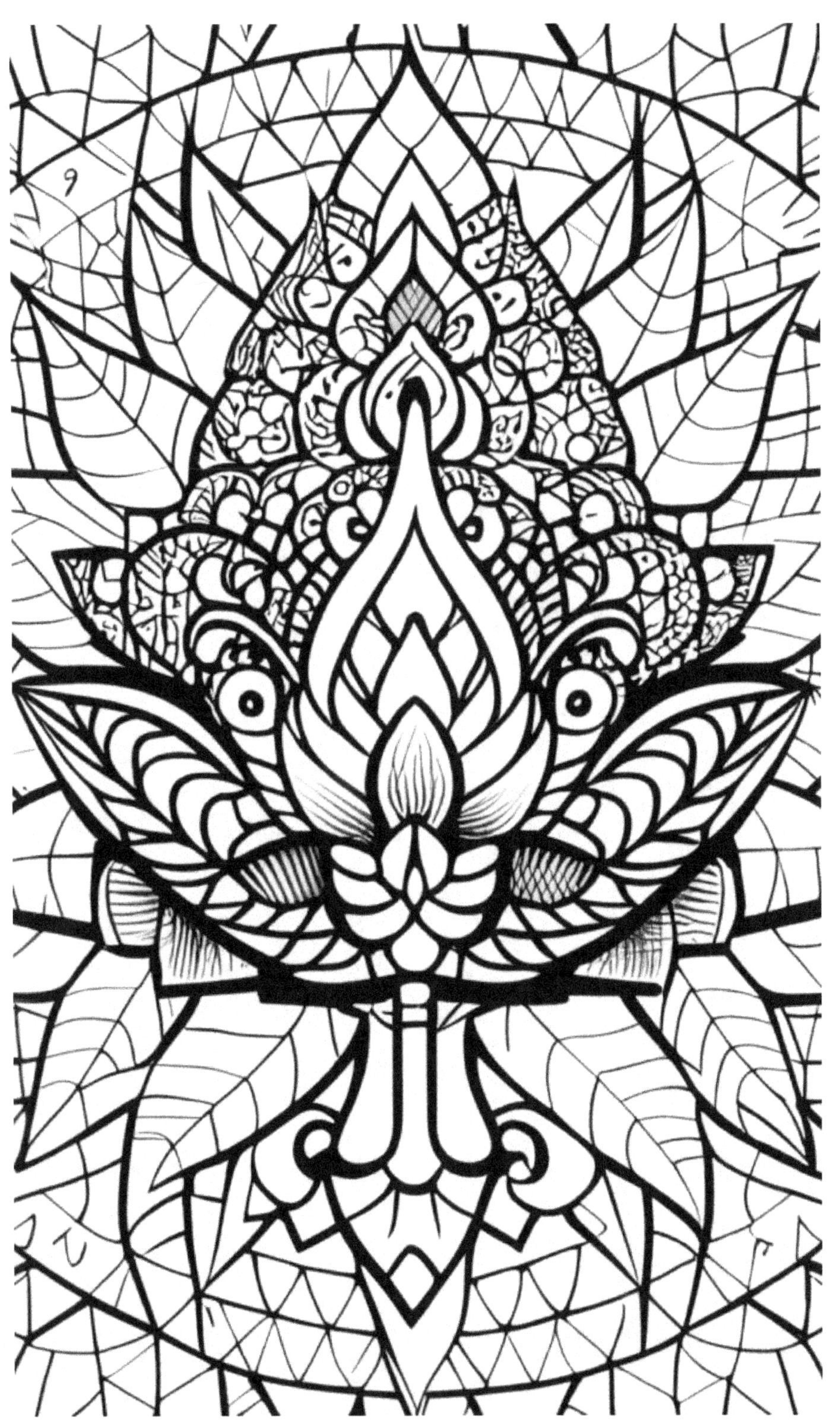

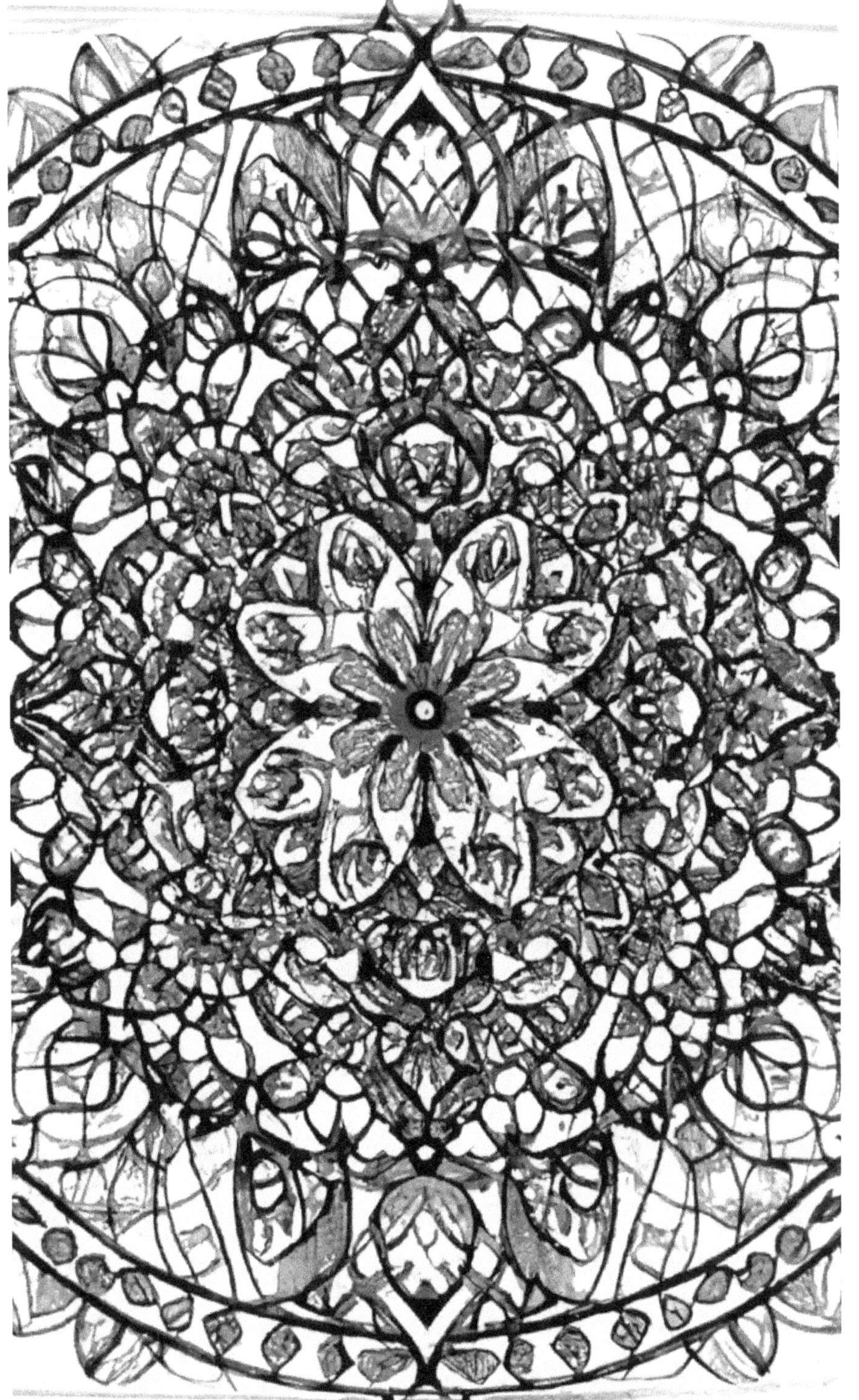

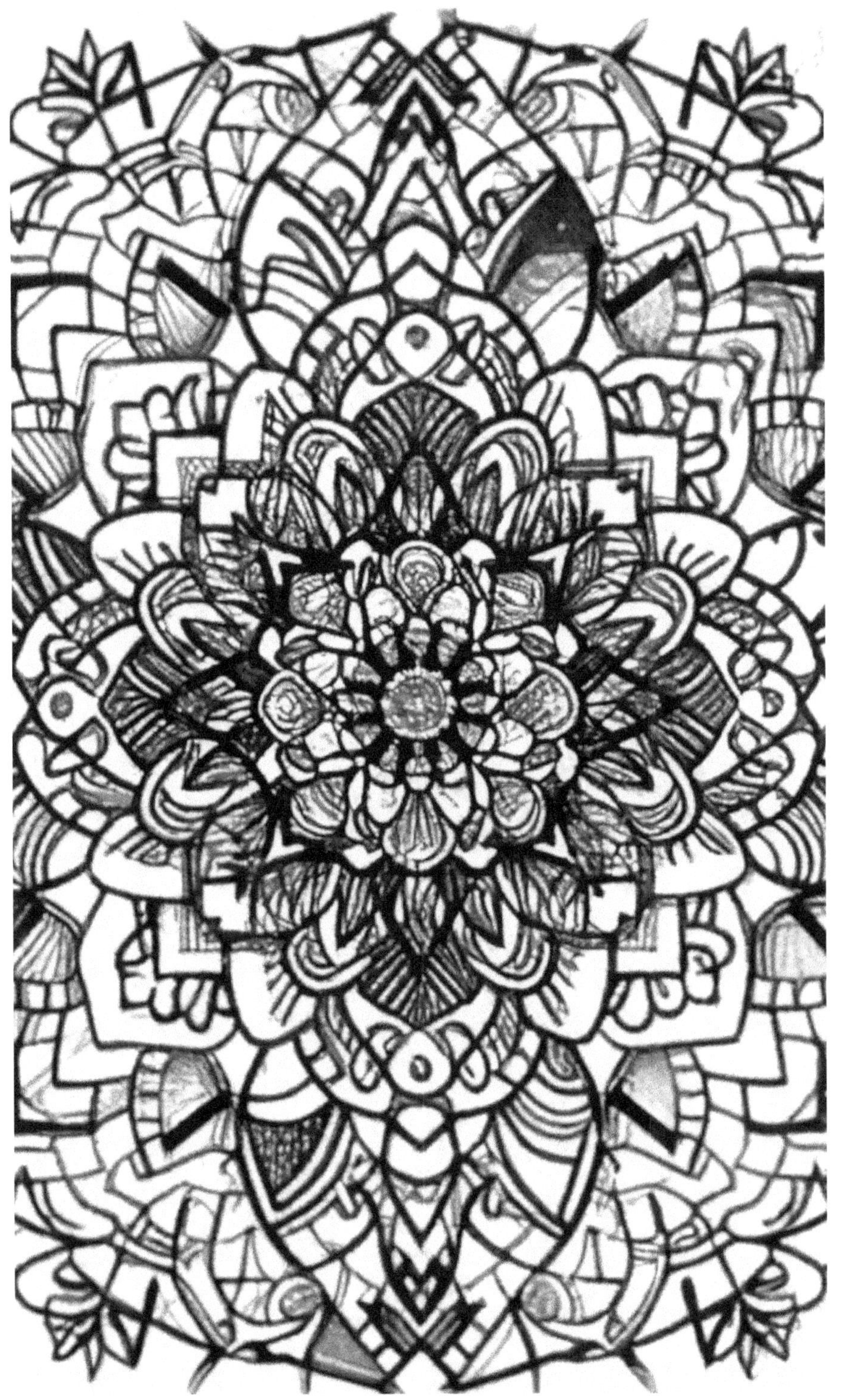

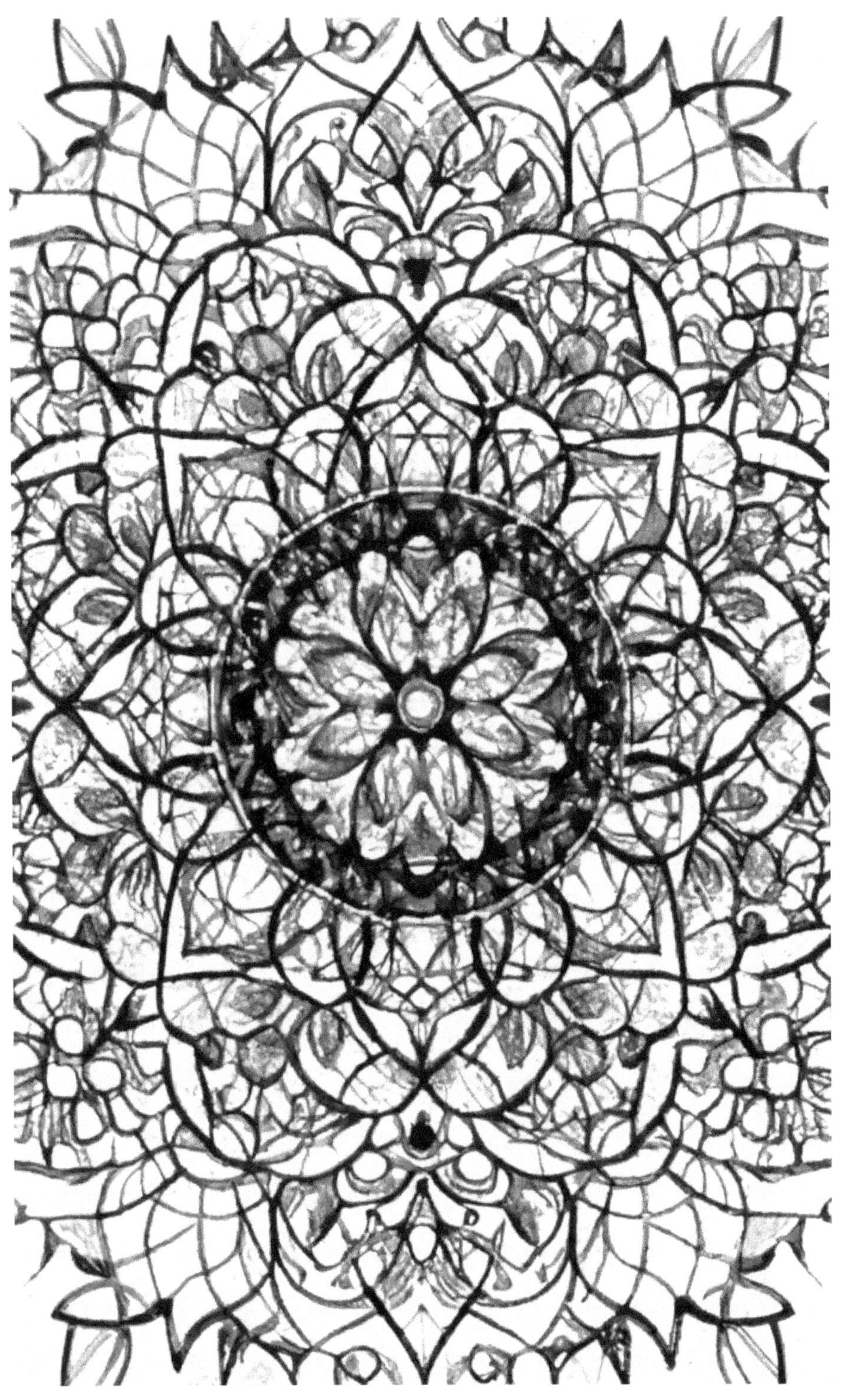

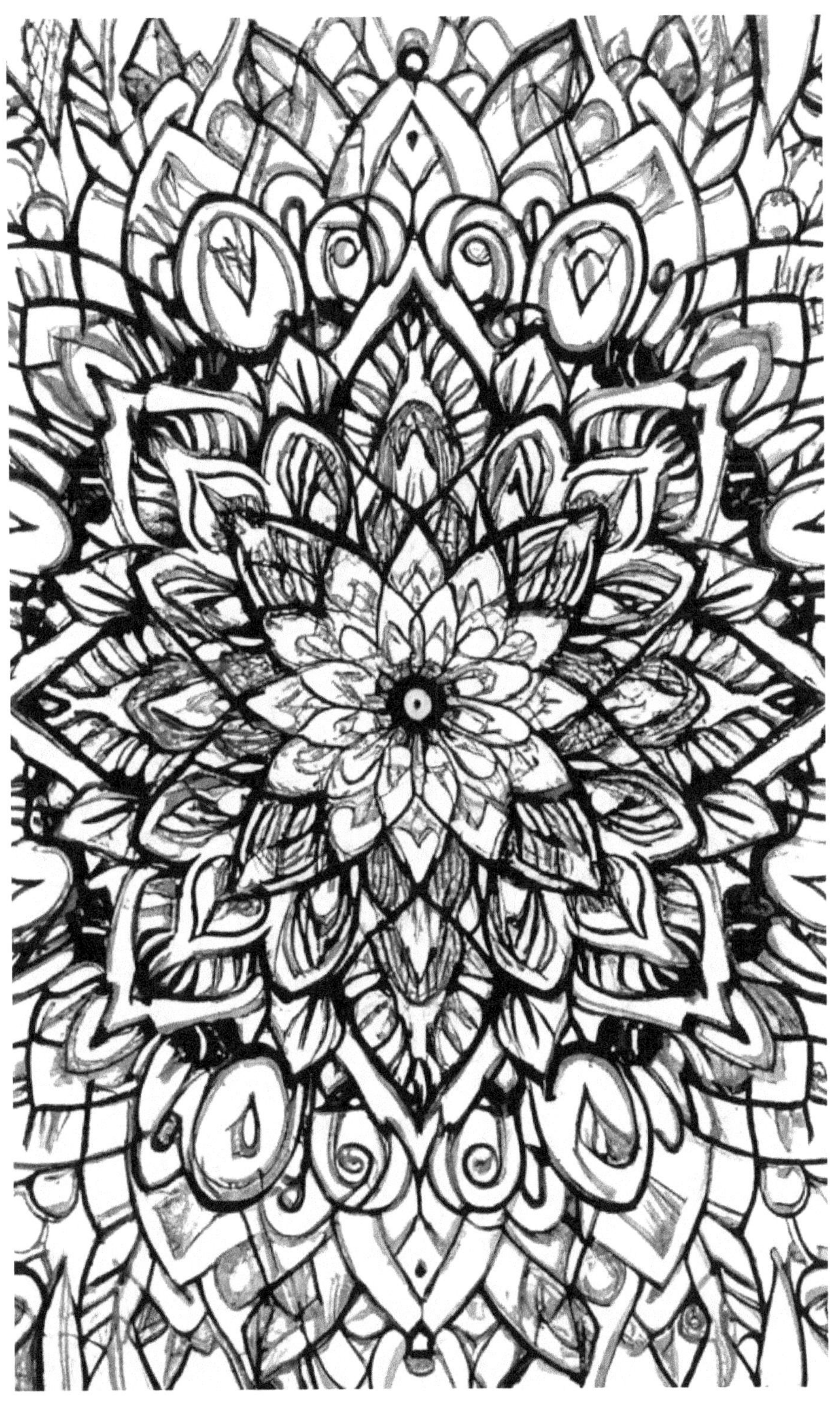

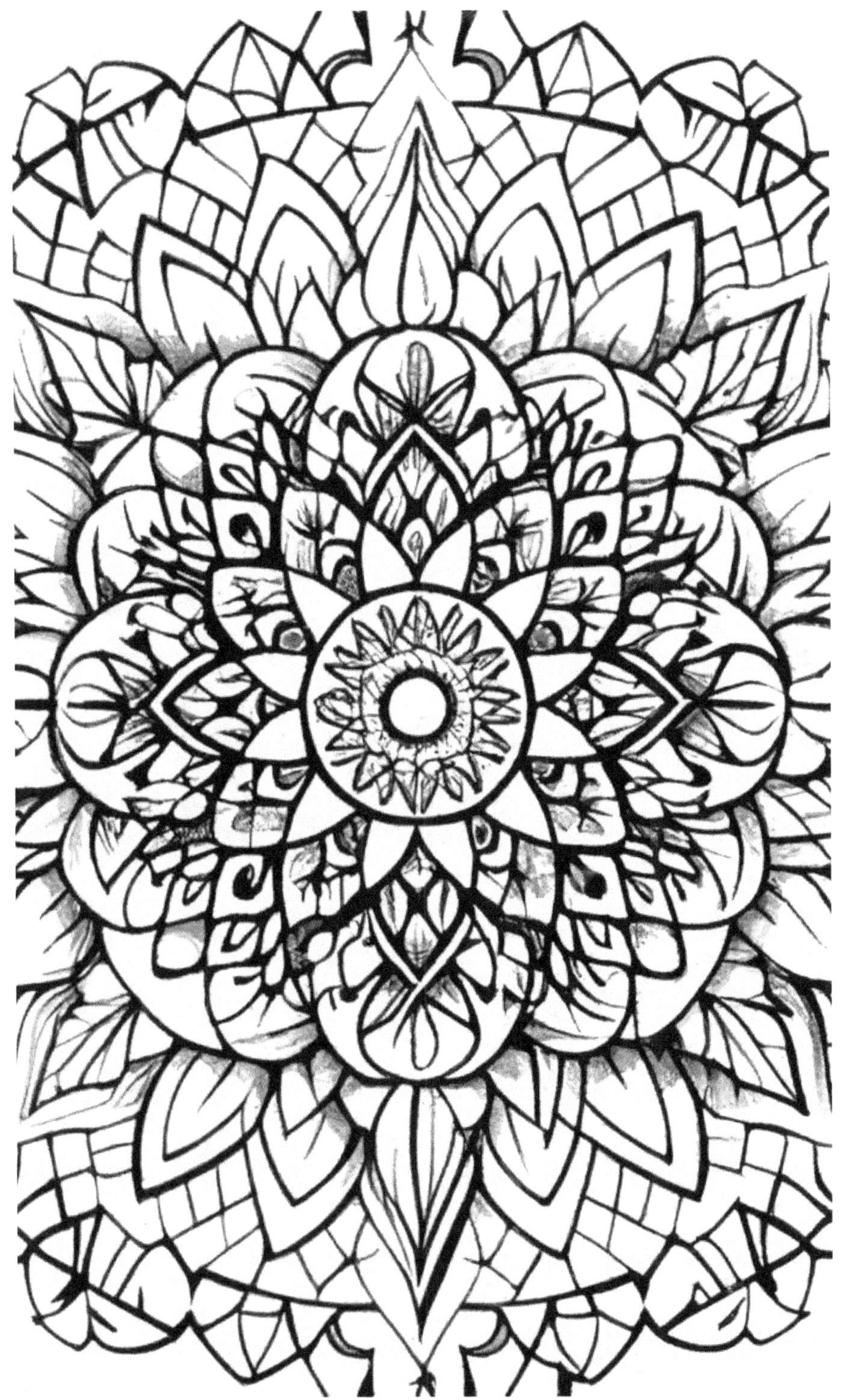

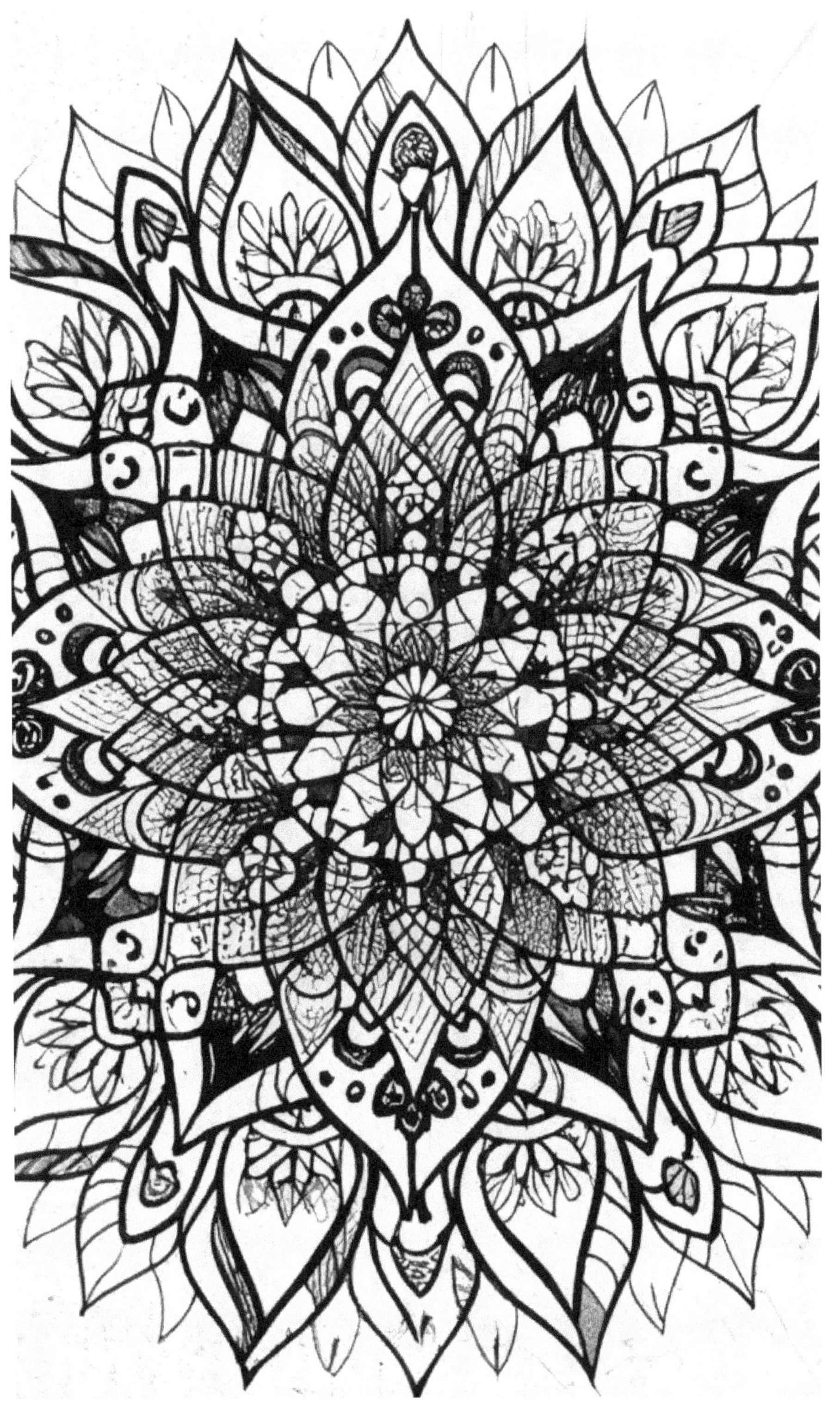

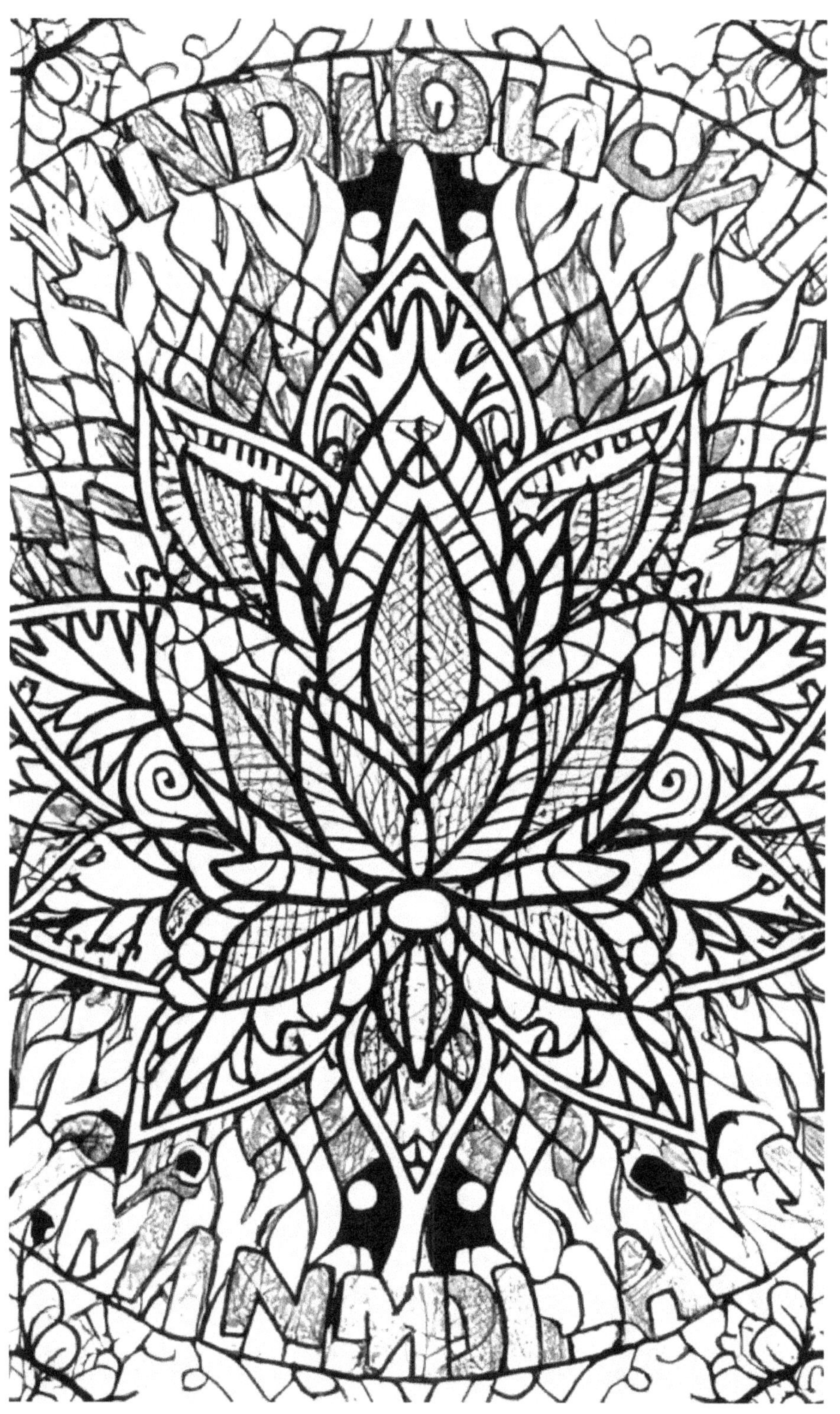

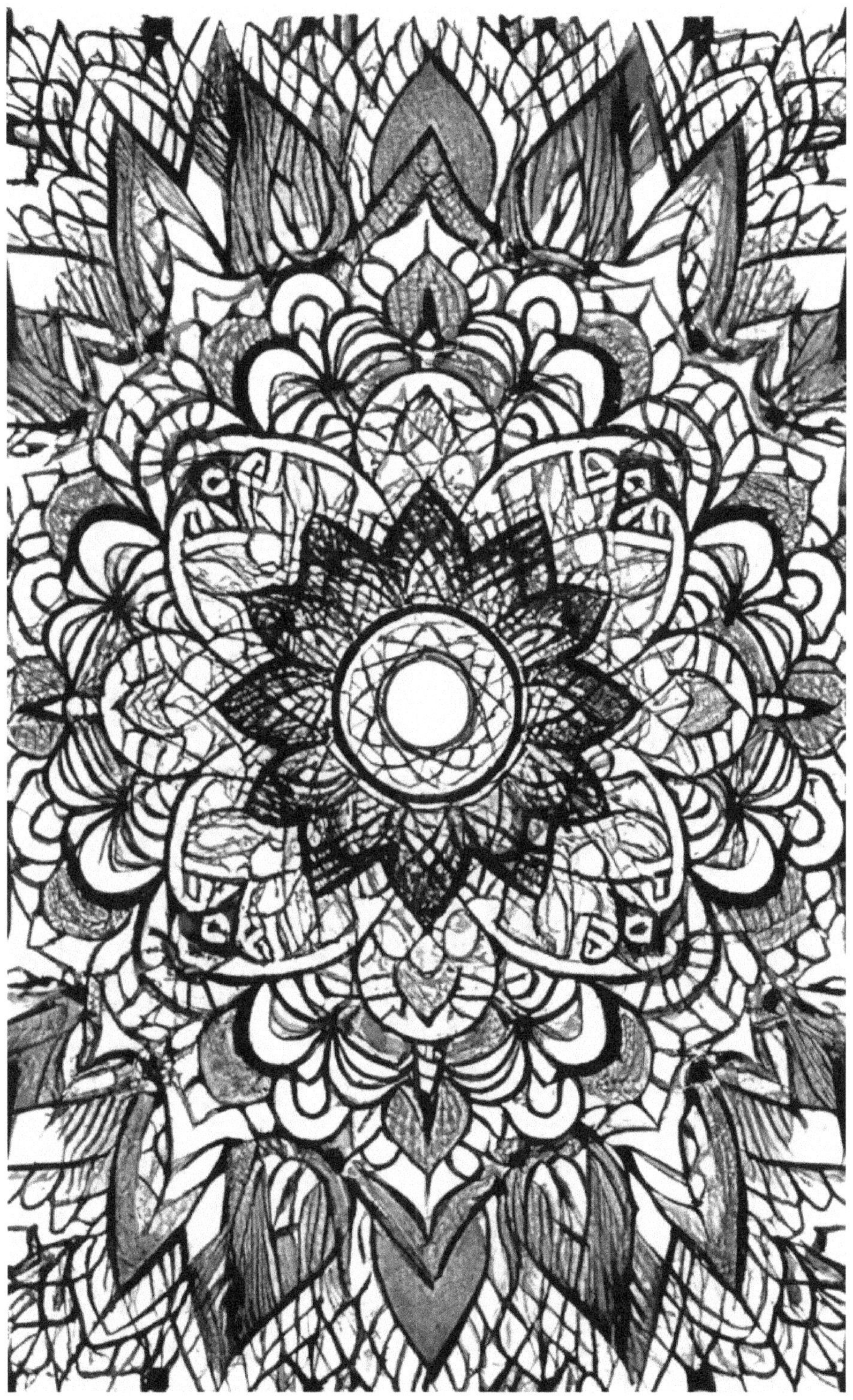

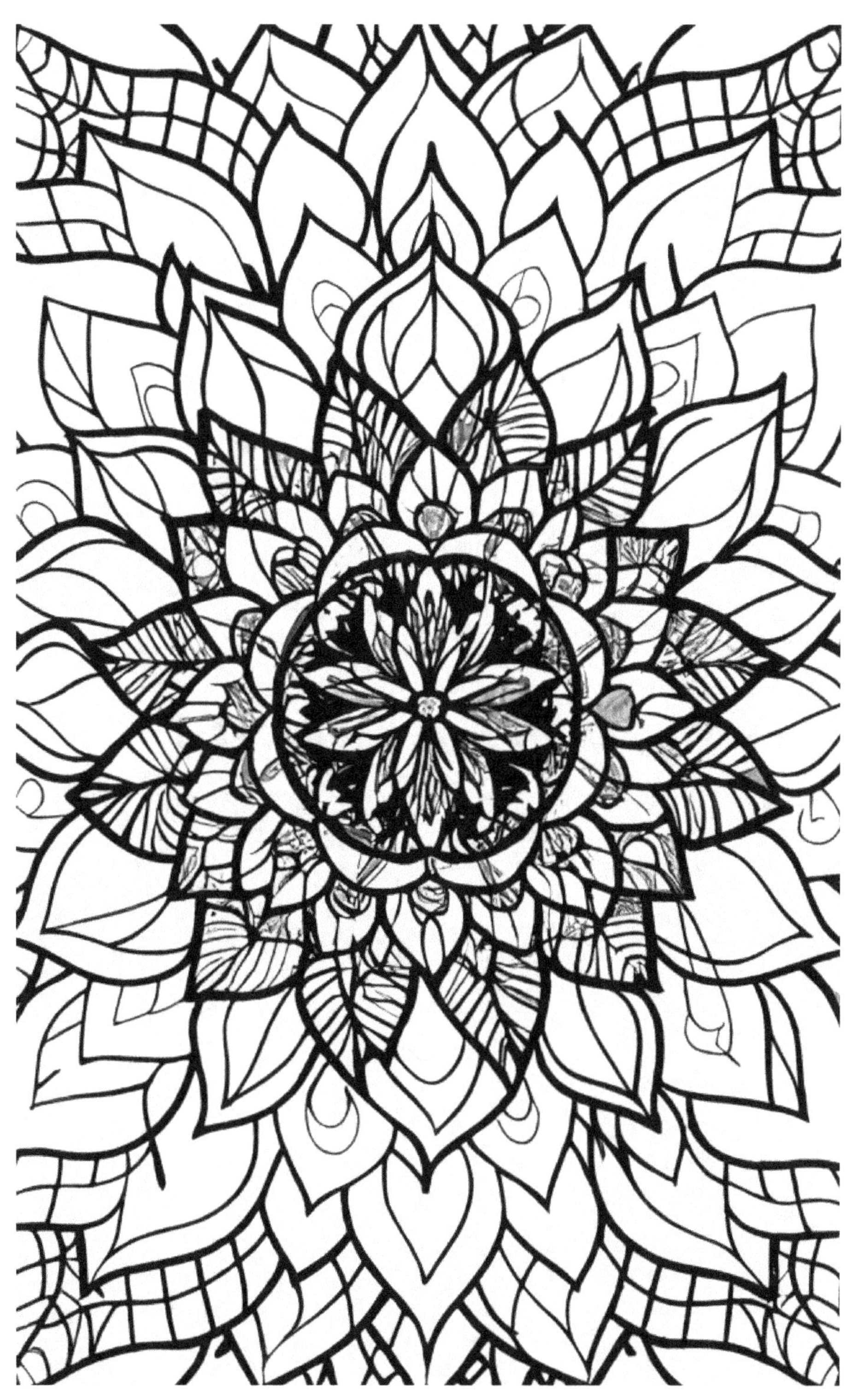

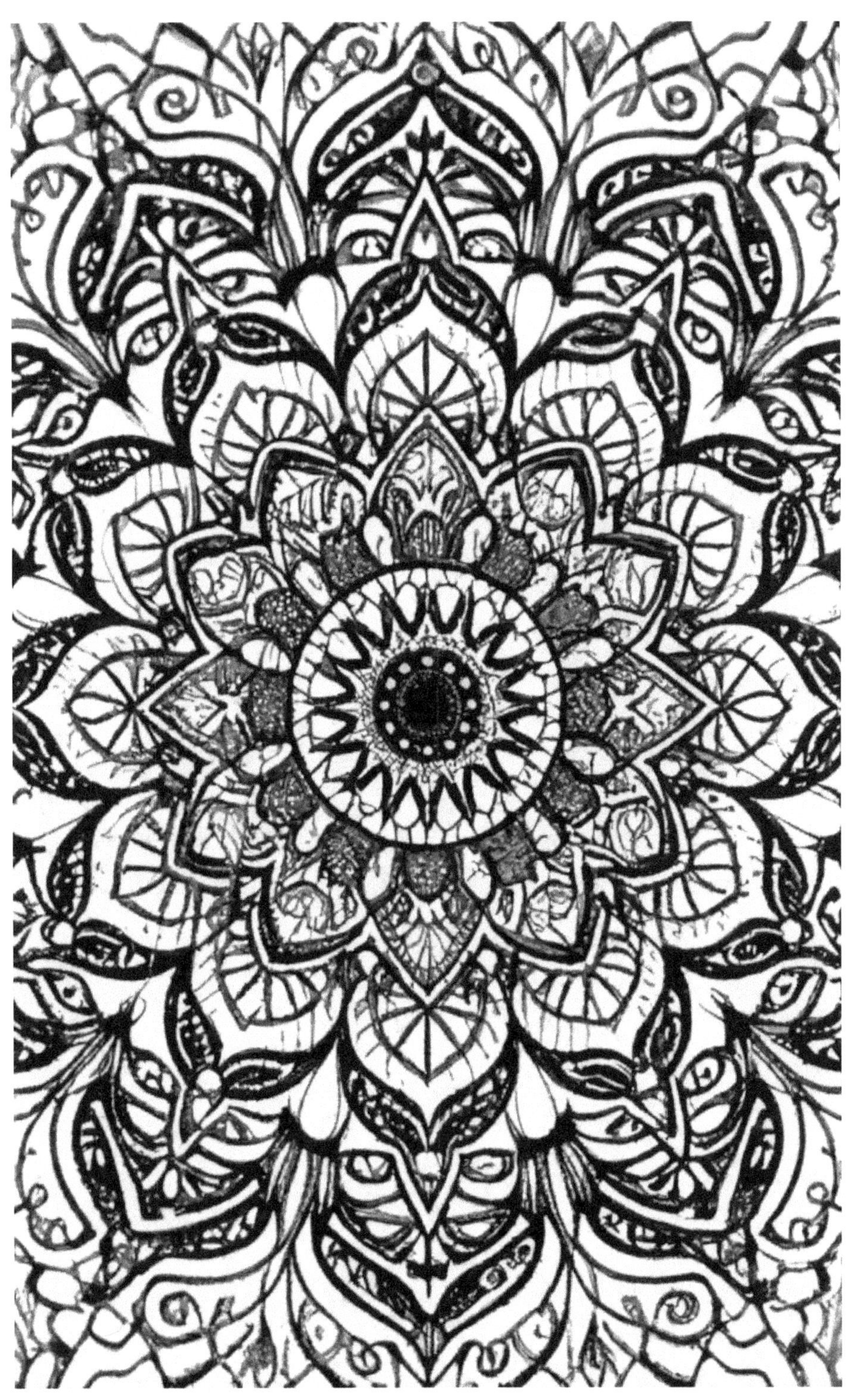

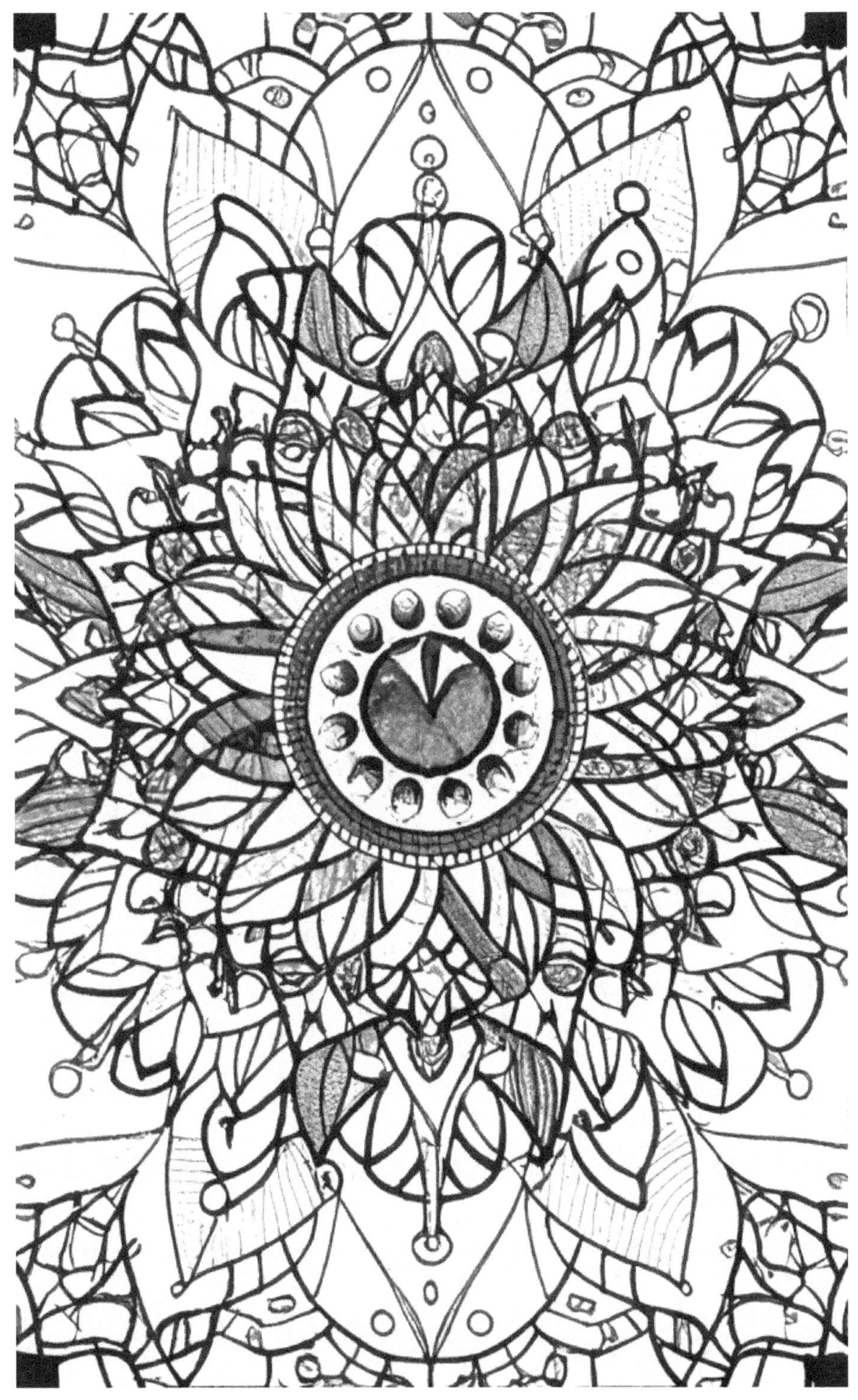

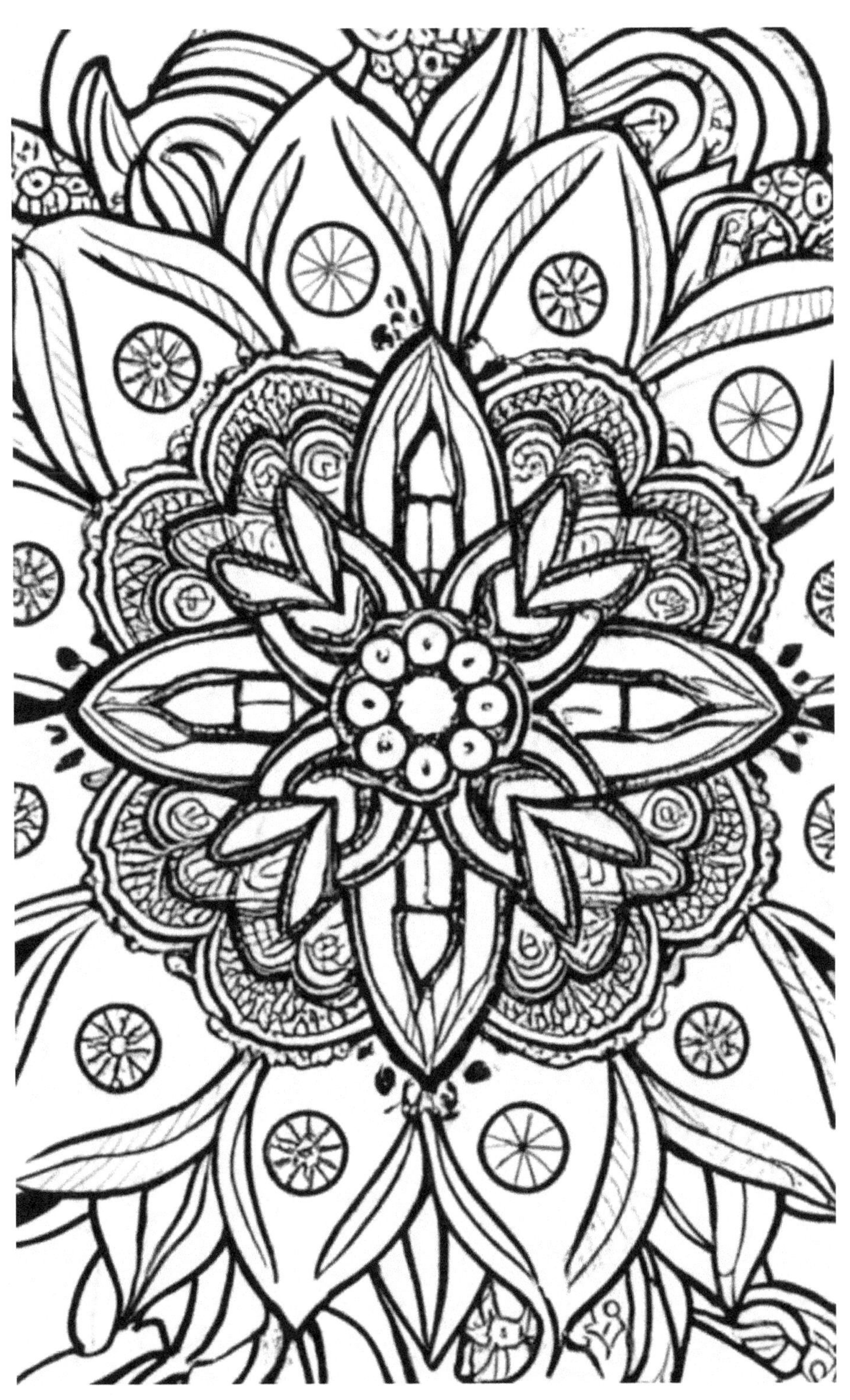

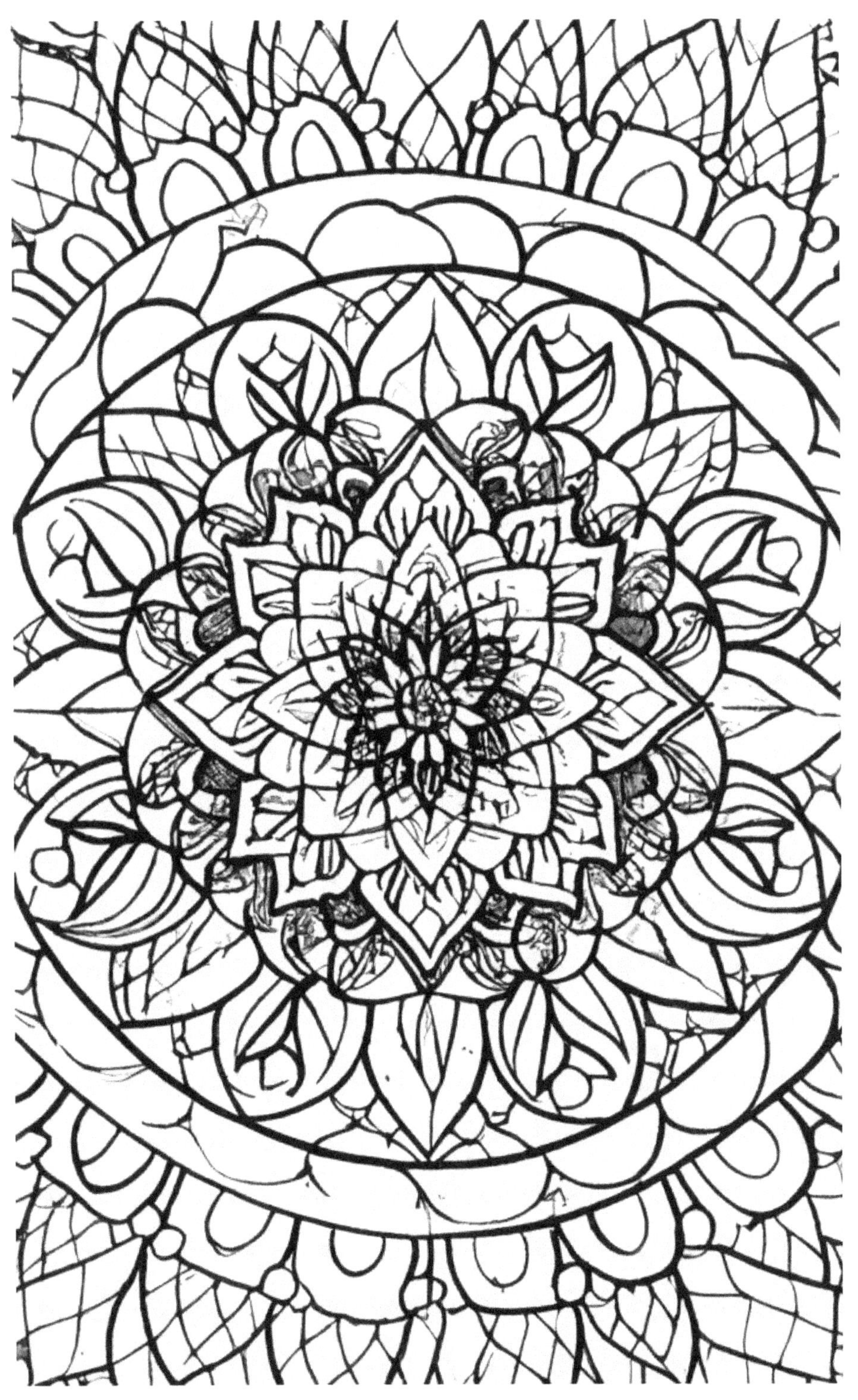

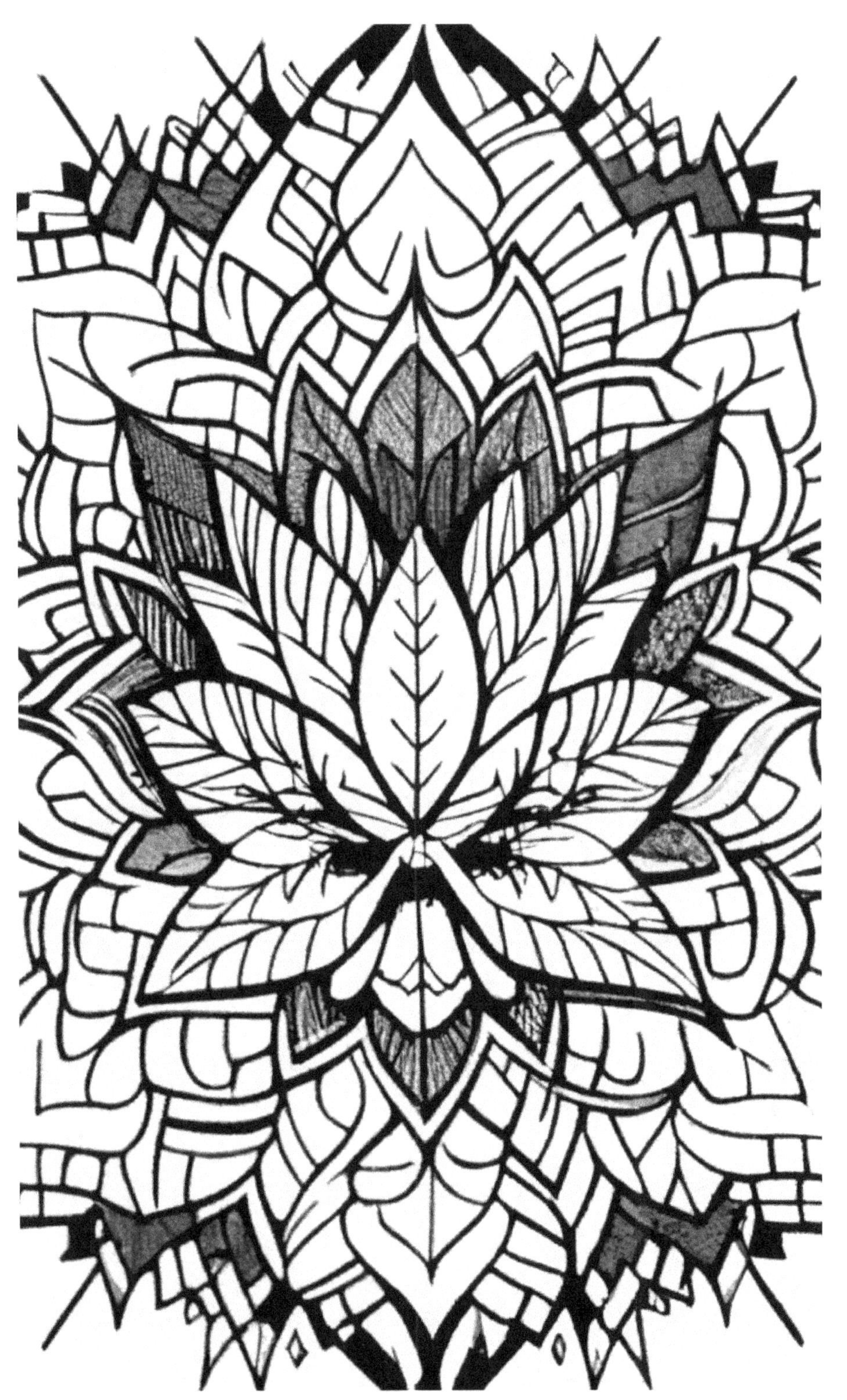

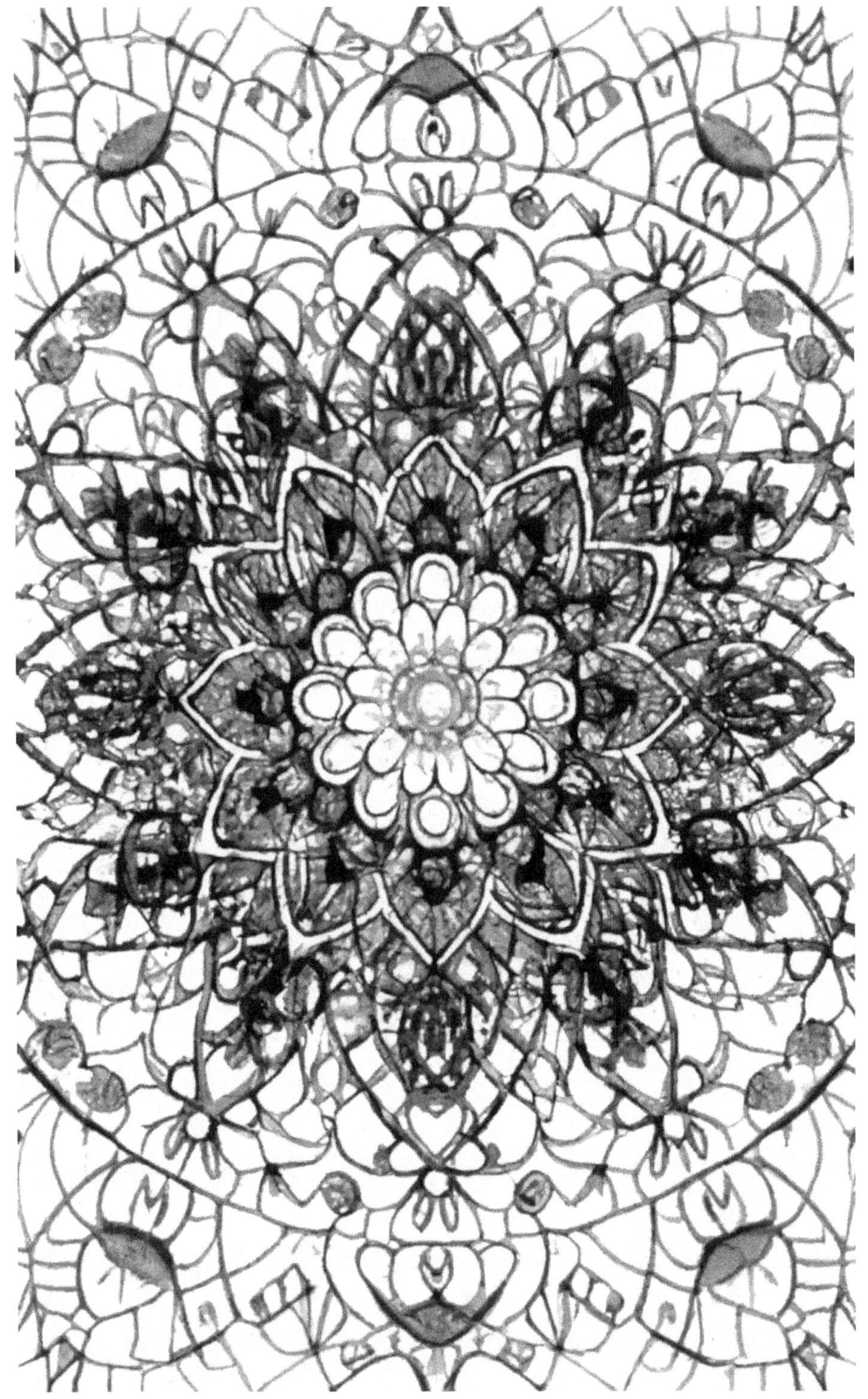

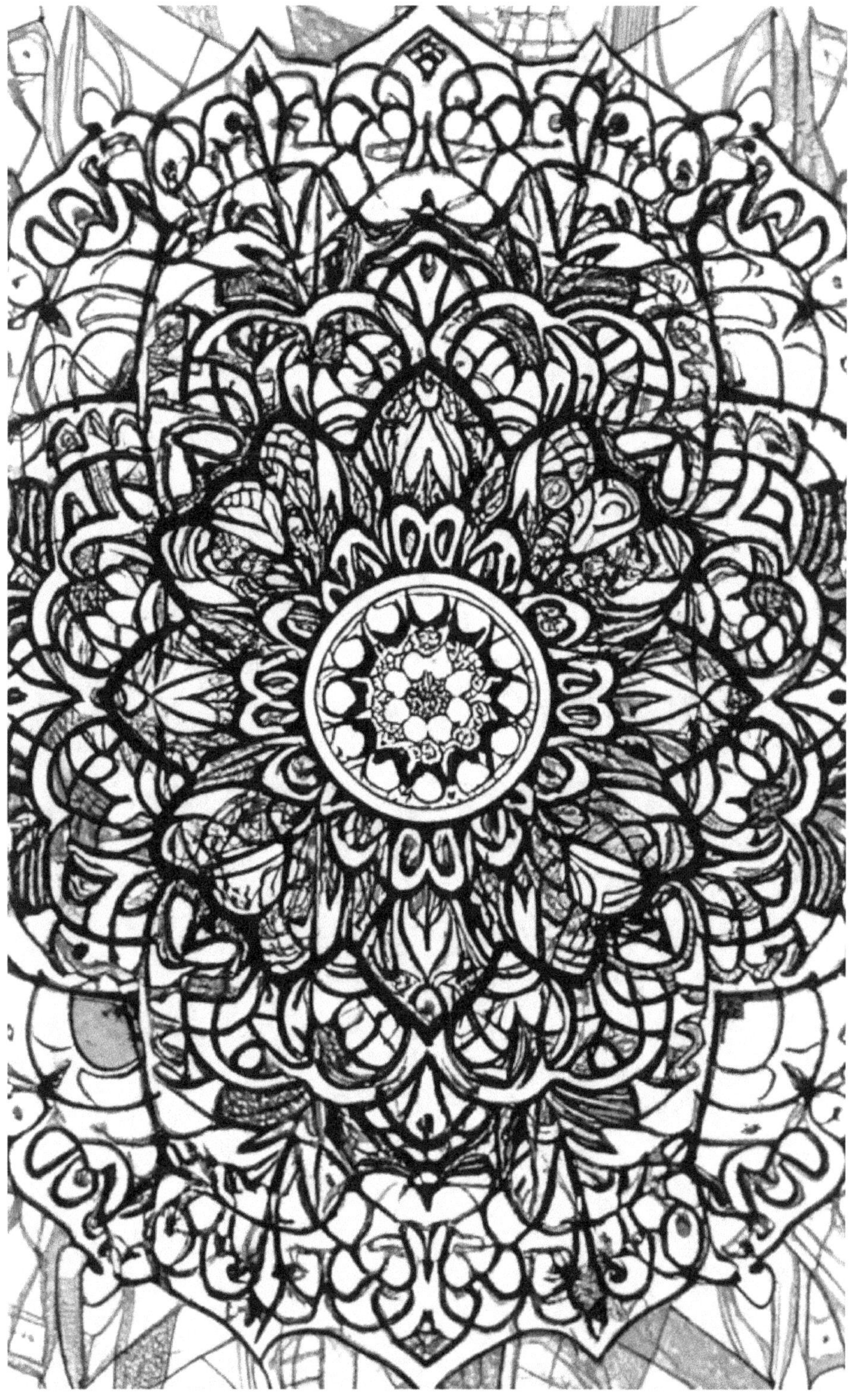

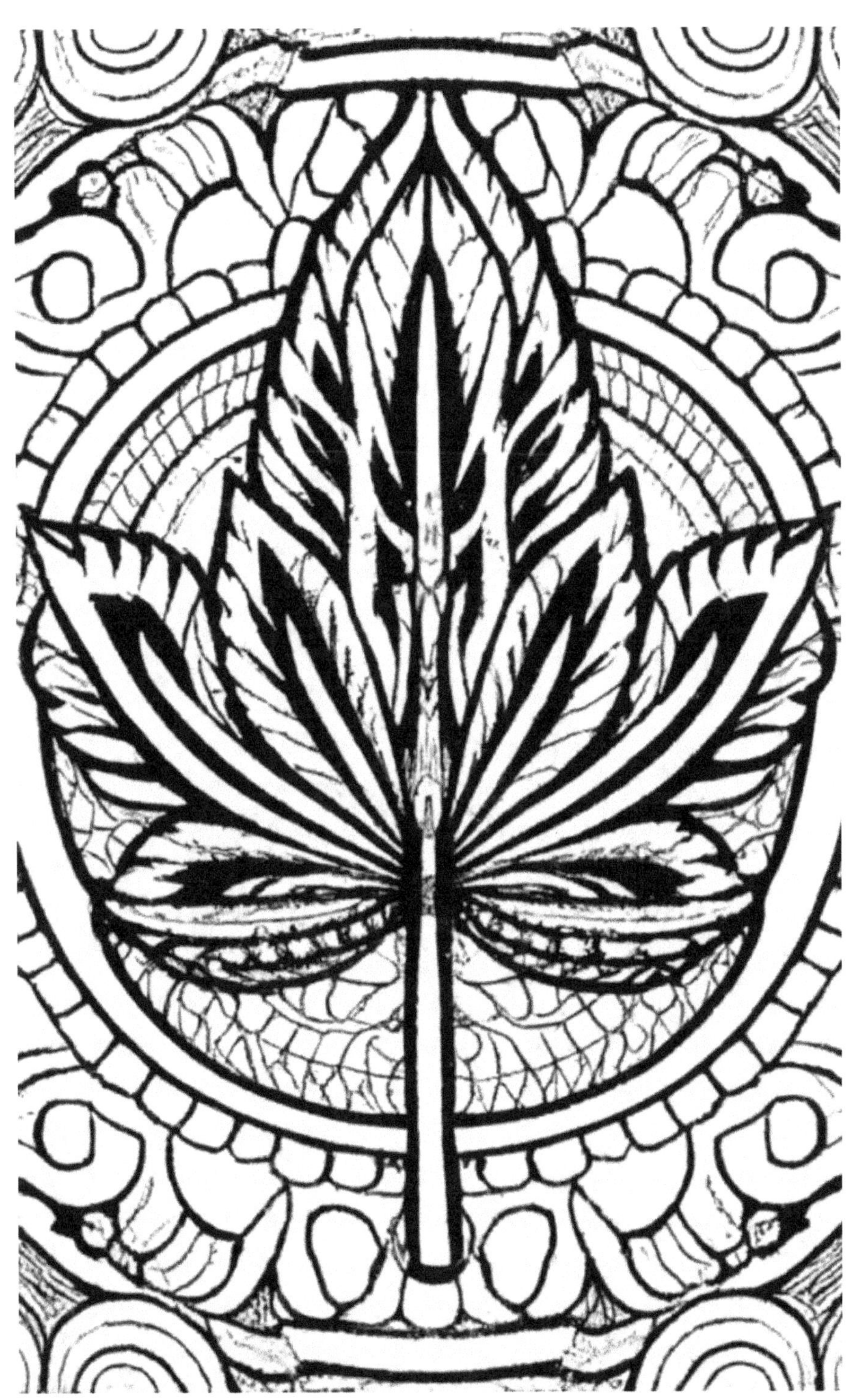

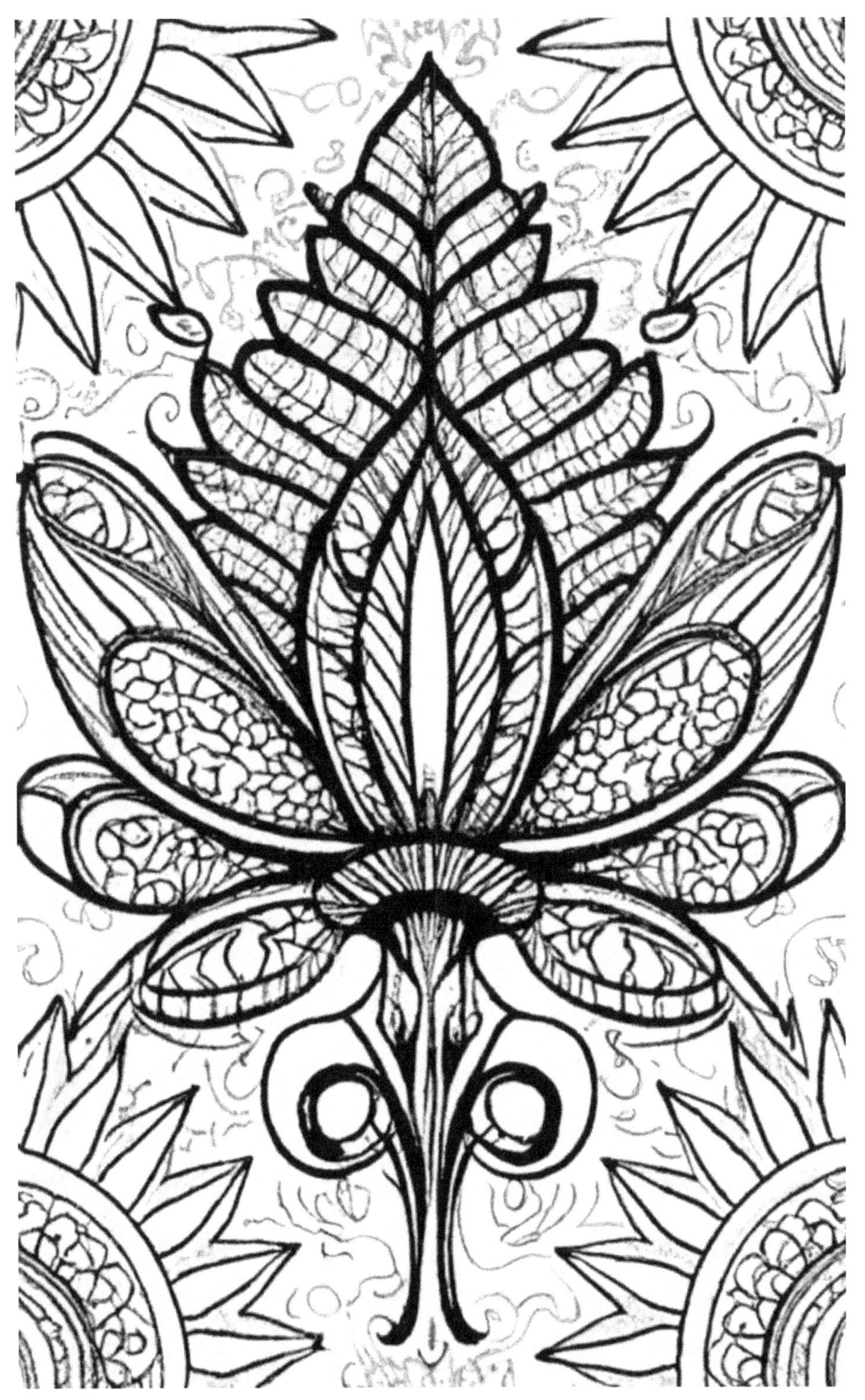

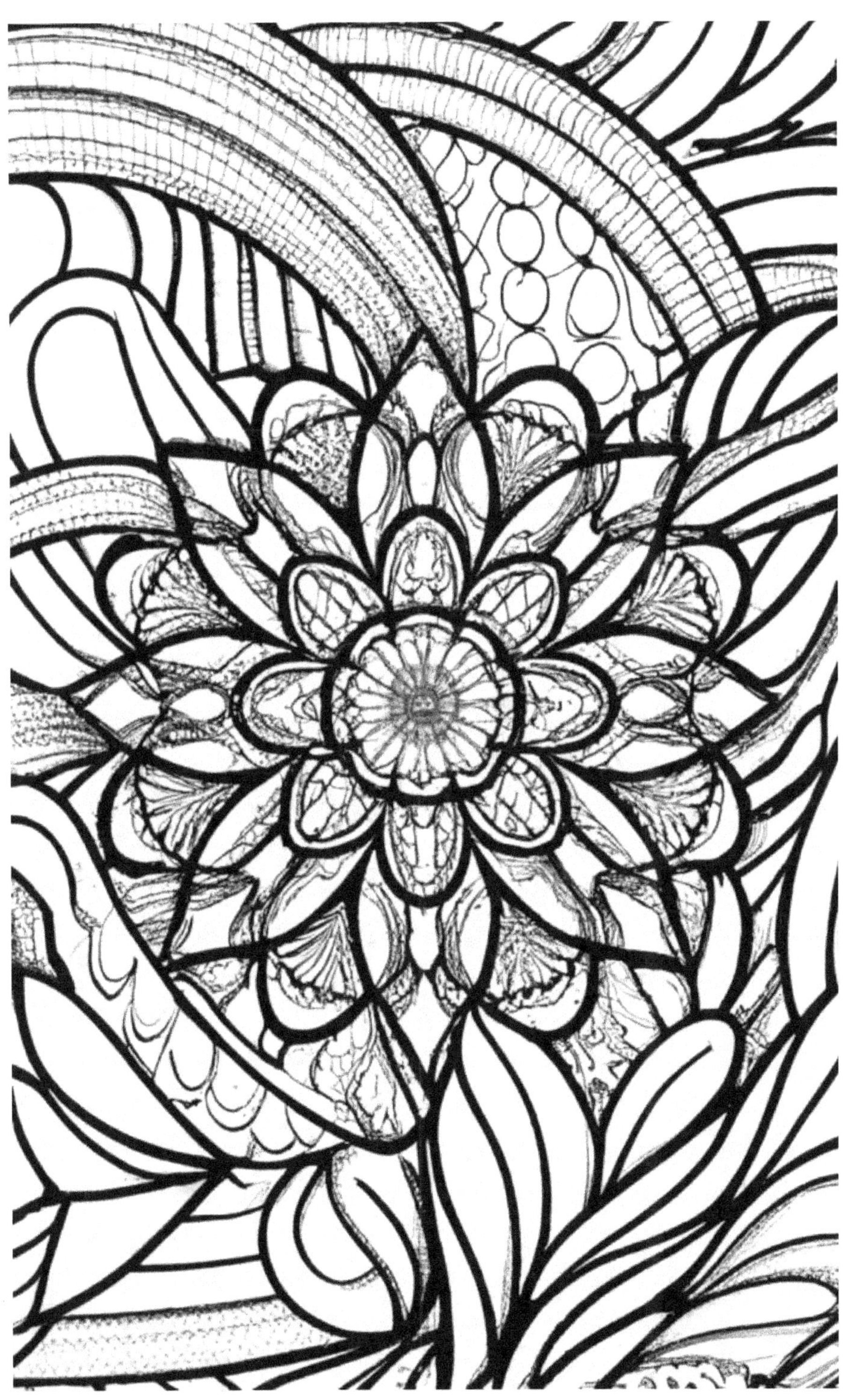

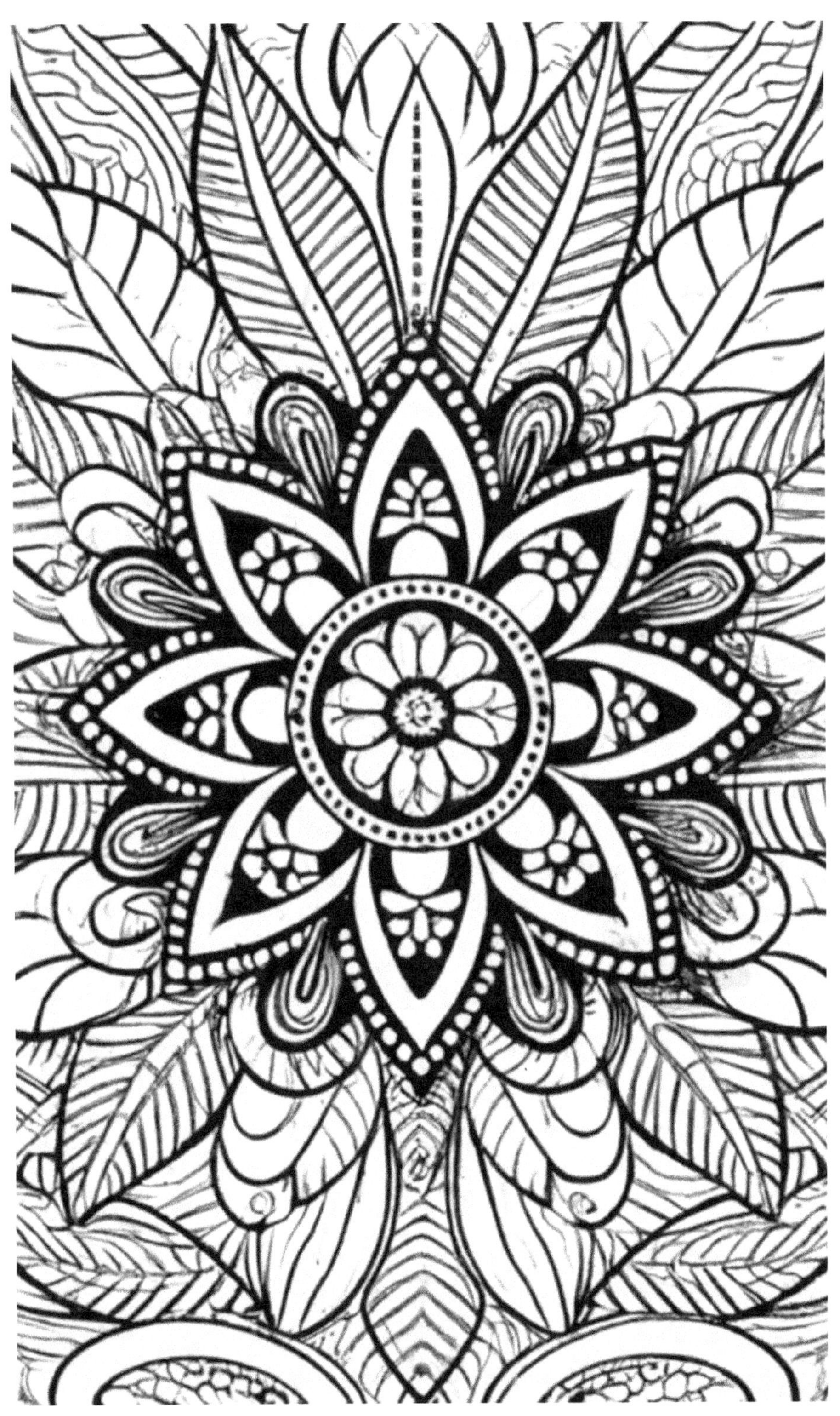

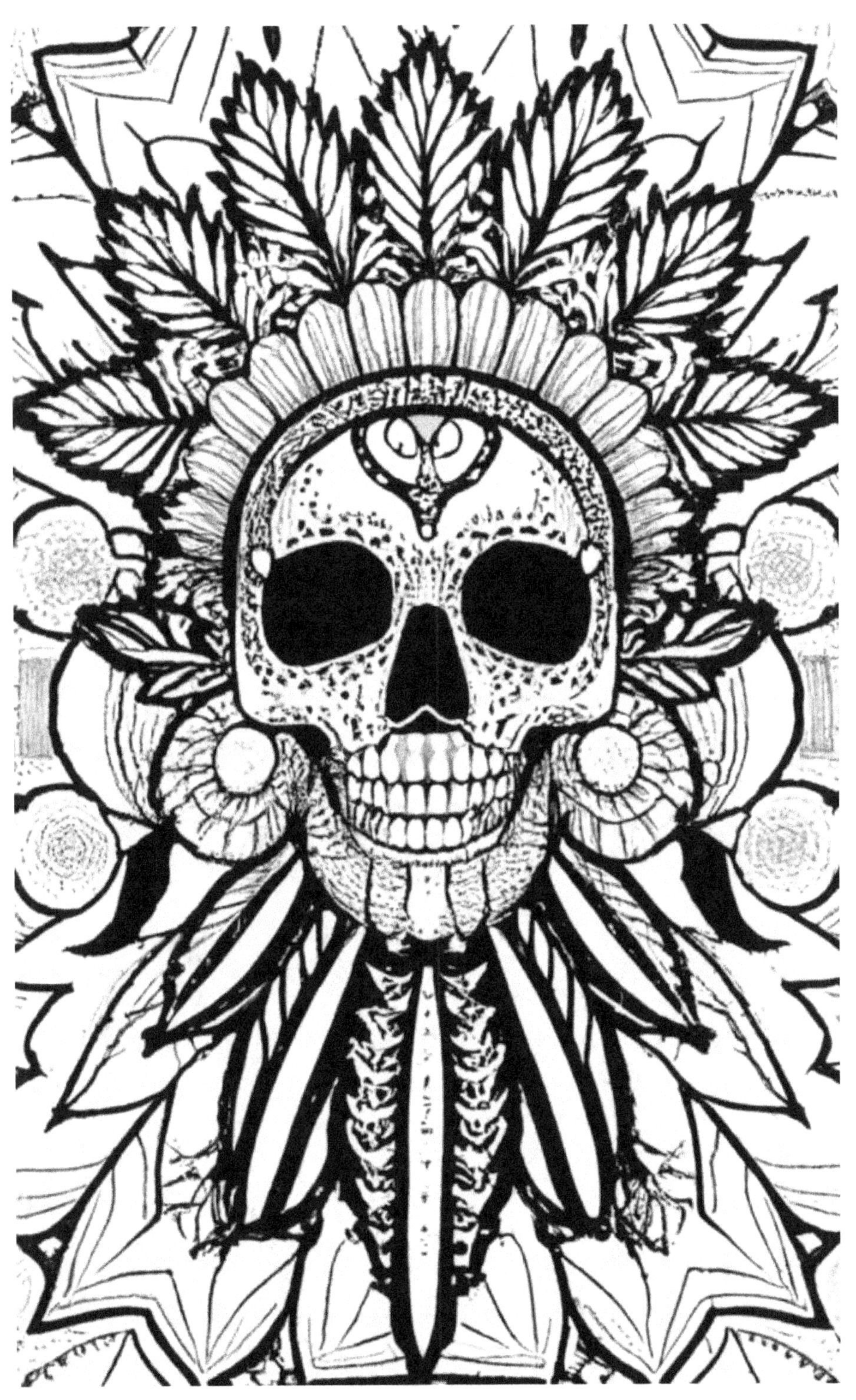

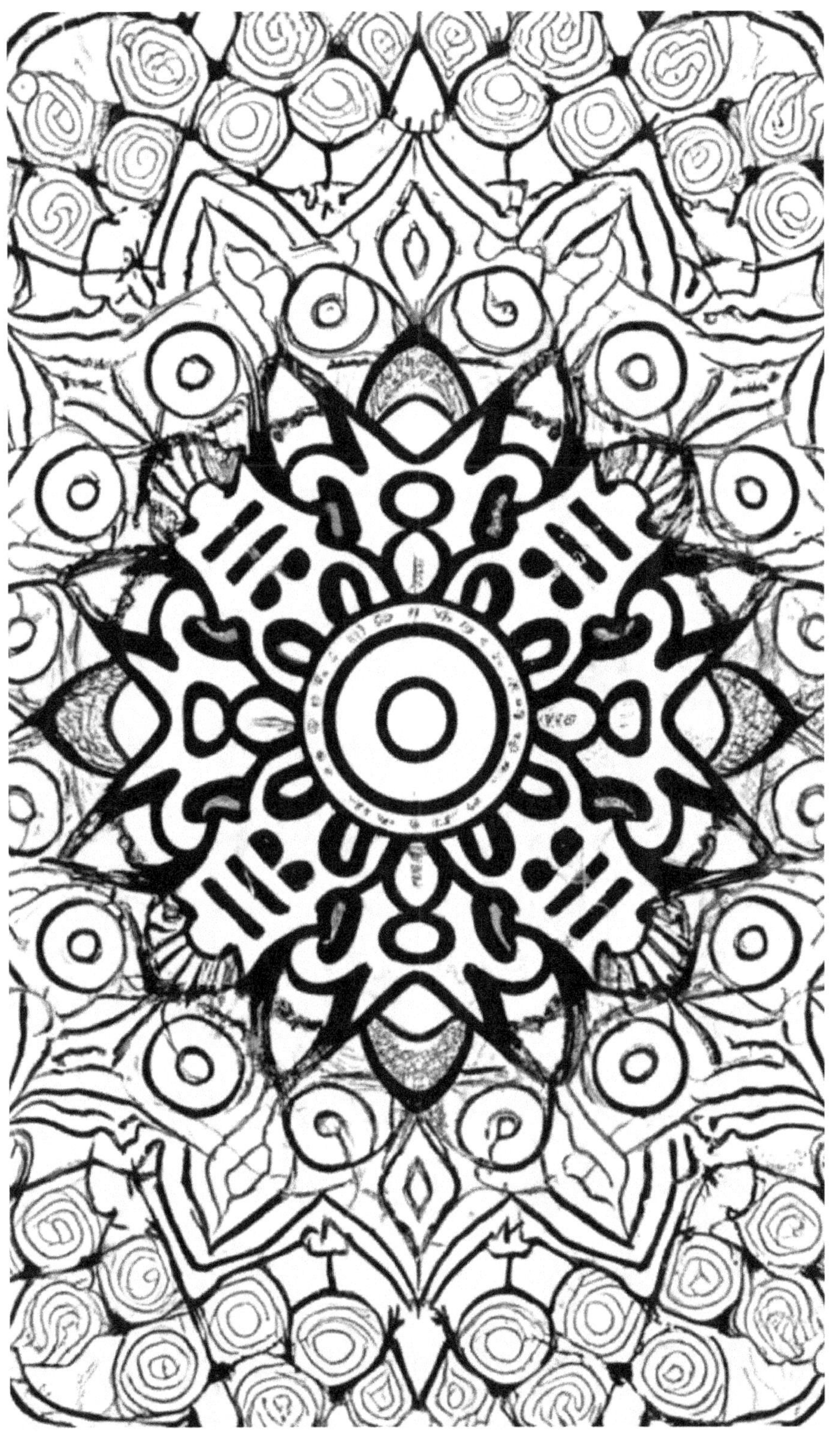

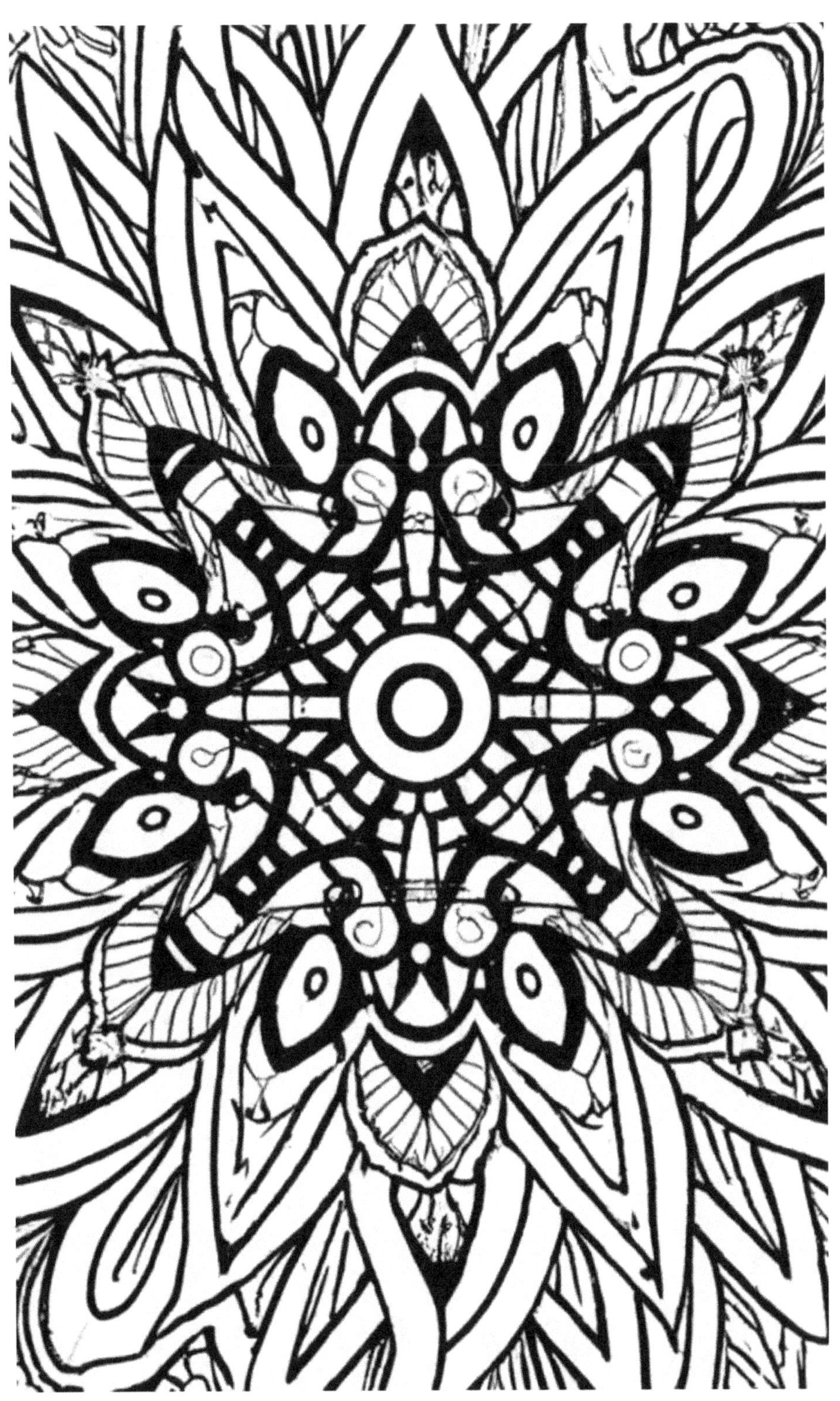

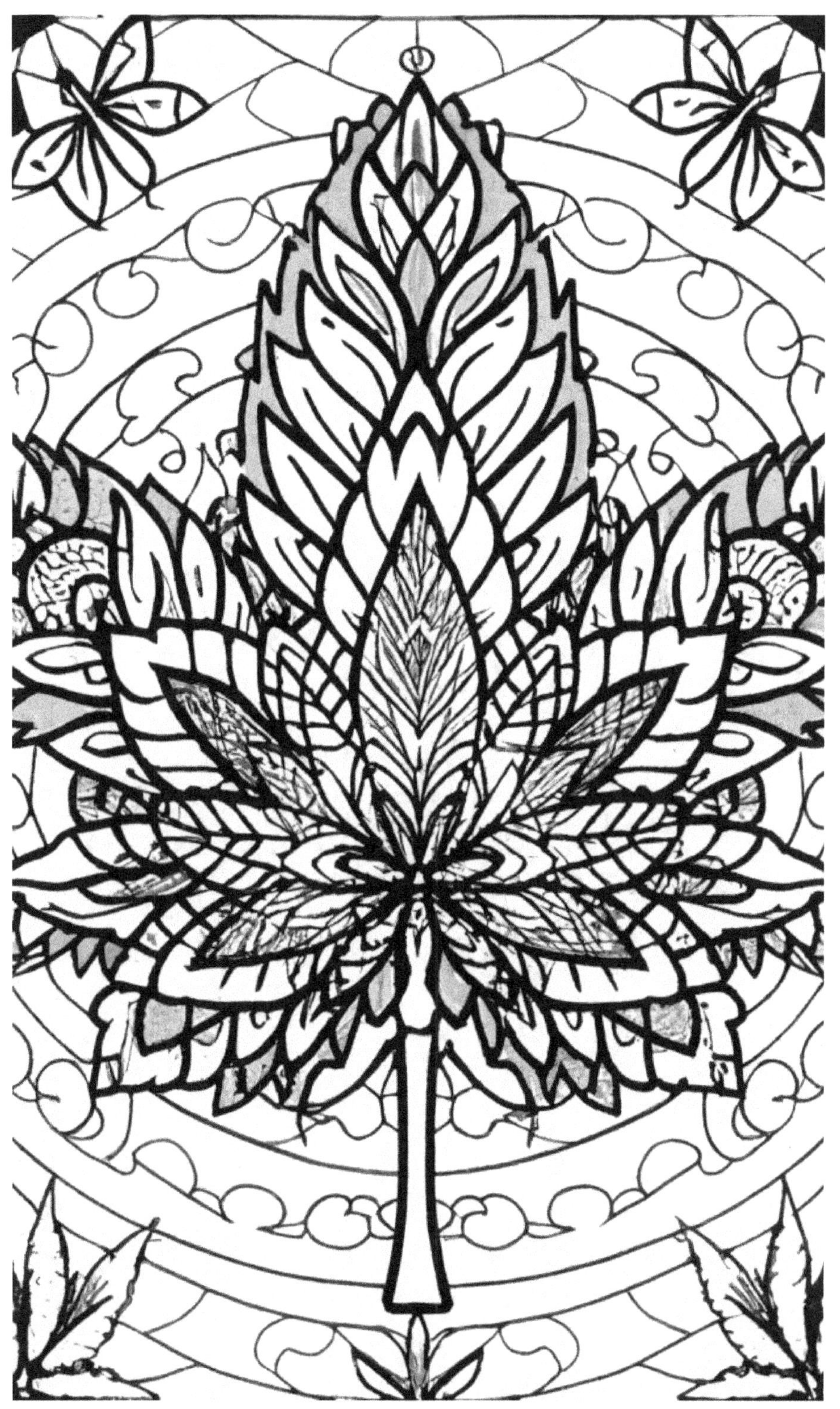

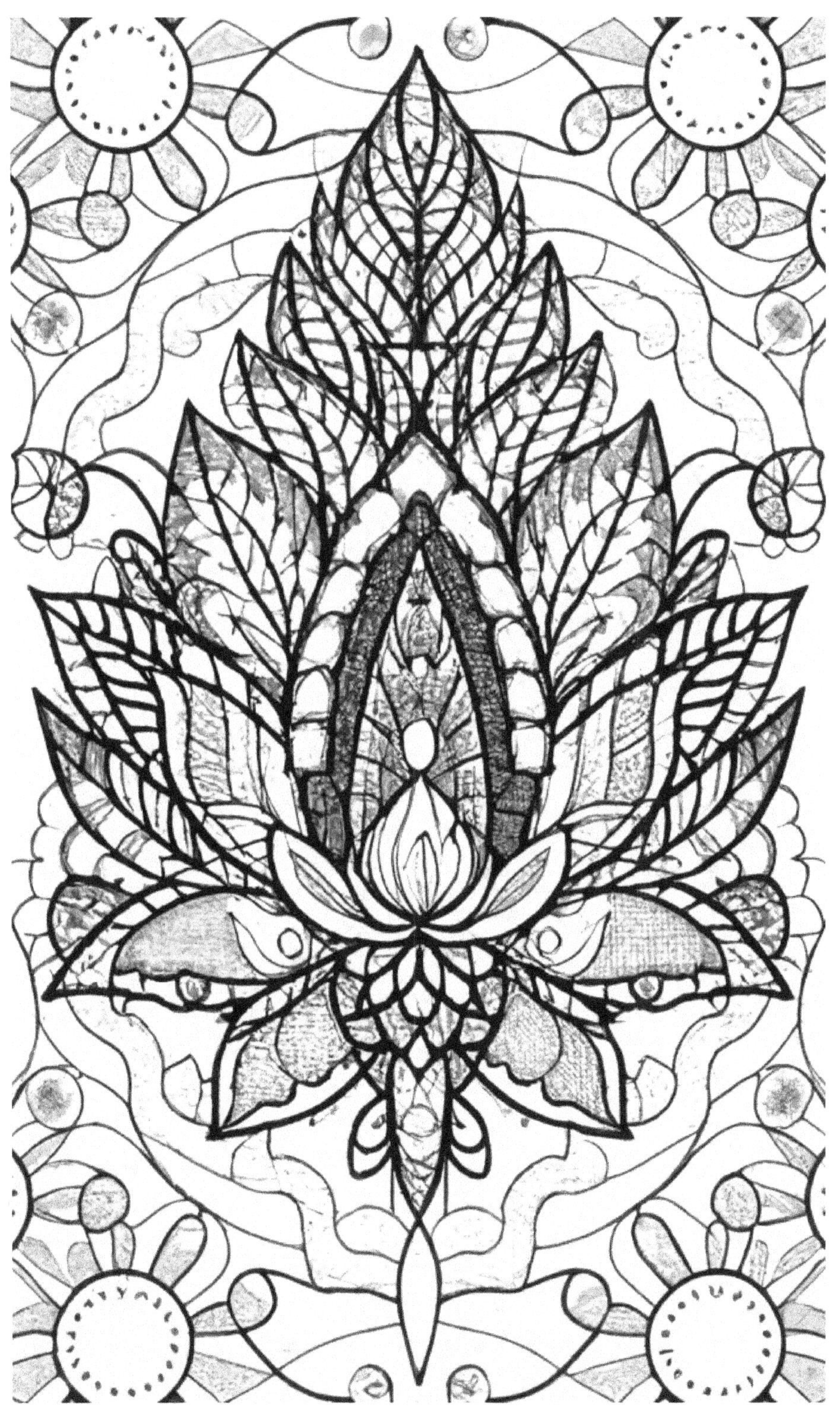

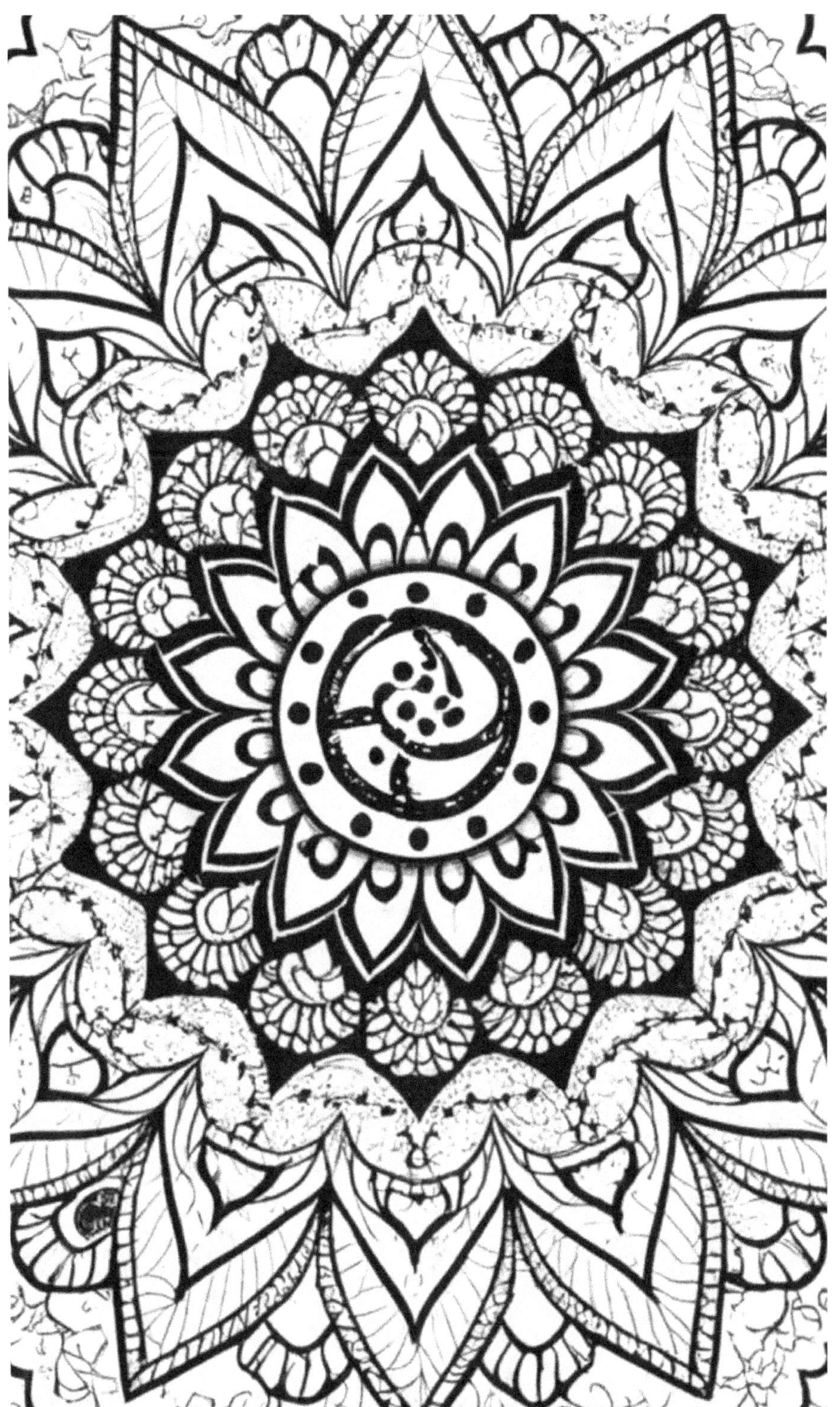

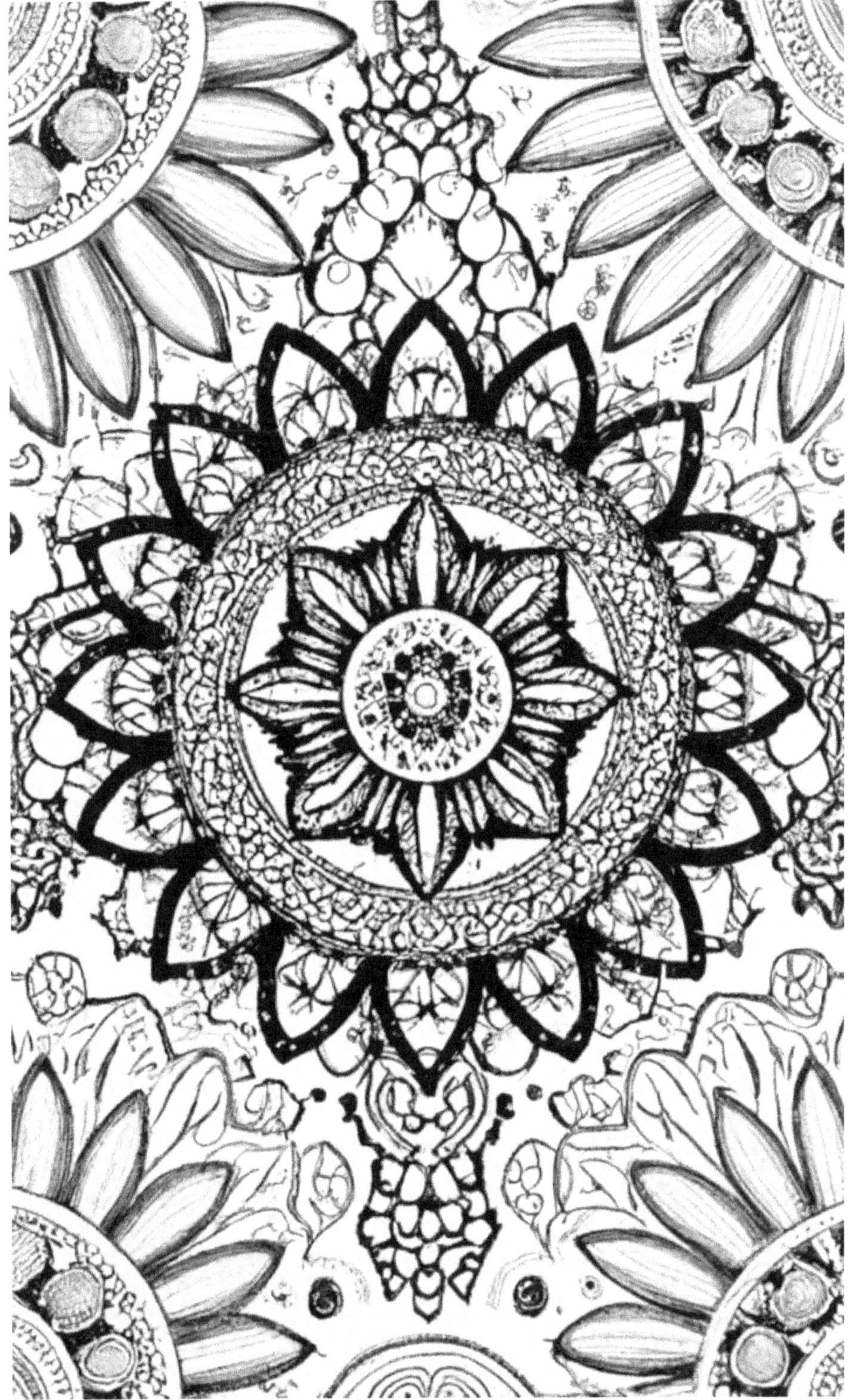

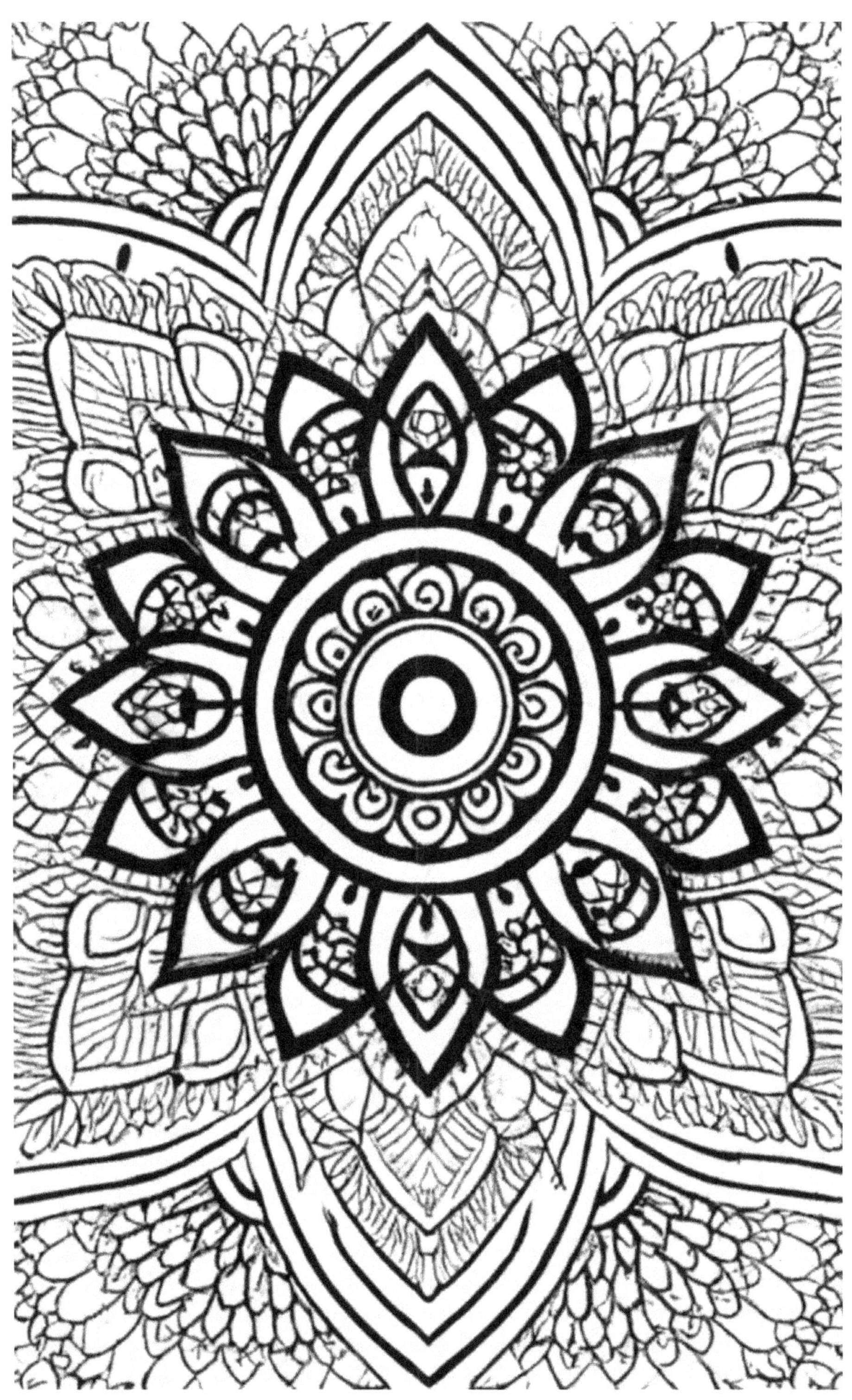

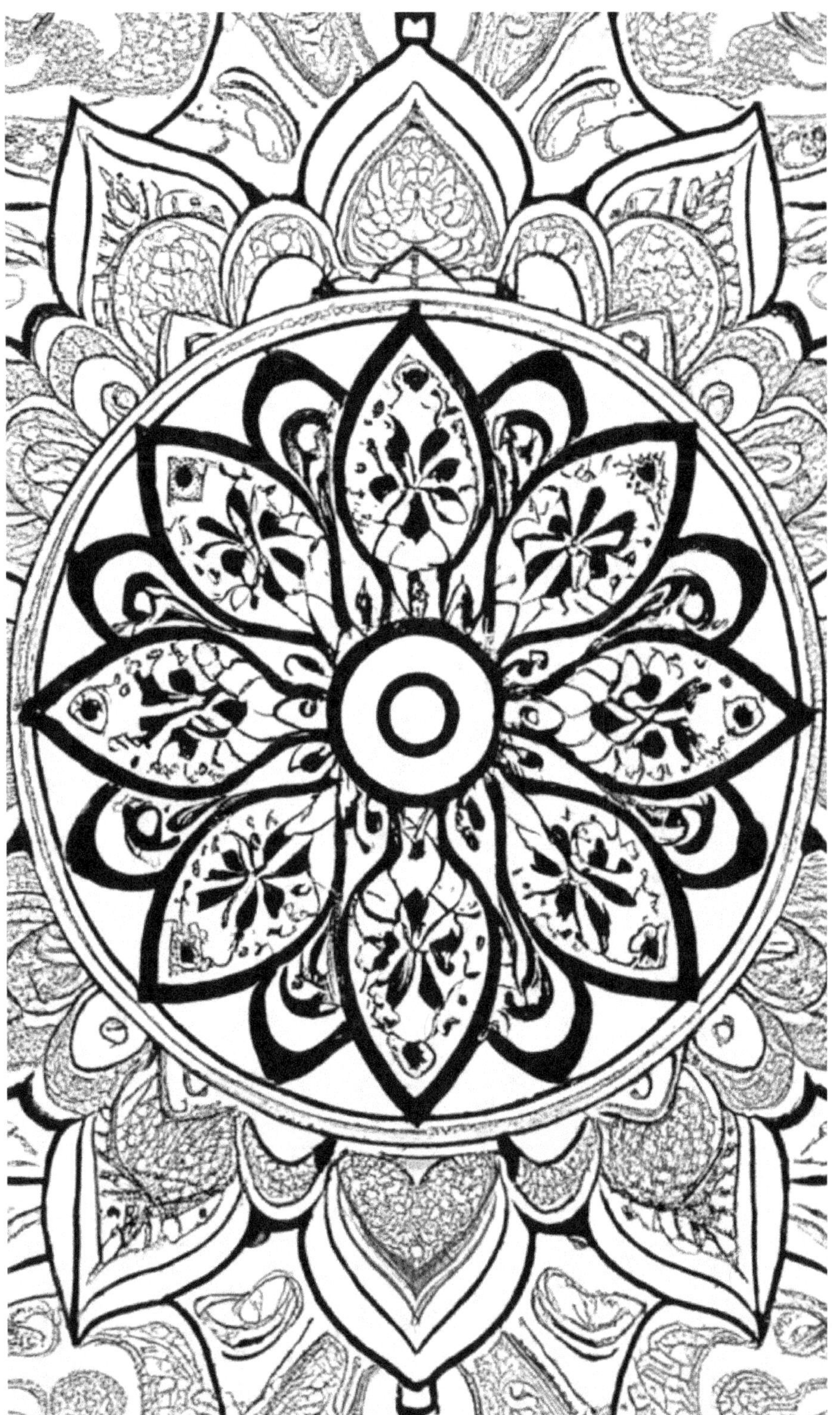

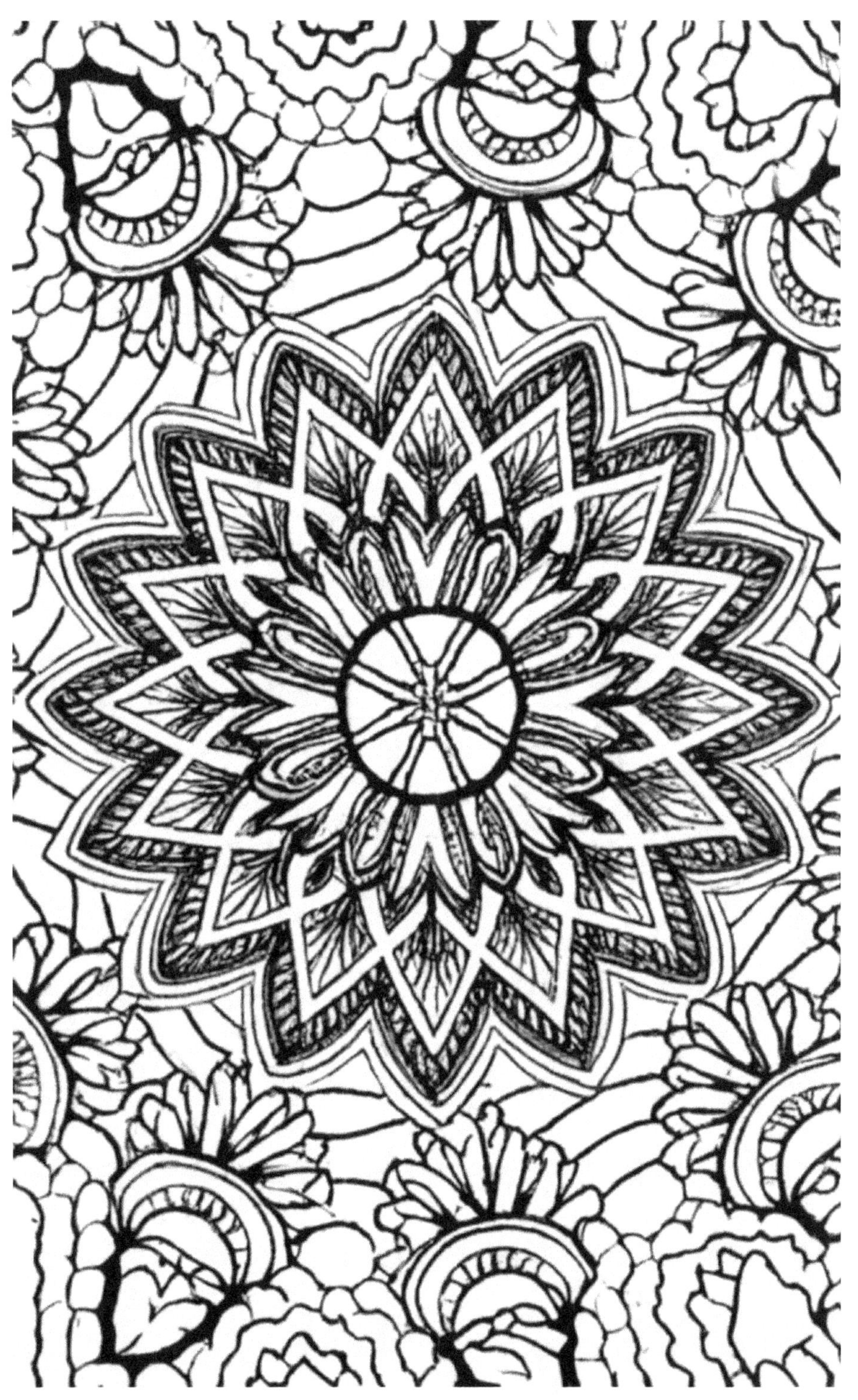

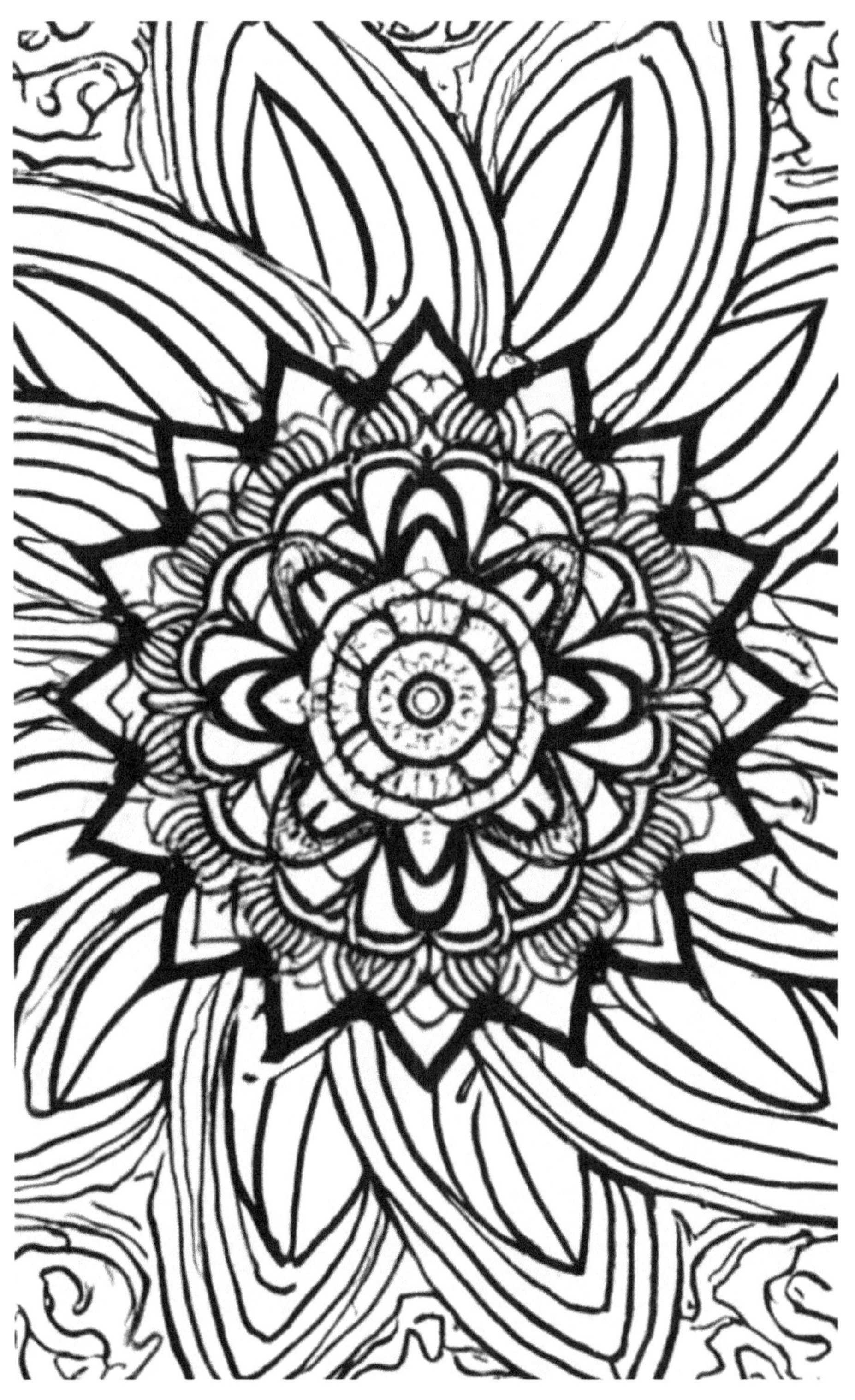

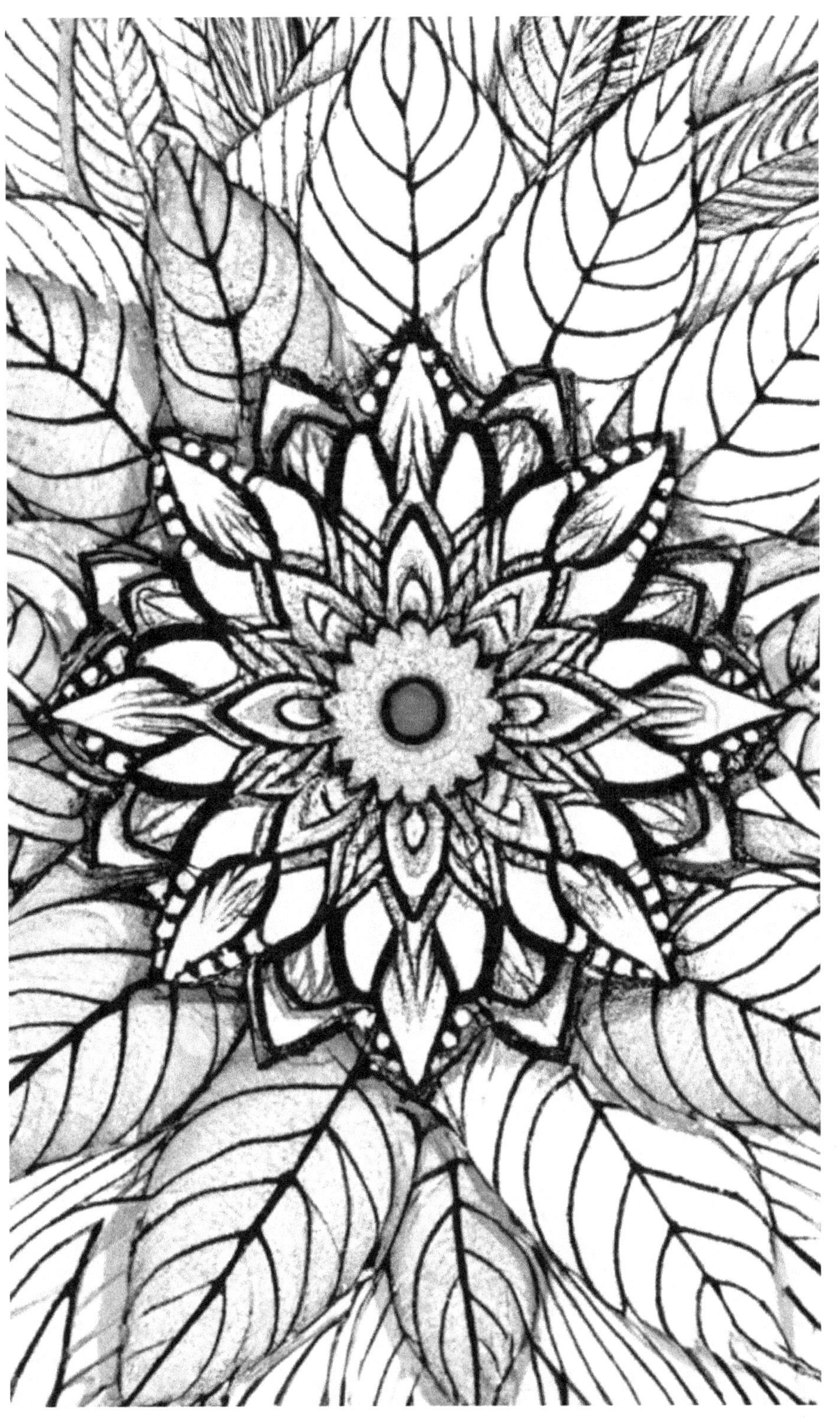

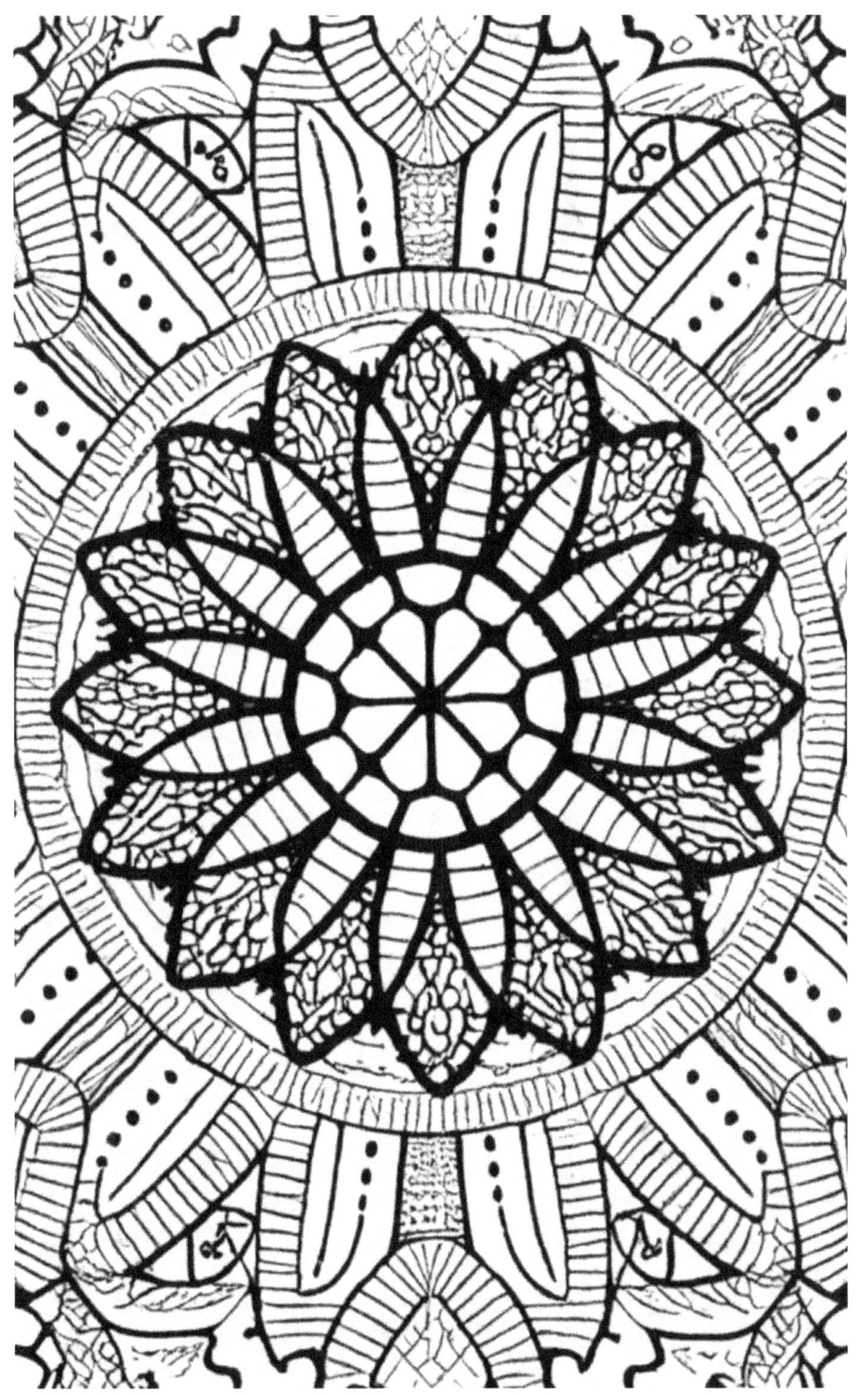